A Search for Synthesis in Economic Theory

A Search for Synthesis in Economic Theory

Ching-Yao Hsieh
and
Stephen L. Mangum

M. E. Sharpe, Inc.
ARMONK, NEW YORK
LONDON, ENGLAND

Library of Congress Cataloging in Publication Data

Hsieh, Ching-Yao, 1917-
    A search for synthesis in economic theory.

    Bibliography: p.
    1. Economics. 2. Classical school of economics. 3. Neoclassical
school of economics. 4. Keynesian economics. I. Magnum, Stephen L.
II. Title.
HB71.H73   1986   330.1   84-29816
ISBN 0-87332-328-9
ISBN 0-87332-329-7 (pbk.)

Printed in the United States of America

To
Courtney Ann and Robert Paul
Stephen James and Jonathan Garth

Contents

List of Figures

Acknowledgments

We wish to express our thanks to James R. Barth for numerous suggestions and constant encouragement. Thanks are also due an anonymous reader for prompting us to clear up some potential ambiguities. A special debt of gratitude is owed Gwen Luke, who typed the original manuscript. Olympus Publishing Company published an earlier version of this book under the title *A Search for Synthesis*. We thank them for believing in us and for being willing to take a chance. The staff at M. E. Sharpe, Inc., has been very supportive in our bringing this updated and expanded edition to publication. We hope their efforts are well rewarded.

Finally we express our love and appreciation to our spouses and families for sacrificing time and convenience to see this effort bear fruit.

A Search for Synthesis in Economic Theory

Introduction

Since the late 1960s the seeming inability of traditional monetary and fiscal policies to combat "stagflation" and address other macroeconomic issues has accelerated the erosion of confidence in the prevailing economic paradigm, the "neoclassical synthesis."* Dissensions among the members of the economics profession on both sides of the Atlantic have grown in number. By the 1970s, a majority of economists had recognized a "crisis" in economic theory. The clarion call was given by Joan Robinson in her Richard T. Ely Lecture entitled: "The Second Crisis of Economic Theory" in 1971.[1] In 1974, Sir John Hicks delivered his Jahnsson Lecture on *The Crisis in Keynesian Economics*.[2] More recently, Daniel Bell and Irving Kristol have edited a collection of essays entitled *The Crisis in Economic Theory*.[3]

Parallel to this development, a crisis has also emerged in the Marxian camp. The failure of Marxian theory to explain the durability of capitalism and the slow growth of the socialist economies has caused deep soul-searching and disillusionment among Marxian economists. This sentiment is reflected in the famous quip of the Maoist Michel le Bris: "God is dead; Marx is dead; and I don't feel too well myself." The most outstanding theoretical criticisms of Marxian theory have been stated by Anthony Culter, Barry Hindess, Paul Hirst, and Athar Hussain in their book, *Marx's Capital and Capitalism Today*, published in 1977.[4]

One salient and common cause for these two "crises" may be traced to the neglect, by both camps, of institutional and social changes in the monetary economy of industrial capitalism. In the case of Marxian

---

*The phrase was coined by Paul Anthony Samuelson. See *The Collected Scientific Papers of Paul Anthony Samuelson*, vol. 2 (Cambridge, Mass: M.I.T. Press, 1966), pp. 111 and 1271. Also see Paul A. Samuelson, *Economics*, 6th ed. (New York: McGraw-Hill, 1964), pp. 360–361.

economics, the four authors of *Marx's Capital and Capitalism Today* point out:

> Marxism currently has no adequate theory of modern monetary forms, of financial capitalist institutions and their different modes of articulation into the financial systems of capitalist national economies, and of the forms of organizations of large-scale, industrial capitalist enterprises and the types of economic calculation they undertake. These deficiencies are real and salient ones. . . . The theorization in *Capital* of, for example, money, credit, capitalist organization and calculation are all seriously inadequate.[5]

In the opinion of the four authors, capitalism is far more complex and resilient than the traditional Marxists had realized. Hence, the labor theory of value is obsolete in explaining pricing decisions of modern corporations.

As for the "neoclassical synthesis," much of past analyses in macro- and microeconomics were based on the foundation of neo-Walrasian general equilibrium. These analyses have failed to consider historical time and the emergence of uncertainty-reducing institutions in a monetary economy. In 1970, Frank H. Hahn admitted: "The Walrasian economy that we have been considering, although one where the auctioneer regulates the terms at which goods shall exchange, is essentially one of barter."[6] As pointed out by Paul Davidson, "The main characteristics of a real world monetary economy are: Uncertainty, Fallibility, Covenants, Institutions, Commerce, Finance, and Trust. These are Seven Wonders on which the Modern World is based."[7]

Implicit in the standard macroeconomic model of the "neoclassical synthesis" is the Walrasian theory of tâtonnement, which is explained simply by the following price-adjustment equation:

$$\dot{P}_i = \alpha[D_i(P_i) - S_i(P_i)], \text{ or } \dot{P}_i = E_i(P_i)$$

where $\dot{P}_i$ is the time derivative of the i-th commodity; $\dot{D}_i$ and $\dot{S}_i$ stand for the demand and supply of the i-th commodity; and E_i denotes the excess demand for that commodity. The equation states that the price of the i-th commodity adjusts in the same direction as excess demand for that commodity.

The validity of the tâtonnement theory has been discarded by general equilibrium theorists since 1960. The difficulties with the theory have been effectively summarized by Franklin M. Fisher in 1983.[8] In the first place, the equation "has nothing directly to do with the question of whether or not trade, consumption, or production takes place out of equilibrium." Secondly, Fisher reiterates Koopmans' 1957 observation to the effect: in a world of price-takers, who changes the price?[9] Indeed, Fisher writes: "We know very little about how individuals do or ought to behave when equilibrium is not present; hence the resort to an aggregate equation."[10] Thirdly, Fisher points out: "Implicit in the assumption that excess demand influences prices is the assumption that they (traders) can take such action which . . . implies that they have something of value which they can and do sell so as to have something to offer when they buy. It also involves . . . the assumption that they do take actions and take them now."[11] Fisher refers to the last assumption as the "Present Action Postulate."

General equilibrium models also assume: (1) that the price system provides full information to the agents, and (2) that all future (forward) markets are open. In the words of Christopher J. Bliss and Roberto F. Cippa, "Decisions are taken once and for all at the beginning of all periods and inconsistencies in plans can be eliminated instantaneously and without costs by price adjustments."[12] "In this sense, the introduction of time does not alter the world of complete certainty."[13] This is the case because the "time" considered in these models is not historical time, which by its nature implies uncertainty. Hence, John D. Hey observes: "General equilibrium theory . . . suffers from two major, and interrelated defects; it ignores uncertainty and it ignores time. It therefore fails to describe the essentially sequential nature of actual economies."[14]

The Post-Keynesians offer an alternative paradigm stressing historical time and the all-pervading influence of uncertainty on economic behavior and economic institutions. Their analyses combine Keynes's insights with the more lasting influences of classical and Marxian economics. It should be noted that some strands of general equilibrium theory have arrived at a position which bears considerable resemblance to the Post-Keynesian view. In 1971, Kenneth J. Arrow and Frank H. Hahn wrote:

> The terms in which contracts are made matter. In particular, if money is the good in terms of which contracts are made, then the prices of goods in terms of money are of special significance.
>
> This is not the case if we consider an economy without a past and without a

future. Keynes wrote that "the importance of money essentially flows from it being a link between the present and the future" to which we add that it is important also because it is a link between the past and the present. If a serious monetary theory comes to be written, the fact that contracts are indeed made in terms of money will be of considerable importance.[15]

We are living in a very exciting age of reconstruction of economic theory. There is now enough common ground among the various schools of thought to make discussion possible. It is this perception that provides the rationale for this book. What are the forces that contribute to the widening common ground? The answer lies in the increasing technical sophistication of economic analysis. Three of the salient common grounds to be considered in more detail in this volume are as follows: the theory of a monetary economy, the disequilibrium foundations of a general equilibrium theory, and a rekindled interest in institutional factors.

(I) The theory of a monetary economy

Frank H. Hahn writes:

> It is now agreed, and it is becoming widely understood, that a minimal requirement for a theory of a monetary economy is that the latter should have trading at every date. Radner . . . has christened such economies sequence economies.[16]

Hahn further observes:

> Since we need a sequence picture as a prerequisite for monetary theory, it now follows that there is no way of avoiding the issue of market expectations either. One of Keynes's claims to the title of great economist is that he saw this more clearly than any of his predecessors had done—and indeed, more clearly than many of his successors. In any case, no monetary theory without sequences, and no sequences without expectations.[17]

In the same vein, Sir John Hicks suggests:

> I have been trying to show that further development of theory, which I agree is required, should begin with an attempt to identify the questions it will have to be concerned with. These, I have tried to show, are in essence

questions of sequential causality. We have so far no more than the beginning of a theory which will help us with such questions; but we do have a beginning. The challenge I am presenting to economists is to go on from it.[18]

These views are shared by the Post-Keynesians. Neo-Marxists also would not reject these views as common ground for further dialogue. As mentioned earlier, some of their serious theoreticians are beginning to see the irrelevance of the labor theory of value in contemporary monetary economies of industrial capitalism.

(II) The disequilibrium foundations of general equilibrium theory

Franklin M. Fisher writes:

> By building a full model of disequilibrium behavior we obtain considerable insight into a number of areas. These include the nature of fixed-price quantity-constrained equilibria, the role of money, the behavior of arbitraging agents and the inclusion of the stock market.[19]

> These matters may be put in perhaps a more striking way. The theory of value is not satisfactory without a description of the adjustment processes that are applicable to the economy and of the way in which individual agents adjust to disequilibrium. In this sense, stability analysis is of far more than merely technical interest. It is the first step in a reformulation of the theory of value.[20]

The search for disequilibrium foundations of general equilibrium theory is ongoing. The outburst of literature on this subject may be grouped under two broad categories: (a) fixed-price quantity rationing models and (b) price adjustment models. Useful surveys of such models have been made in 1977 by Jean Michel Grandmont and in 1980 by Allan Drazen.[21] A representative model of the first is that of Jean-Pascal Benassy.[22] The scholarly work of Franklin M. Fisher in 1983 provides a new approach to ongoing research in the second. Both of these models will be considered in Part 4 of this book.

The disequilibrium theorists' emphasis on non-Walrasian states is shared not only by Post-Keynesian writers but also by Janos Kornai. In his path-breaking work, *Anti-Equilibrium* (1971), Kornai made a persuasive argument against the traditional equilibrium analysis. More recently in 1982, Kornai writes:

At this point I wish to enter into a controversy with my "predecessor"—
E. Malinvaud who gave the Jahnsson lectures in 1977. His study contains—as do all his works—a number of interesting and important ideas,
formulated in the lucid and precise manner that is characteristic of him.
We share a common interest in non-Walrasian states of economic systems.
There are, however, a few matters in which my views *differ* from his, as
well as from the widely represented school to which he refers, associated
with the names of Barro, Grossman, Benassy and others.[23] (italics supplied)

The common ground for continued dialogue is clearly visible in the
above passage.

Returning to the Post-Keynesian camp, we note that in 1981 James
Cicarelli and John Stuck cite a survey of economists on the subject of
"breakthroughs" and developments likely to occur in economics within the next twenty years or so. One of the predicted developments is
"greater emphasis on disequilibrium analysis in micro and macro theory and less on equilibrium analysis."[24]

(III) A rekindled interest in institutional factors

Sixteen years ago (in 1970), Martin Shubik made the following prediction:

> Since the defeat of the institutionalists, there have been many new devel-
> opments in economics that I believe are going to result in a joining
> together of detailed institutional studies, advanced mathematical econom-
> ic theory and political economy. I expect that a new microeconomics is
> about to emerge. It can be described (in a ponderous manner) as mathema-
> tical-institutional-political economy.[25]

Recent developments prove that the Shubik prediction is not an impossible dream. The Post-Keynesians have always stressed the importance
of institutional factors. As pointed out by Alfred S. Eichner, "Post-
Keynesian theory is meant to describe an economic system with advanced credit and other monetary institutions—all of which play a
fundamental role in the dynamic processes being analyzed."[26] In the
same vein, John Cornwall writes:

> In summary, post-Keynesian macrodynamics can be seen as an attempt to

incorporate both the institutional framework of an advanced market economy and the manner in which this institutional framework changes over time into the explanation of growth and cyclical processes.[27]

The general equilibrium theorists likewise have paid increasing attention to institutional developments. For instance, Jean-Pascal Benassy writes:

> The study of fixprice models will nonetheless be extremely rewarding for a number of reasons:
>
> First, some countries, notably socialist countries, do indeed have prices that are fixed by central decisions for a fairly long period of time. The model thus applies directly to these countries.
>
> Second, it is certainly the tradition of Keynesian theory and of many macroeconomic models to assume that quantities (that is, income in most Keynesian models) react faster than prices. This assumption is based on the observed sluggishness of some prices and wages—in particular, their downward rigidity. Accordingly, fixprice models can be thought of as modeling the very short run.
>
> Finally, at a theoretical level, the study of fixprice equilibria will be a useful preliminary to the study of other non-Walrasian equilibrium concepts that include more price flexibility: we shall show that fixprice equilibria exist for all positive prices under fairly standard assumptions.[28]

These and other areas of common ground suggesting convergent tendencies in economic theory will be explored at length in the pages that follow.

This book consists of four parts. The major tenets of classicism are considered in Part 1. The discussion is confined to three representative writers; Adam Smith, David Ricardo, and Robert Thomas Malthus. No attempt is made to give a chronological survey of the development of classical political economy from Quesnay to John Stuart Mill and Marx. That is the task of traditional textbooks on the history of economic thought. Our objective is to highlight the links between classical theory and modern economics. The similarities and crucial differences between the writings of Adam Smith and contemporary "supply-side" economics are discussed first. Next, the influence of Ricardian economics on Post-Keynesian economics as well as on the "new classical

macroeconomics" is considered.* The link between Ricardo and contemporary "supply-side" economics is also under the purview of Part
1. In surveying the lasting influences of Ricardo, Piero Sraffa's prelude
to a critique of neoclassical price theory is highlighted.[29] The closing
chapter of Part 1 deals with causality in classical theory. The discussion
is presented in the light of Sir John Hicks's 1979 exposition.[30]

The "neoclassical synthesis" and its critiques are the subject of Part
2. A macroeconomic model is first introduced to illustrate the basic
tenets of this paradigm. The model uses the IS-LM framework originally introduced by Sir John Hicks. Its microfoundation is Walrasian
general equilibrium theory. The equilibrating mechanism is limited to
prices. Next, the theoretical heritage of the "neoclassical synthesis" is
traced, followed by a brief survey of some of the important criticisms
of the "neoclassical synthesis" from four sources: (1) disequilibrium
macroeconomics, (2) monetarism, (3) rational expectations, and (4)
neo-Austrian economics. Part 2 concludes with a discussion of causality in the "neoclassical synthesis."

The Post-Keynesian paradigm is the subject matter of Part 3. The
explicit role played by investment emerges as a common thread tying
the various theories together. In its macroeconomics, as pointed out by
Alfred S. Eichner, "Post-Keynesian theory offers an explanation of
economic growth and income distribution—with the two viewed as
being directly linked to one another. The key determinant is the same
for both. This is the rate of investment, whether measured against total
national income or viewed as the percentage change over time."[31] In
microeconomics, the Post-Keynesian theory of prices is dynamic. Pricing decisions are viewed as dominated by a long-term perspective
reflecting the overriding goal of the large corporation: continuous and
accelerating growth. Expansion requires investment; investment needs
financing. Hence a target rate of profit is incorporated into the cost-
determined prices. Here again the central role of investment is made
explicit. Part 3 closes with a chapter on "sequential causality" in Post-
Keynesian economics.

---

*The leading writers of the "new classical macroeconomics" are Robert Lucas,
Thomas Sargent, Neil Wallace, and Robert Barro. The leading writers of Post-
Keynesian economics are Joan Robinson, N. Kaldor, J. A. Kregel, L. Pasinetti,
D. M. Nuti, Piero Sraffa, J. Eatwell, G. C. Harcourt, and others in England;
P. Garegnani and A. Roncaglia in Italy; K. R. Bharadwaj and A. Bhaduri in India;
T. K. Rymes and A. Asimakopulos in Canada; and E. J. Nell, Paul Davidson, S.
Weintraub, A. S. Eichner, Basil J. Moore, and others in the United States.

Part 4 begins with a discussion of the predecessors of the Benassy model. Next, the basic logic of the Benassy model is explained in less technical terms, making the complicated analysis less forbidding to non–technically oriented readers. We then proceed to consider Franklin M. Fisher's important contributions to ongoing research in the disequilibrium foundations of equilibrium theory. The book closes with a survey of some other non-Walrasian models such as Harvey Leibenstein's X-Efficiency theory of the firm, behavioral theories of the firm, Post-Keynesian price adjustment models, and implicit contracting theory.

This book is designed for graduate and advanced undergraduate students in economics though a conscious effort has been made to keep basic concepts understandable to a wider audience. The objective is to assist such students to have a better perspective and understanding of the alternative paradigms in their field and the historical development of these paradigms. Secondly, this approach will help them to integrate their studies of micro- and macroeconomics into an understandable whole in preparation for comprehensive examinations in macroeconomics and any further work in the field. By presenting the history of economic thought in the context of lessons for today, and the future, we believe that this book will be a useful organizing device for any student of economics and a useful text in courses such as macroeconomics and the history of economic analysis.

Part I

Contemporary Reinterpretations of Classicism

CHAPTER 1

The "Supply-Side" Economics of Adam Smith

Classical economics and contemporary "supply-side economics"

Contemporary "supply-side economics" emerged as one possible response to the vexing stagflation and other economic problems of our time.[1] The immediate policy concern of contemporary supply-siders has been to redress what they consider to be the destructive effects of demand management and excessive regulatory policies since the 1960s. As stated by James R. Barth, the specifics of contemporary supply-side economics have been "reductions in marginal tax rates, cuts in government spending, a slow and steady growth in the money supply, and regulatory reform."

Almost immediately, most economists realized that the so-called "supply-side emphasis" was not a revolutionary doctrine, nor was it the innovation of the Reagan Administration. Long before the rise of contemporary supply-siders, the general equilibrium models of Patinkin, Hicks, and others under the paradigm of the "grand neoclassical synthesis" had an implicit "supply-side emphasis." These models generally highlight the price system as the equilibriating mechanism and relegate demand management arguments to the background. Individuals most sympathetic to the contemporary version of "supply-side economics" would go further and view it as a reaffirmation of traditional "supply-side" policies to increase the wealth of nations and to achieve an efficient allocation of resources. They would point to the classical economists from Adam Smith to John Stuart Mill and their policies for promoting economic growth.

The major focus and interests of the classical writers were the viability of the economy and the process of economic growth. Viability requires the equality of inputs and outputs. Otherwise, the economy will not be self-sustaining. Growth depends upon the surplus of outputs over inputs and upon the best utilization of the surplus or net product. These ideas are best stated by Vivian Walsh and Harvey Gram:

> [In the classical model] inputs are produced commodities which are treated as variables, and not as parameters. Commodities are produced by means of commodities so that time enters essentially into the economic problem. [The simplest way to illustrate the classical theory is in the context of a one-sector corn model. The economic question would then be:] will the corn produced this year be enough to provide the necessary inputs for next year's production? Here the fundamental concepts are viability and surplus, and the problem of allocating the surplus between the accumulation of capital and luxury consumption over and above subsistence comes to the fore.[2]

As Walsh and Gram document, the classical writers show that, for an economy to be capable of growth, the technology of production must yield a net output over and above inputs. Hence, technology of production emerges as the central concept in classical analysis. It determines not only viability and surplus, but also the natural price and the natural rate of profit in the spirit of von Neumann.[3] Their basic models implicitly assume that the production function is a linear process. If constant returns to scale are assumed, "it is then possible to present the technology for producing corn by a single 'coefficient': the fraction of a unit of corn needed to produce a unit of corn a_{cc}."[4] In the Ricardian subsistence-wage model, workers' consumption is included as part of the means of production, hidden within the technical coefficient a_{cc}. The one-sector corn model may be stated as follows:*

Let Y_c stand for the gross output of corn and $a_{cc}Y_c$ denote the input of corn required for the production of Y_c units of corn. A viable corn economy in which surplus is positive may be characterized by the following equations:

(a) $$a_{cc}Y_c < Y_c, \text{ or, } 1 - a_{cc} > 0$$

(b) $$Y_c = a_{cc}Y_c + ga_{cc}Y_c + \lambda_c Y_c, \text{ or,}$$
        $$a_{cc}Y_c + ga_{cc}Y_c = Y_c - \lambda_c Y_c,$$

*It should be noted that the classical corn model is the prototype of one-sector growth models, such as the Harrod–Domar model and Solow and Swan's neoclassical growth models.

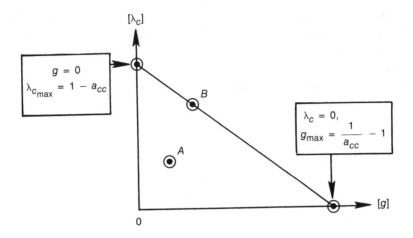

Figure 1.1

The consumption–growth trade-off

where $a_{cc}Y_c$ represents replacement investment; $ga_{cc}Y_c$ represents net investment; and $\lambda_c Y_c$ defines consumption of corn over and above subsistence. The symbol λ_c denotes the fraction of gross output of corn allocated for luxury consumption. Equation (b) is simply the familiar identity equation, $Y = C + I$, or $I = Y - C$.

Dividing both sides by Y_c, we find that equation (b) is transformed into:

(c) $a_{cc} + ga_{cc} = 1 - \lambda_c$, or, $\lambda_c = -a_{cc}g + (1 - a_{cc})$.

This equation describes the consumption–growth trade-off in the corn model, which is illustrated by Figure 1.1.

Maximum luxury consumption, $\lambda_{c_{max}} = 1 - a_{cc}$ (if $g = 0$), is indicated by the limiting point on the vertical axis which measures λ_c. The maximum growth rate of output, $g_{max} = 1/a_{cc} - 1$ (if $\lambda_c = 0$), is represented by the limiting point on the horizontal axis which measures the growth rate, g. The mercantilist misuse of surplus may be represented by a point such as A inside the trade-off line. A high consumption economy may be depicted by point B on the trade-off line. The corn model clearly demonstrates that viability and the rate of growth of output depend entirely on the technology of production.

There is a tendency, when discussing the emphasis of classical economics on economic freedom and the laissez faire approach to economic policy, to minimize, in fact ignore, any real role for government. The classicists did not conceive the market mechanism and the system of economic freedom as arising in a vacuum. Government was to determine and enforce the legal framework necessary for the exercise of economic freedom.* Lionel Robbins observes:

> The invisible hand which guides men to promote ends which were no part of their intention, is not the hand of some god or some natural agency independent of human effort; it is the hand of the law giver, the hand which withdraws from the sphere of the pursuit of self interest those possibilities which do not harmonize with the public good. There is absolutely no suggestion that the market can furnish everything; on the contrary, it can only furnish anything when a host of other things have been furnished another way.[5]

Even the acrimonious critic of the market mechanism Karl Polanyi asserts that "laissez faire was planned; planning was not."[6] Polanyi points out that, although the idea of the self-regulating market mechanism was conceived during the Enlightenment, it was only in the 1820s that the liberal creed began to assume its evangelical fervor. The three basic tenets of this militant liberal creed were: (1) the establishment of a competitive labor market, which was brought into existence for the first time by the Poor Law Amendment Act of 1834, (2) the restoration of the automatic gold standard, which was accomplished by Peel's Bank Act of 1844, and (3) the enforcement of international free trade, which became a reality after passage of the Anti-Corn Law Bill of 1846.†

*Ricardo expressed this idea well:

> To keep men good you must as much as possible withdraw from them all temptations to be otherwise. The sanctions of religion, of public opinion, and of law, all proceed on this principle, and that State is perfect in which all these sanctions concur to make it in the interest of all men to be virtuous, which is the same thing as to say, to use their best endeavor to promote the general happiness. (J. R. McCulloch, editor, *The Works of David Ricardo* [London: John Murray, 1881], p. 554)

†See Karl Polanyi, *The Great Transformation* (Boston: Beacon Press, 1957), Chapter 12. Polanyi argues that these pieces of legislation, passed under the pressure of the philosophic radicals, established laissez faire. Laissez faire is therefore manmade, rather than incumbent in the workings of natural law. In fact, Polanyi asserts that laissez faire is most unnatural. Just as the human body develops systems to protect itself from disease, so do economic systems and economic agents. Economic protectionism is natural in Polanyi's view; unions are a natural response to worker uncertainty. Laissez faire and the legislation by which it was spawned tore apart what was natural. Laissez faire in his view is therefore unnatural.

A simplistic explanation of the invisible hand concept often implies a degree of social harmony that seems most unbelievable in reality. But to believe such harmony was inevitable was not what the classicists were saying. Indeed, they argued that such harmony, a very limited kind of harmony, would have to be created by a system of social control. The classicists envisioned such social control as being established through government and what Warren Samuels has termed "the nonlegal or nondeliberative forces of social control" such as morals, religion, customs, and education. As Samuels states:

> . . . not only did the classicists recognize the created character of the social order . . . but also they were cognizant of the roles of both the legal and nonlegal or nondeliberative forces of social control . . . moreover, and this fact is of great importance, the classicists' case for the relative de-emphasis of the legal forces, i.e. the role of the government in the economy, was in effect premised on the effective operation of the nondeliberative forces of social control.*

The main theme of *The Wealth of Nations*

Adam Smith's major work, *The Wealth of Nations*, is a theoretical attack on mercantilism, showing that mercantilism's incumbent misallocation of economic surplus is harmful to economic growth and must be replaced by a policy of laissez faire. The main theme of the book is economic growth and a subsidiary theme is the efficient allocation of given resources. Contrary to popular belief, Smith discusses the competitive market mechanism and optimal allocation of given resources

---

*Warren J. Samuels, *The Classical Theory of Economic Policy* (Cleveland: The World Publishing Company, 1966) p. 23. Samuels does a superb job of reviewing the classical writers such as Smith, Ricardo, Bentham, J. S. Mill, and others for reference to nonlegal sanctions. In Chapter 2 Samuels presents strong evidence, through quotations, that Smith viewed religion as a force "restricting and channelling behavior" (p. 34); Ricardo's mentioning religion as "one of the forces directing behavior to the virtues promotive of the general happiness" (p. 39); and Mill's "inculcation of morals as a constraint upon behavior" (p. 51). In *The Theory of Moral Sentiments* Smith writes, "When custom and fashion coincide with the natural principles of right and wrong, they heighten the delicacy of our sentiments, and increase our abhorrence for everything which approaches to evil" (pp. 60–61). Samuels presents evidence that the main body of classicists viewed education to be "a social contract operating through the inculcation of individuals in the prevailing moral code, training individuals for a place in the status quo, and impressing upon individuals the existent cosmology within the constraints of which private thought takes place" (p. 66).

according to consumer wants in only two chapters, Chapters 7 and 9 in Book 1. Even these microeconomic writings are growth-oriented. The main theme is aptly reinterpreted by Hla Myint as follows:

> The central principle, which successfully unifies the various classical economic doctrines from Adam Smith to J. S. Mill, embodies the following fundamental proposition: viz. the economic welfare of society can be more effectively promoted by (i) increasing the physical productivity of labour, and (ii) increasing the total volume of economic activity, rather than tamely accepting the given quantity of productive resources and making refined adjustments in allocating them among different industries. From this follow the two major canons of classical economic policy, (i) free trade which extends the scope of the division of labour and brings fresh resources into the productive framework, and (ii) capital accumulation which enables society to maintain a greater quantity of labour.[7]

The fundamental Smithian theme may be illustrated by the following simplified version of Irma Adelman's growth model.[8]

$$(1) \qquad\qquad Y = F(K, L, N).$$

Equation (1) is the aggregate production function. Smith recognized the existence of three factors of production: capital or "stock," which is designated by the symbol K, labor, represented by the symbol L, and land, designated by the symbol N. And Y stands for aggregate output. It should be noted that behind the symbol L is the Smithian doctrine of productive labor. The wealth of nations (Y) is treated as a product of labor productivity and the employment of productive labor. As pointed out by Sir John Hicks, "There is no fixed capital in Smith's (formal) model; but he does have something that corresponds to gross investment . . . The labour which is employed in this 'gross investment' he calls 'productive labour.' Thus it is productive labour that plays the same part in his system as gross investment does in ours."*

Smith saw the productivity of labor as depending on the division of labor which is limited by the extent or size of the market. A liberal

---

*See John Hicks, *Capital and Growth* (New York: Oxford University Press, 1965), p. 37. Productive labor is that which is investment oriented, increasing future output. In contrast, unproductive labor according to Smith can be thought of as that employed in production of consumption goods.

economic policy and an end to mercantilism were viewed as the means of widening the market, promoting the division of labor, and spurring capital accumulation.

It should be noted that the Smithian production function is not subject to the restriction of diminishing marginal returns. Smith was not a "dismal scientist." He optimistically assumed an automatic flow of technological progress permitting continued growth in output and productivity. However, Smith did share with his successors the view of the eventual coming of the stationary state.*

The Smithian aggregate production function nevertheless has two restrictions:

$$(2) \qquad \frac{\partial F}{\partial K} = g(K,\ U),\ \text{and}$$

$$(3) \qquad \frac{\partial F}{\partial L} = h(K,\ U).$$

Equation (2) states that the marginal productivity of capital depends upon the quantity of capital employed and upon the institutional framework of the economy, depicted by the symbol U. Equation (3) refers to the functional relationship between the marginal productivity of labor and the same two independent variables.

Smith believed that the institutional framework was given exoge-

---

*Irma Adelman selects the following passage from *The Wealth of Nations* to demonstrate Smith's belief in the stationary state:

> In a country which has acquired the full complement of riches which the nature of its soil and climate, and its situation with respect to other countries, allowed it to require; which could, therefore, advance no further, and which was not going backwards, both the wages of labour and the profits of stock would probably be very low. In a country fully peopled in proportion to what either its territory could maintain or its stock employ, the competition for employment would necessarily be so great as to reduce the wages of labour to what was barely sufficient to keep up the number of labourers, and the country being already fully peopled, that number could not be augmented. In a country fully stocked in proportion to all the business it had to transact, as great a quantity of stock would be employed in every particular branch as the nature and extent of trade would admit. The competition, therefore, would everywhere be as great, and consequently the ordinary profit as low as possible. (Adam Smith, *The Wealth of Nations* [New York: Random House, 1937], p. 53)

nously. This framework can be thought of as an autonomous policy variable which can shift the production function. Thus, we may write:

$$(4) \qquad\qquad U = \bar{U}.$$

One justification for this equation is the classical writers' belief in the positive role of the state. As pointed out by Lionel Robbins, there were two different strands of thought in the great liberal movement of the eighteenth and nineteenth centuries.[9] The Physiocrats and Frédéric Bastiat represent one strand originating in the tradition of natural law and natural right. The philosophy of natural law stresses that the rational order of nature is the embodiment of justice and that it is eternal, unchanging, and independent of man's private reason. Hence, it is ascertainable by reason.[10] Accordingly, Mercier de la Rivière and Bastiat believed the criterion of economic policy should be conformity with the natural order at all times and in all places. In this view the functions of the state should be minimal. The English classical economists, on the other hand, followed the Utilitarian tradition of Hume and Bentham, in the words of Robbins, "according to which all laws and rights were to be regarded as essentially man-made and to be evaluated according to their effects on the general happiness, long term and short. Smith frequently uses the terminology of 'Naturerecht,' but his arguments are consistently utilitarian in character."[11]

$$(5) \qquad\qquad \frac{dN}{dt} = 0.$$

This equation states that land is fixed in quantity, which is implied by Smith in his statement that land rent is a monopoly price. Therefore the aggregate production function may be written more simply as:

$$(6) \qquad\qquad Y = F(K, L).$$

The growth rate of the annual flow of output may be obtained by differentiating equation (6) with respect to time. Doing so one obtains:

$$(7) \qquad\qquad \frac{dY}{dt} = \frac{\partial F}{\partial K} \frac{dK}{dt} + \frac{\partial F}{\partial L} \frac{dL}{dt} .$$

By substituting equations (2), (3), and (4) into (7), we derive the following expression:

$$(8) \qquad \frac{dY}{dt} = g(K, \bar{U})\frac{dK}{dt} + h(K, \bar{U})\frac{dL}{dt} .$$

The term dK/dt (capital accumulation) is determined by the rate of savings, or parsimony. Smith believed that under normal conditions savings would always be invested and that savings rather than consumption promotes growth. It should be noted that the Smithian theory of savings and investment, together with his real sector analysis (his basic model did not make money a causative factor in the economic process), represents three important features of Say's law. [12]

As to the allocation of aggregate output between savings and consumption, Smith argued that the rate of saving depends crucially upon the rate of profit. As long as there is a positive rate of profit, savings and capital accumulation would continue. This doctrine may be stated symbolically as:

$$(9) \qquad \frac{dK}{dt} = k[r - \bar{r}, Y].$$

where the symbol r represents the rate of profit at time t, $\bar{r}$ symbolizes the minimum value of the rate of profit which covers compensation for risks, and Y represents aggregate output, the source of savings. What determines the rate of profit? Here, Smith brought in his view of the positive function of the state. The rate of profit, he contended, is regulated by the institutional environment, i.e., the degree of monopoly or competition, the extent of regulation of business, the control of international trade, taxation, and so forth. Being an optimist, Smith asserted that liberal economic policy (U) would always ensure a positive rate of profit. The Smithian view is summarized as follows:

$$(10) \qquad r - \bar{r} = m(K, \bar{U}),$$

where

$$\frac{\partial M}{\partial K} < 0.$$

Smith explained the rate of growth of the labor force by his theory of population, which anticipates that of Malthus. Equation (11) depicts the Smithian theory of population.

$$(11) \qquad \frac{dL_s}{dt} = q(w - \bar{w}).$$

The symbol dL_s/dt designates the rate of growth of labor supply, which varies with the difference between the market wage rate w and the subsistence wage rate $\bar{w}$. If the market wage exceeds the subsistence wage, the supply of labor will increase and vice versa. The subsistence wage is that wage rate which keeps the existing labor supply constant, neither increasing or decreasing.

The rate of increase in the demand for labor in Smithian population theory is represented by the following equation:

$$(12) \qquad \frac{dL_d}{dt} = a\frac{dK}{dt} + b\frac{dY}{dt}$$

The term dL_d/dt represents the rate of growth of the demand for labor. The symbols a and b represent the contributions to the rate of growth of the demand for labor by capital accumulation and by the rate of growth of output. Behind the demand for labor function is the well-known wages fund doctrine, which is an integral part of the classical economists' concept of capital. Robert V. Eagly observes.

> Following Quesnay's lead, classical economists defined capital quite comprehensively to include command of all the reproducible inputs used in production, i.e., machinery, raw materials, and labor. The degree of abstraction in the capital concept was considerable. To consider the initial allocation process, the total capital stock was conceptualized to consist not of use specific commodities but of abstract commodities ''in general,'' a malleable putty-like commodity unit that could be allocated either to the wages fund or to the stock of machinery. Such an abstraction permitted classical analysis to concentrate on the problem of capital allocation.*

*See Robert V. Eagly, *The Structure of Classical Economic Theory* (New York: Oxford University Press, 1974), p. 34. Samuel Hollander points out that the British

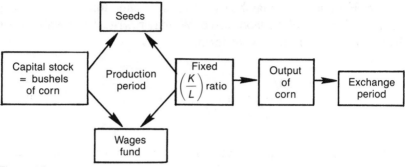

Figure 1.2

Capital stock allocation in classical theory

Let us assume that the homogeneous output in the Smithian model is corn. Capital stock then consists of bushels of corn kept in storage which are saved from the previous production period. This capital stock is divided into two components during the production period: (a) the means of production (seeds) and (b) the means of subsistence for the laborers employed in the production of corn. This second component is the wages fund. Given implicitly the fixed capital–labor ratio which is determined exogenously by technology, capital and labor are jointly demanded. It is in this way that the demand for labor becomes a function of capital accumulation. The allocation of capital stock in classical theory is depicted schematically in Figure 1.2.

(13)
$$\frac{dL_s}{dt} = \frac{dL_d}{dt} .$$

Equation (13) is based on the Smithian assumption that in the long run the supply of labor will be in proportion with the demand for labor.

---

economy of Smith's day was not basically "agricultural." "The agricultural sector itself was actually one of the most capital intensive sectors, and structural change within the manufacturing sector was transforming the nature of the economy. It is clear from Smith's account both of the industry structure and technological change that he was aware of the beginnings of a transition; and it is the trend which matters." See Hollander's *Economics of Adam Smith* (Toronto and Buffalo: University of Toronto Press, 1973), pp. 311–312.

Hence, Equation (12) may be used to describe the forces determining the rate of growth of the labor force. We may rewrite the growth rate of labor supply in the following form:

$$(14) \qquad \frac{dL}{dt} = a\frac{dK}{dt} + b\frac{dY}{dt} .$$

If we substitute equation (14) into the equation for the annual flow of output (equation 8), the following expression is derived:

$$(15) \qquad \frac{dY}{dt} = g(K, \bar{U})\frac{dK}{dt} + h(K, \bar{U})\left(a\frac{dK}{dt} + b\frac{dY}{dt}\right) .$$

By collecting the dy/dt terms on the left-hand side of equation (15) and factoring out the terms in dK/dt on the right-hand side, we obtain the solution of the model:

$$(16) \qquad \frac{dY}{dt} = \frac{dK}{dt}\left\{\frac{g(K, \bar{U}) + ah(K, \bar{U})}{1 - bh(K, \bar{U})}\right\} .$$

The solution succinctly summarizes the main theme of *The Wealth of Nations*. It points out that the rate of growth of output crucially depends upon two elements: (a) capital accumulation and (b) liberal economic policies. Equation (16) not only brings forth the "supply-side emphasis" of Adam Smith in bold relief, but also clearly demonstrates that capital accumulation is the unifying principle tying together the various specific doctrines (viz., the theory of savings and investment, population theory, the wages fund doctrine, the principle of free trade, the theory of value, monetary theory, public finance, and the concept of economic welfare) in one "magnificient dynamics."* Some of these growth-oriented doctrines will be considered in the following section.

*The expression "magnificient dynamics" is coined by William J. Baumol. See his *Economic Dynamics* (New York: The Macmillan Company, 1951), Part 1.

Growth-oriented specific doctrines

Microeconomics

Smith's microeconomics, like his macroeconomics, reflects a preoccupation with the issues of viability and growth. Smith (and other classical economists) divided the problem of price determination into two parts: (a) the natural price and (b) the market price. The natural price is inherent in the production process itself. In the modern terminology of linear programming it is the dual of the primal problem of output maximization. This concept may be explained in the context of the corn model.

The Primal	The Dual
(i) $\lambda_c = (1 - a_{cc}) - a_{cc}g$. (ii) $\lambda_c = 0$, $g_{max} = \dfrac{1}{a_{cc}} - 1$.	(iii) $P_c a_{cc} + r P_c a_{cc} = P_c$ (iv) $a_{cc}(1 + r) = 1$. (v) $r = \dfrac{1}{a_{cc}} - 1$.

Equation (i) (see box) states the trade-off between luxury consumption and growth. Equation (ii) defines the maximum growth rate of output. Turning to the dual problem, equation (iii) describes the production price of corn. The symbol P_c stands for the price of corn; $P_c a_{cc}$ represents the money cost of replacing the means of production; and r is the rate of profit on the value of the capital investment, viz., $P_c a_{cc}$. It should be noted that, in any one-sector model, there is no problem of determining relative prices, for the price of corn in terms of itself is unity. Therefore, after dividing through by P_c and factoring out a_{cc} equation (iii) is transformed into equation (iv). Equation (v) is obtained by rearranging terms in (iv).

Equation (iii) depicts the natural (production) price of corn independent of market exchange. The natural price is embedded in the technology of production and reflects the viability and surplus of the system of production as a whole. It is analogous to the shadow price (accounting price) in linear programming. The dual relationship is shown by the equality of the maximum rate of growth of output

$$g_{max} = \frac{1}{a_{cc}} - 1$$

and the natural rate of profit

$$r = \frac{1}{a_{cc}} - 1.$$

This equality shows simply that the rate of increase of output must exactly cover the interest cost of investment in inputs. The same theorem was derived by von Neumann in his seminal paper ''A Model of General Economic Equilibrium.'' In both the classical corn model and the disaggregated capital (multicommodity) model of von Neumann, the maximum rate of growth of output and the corresponding rate of profit are determined by the technology of production. In the corn model, the technology of production is denoted by the coefficient a_{cc}.

The classical exchange process (including that of Smith) is best illustrated by a heterogeneous commodity model. As in the corn model, the capitalists own the entire capital stock (the means of production) at the beginning of the production period. The existing technology of production determines the allocation of the capital stock. The capitalists also own all of the commodities produced at the end of the production period. Then the market exchange period begins, an exchange envisioned as the exchange of produced goods among capitalists. The purpose of the exchange process is to obtain the inputs required by the next production period. The prices involved in this process are market prices. There need not be immediate conformity with the natural price. When market prices deviate from natural prices, it is a manifestation that conditions of viability and growth of the economy have not been fulfilled.

Competition among the capitalists eventually will bring the market prices in conformity with natural prices. As observed by David P. Levine, ''The market acts exclusively to 'execute' the laws of the production system as those laws are expressed in the production price.''[13] The equilibrating mechanism in the classical system is the movement of capital among the industries, seeking the highest rate of return. As a result of such movements market prices will change; consequently the rate of profit will change also. The optimal set of relative prices, those in conformity with natural prices, is reached when the rate of profit is uniform across all sectors of the economy. Robert V. Eagly observes: "The uniform profit criterion thus makes relative prices dependent upon the size, productivity and distribution of the economy's total capital stock—evidence once again of the all-pervasive importance of capital in classical theory."[14] This is clear evidence of the growth-oriented microeconomics of Smith and the classical economists.

Welfare economics

The welfare economics of Adam Smith is as preoccupied with capital accumulation and economic growth as is his microeconomics. The classical index of economic welfare was stated by Smith in the *Wealth of Nations*, Book 1, Chapter 5. Although the title of the chapter is "Of the Real And Nominal Price Of Commodities, Or Of The Price In Labour, Or Their Price In Money," it, in the words of Mark Blaug, "is not concerned with value theory but with welfare economics, and, in particular, with the problem of index numbers of welfare."[15]

Smith first pointed out that labor "is the real measure of exchangeable value of all commodities."[16] He then elaborated further:

> The real price that every thing costs to the man who wants to acquire it, is the toil and trouble of acquiring it. What every thing is really worth to the man who has acquired it, and who wants to dispose of it or exchange it for something else, is the toil and trouble which it can save to himself, and which it can impose upon other people.[17]

Here Smith considered subjective utility (or the disutility of the "toil and trouble" of labor) as the index of economic welfare. Thus Hla Myint observes: "This passage would suggest that Smith considered the essence of man's struggle against nature as consisting in the outlay of subjective disutility rather than, as Ricardo would say, in the physical unit of labour. Since outlay and return must be comparable, the statement implies that Smith was trying to arrive at a subjective concept of income as distinct from Ricardo's concept of objective physical output.[18]

However, Smith's focus of attention soon shifted from the subjective utility approach to the objective approach of physical output. The reason for this shift was his preoccupation with capital accumulation and economic growth. In the words of Sir John Hicks: "There can be little doubt that Smith intended this chapter [Book II, Chapter III, "Of The Nature, Accumulation, And Employment of Stock"] to be regarded as the center-piece of his whole work. Book I and the earlier chapters of Book II lead up to it; the rest of the work consists, in large, of the application of it."[19] In order to rationalize this change of focus, Smith seems to assume that subjective satisfaction is roughly proportional to the quantity of physical output. His classical successors generally accepted this assumption without modification.

It has generally been taken for granted that the fundamental assumption of classical welfare economics is that consumer sovereignty guided by the "invisible hand" would teleologically achieve a social optimum. However, the main textual evidence of the classical discussion of perfect competition as the efficient allocator of given resources was confined to Book 1, Chapters 7 and 10, of *The Wealth of Nations*. The competitive equilibrium in output markets was considered by Smith in Chapter 7; the competitive factor market equilibrium was discussed in Chapter 10. The only other textual evidence for efficient allocation of given resources is the familiar Ricardian comparative cost doctrine in the theory of international trade. From these scanty sources, one would conclude that the allocative concept of perfect competition is a subsidiary theme in classical economics.

The role of money

Smith also viewed the role of money within a growth-related framework. This is evidenced by his treatment of the nominal quantity of money as an endogenous variable. Smith wrote:

> The quantity of money . . . must in every country naturally increase as the value of the annual produce increases. The value of the consumable goods annually circulated within the society being greater, will require a greater quantity of money to circulate them. A part of the increased produce, therefore, will naturally be employed in purchasing, wherever it is to be had, the additional quantity of gold and silver necessary for circulating the rest. The increase of those metals will in this case be the effect, not the cause, of the public prosperity.[20]

A cursory reading of this passage gives the impression that Smith sounded like the nineteenth-century anti-bullionists. This impression is reinforced by his "real bills doctrine." However, as pointed out by David Laidler:

> Smith was a proponent of banking and paper money, and was in no sense an adherent of any type of "money does not matter" doctrine. His advocacy here hinged on *supply-side considerations* of a type analyzed in the 1960s literature dealing with the influence of money on growth and economic welfare. The issues involved here are clearly long run in nature. . . . Smith's treatment of banking was an integral part of his treatment of the process of economic growth.[21]

As to the Smithian "real bills doctrine," Laidler argues:

> . . . although there can be no doubt that Smith espoused the Real Bills Doctrine, he was not led to argue, as were many later adherents of the fallacy, that the banking system could safely be left to its own devices, even in the absence of specie convertibility. It was not, therefore, a fundamental component of his analysis of banking policy in the same sense as his insistence upon the importance of convertibility. Nothing illustrates this point more clearly than the fact that it was specie convertibility, not any limitation on the type of loans that banks might make, that Smith wished to see written into law.[22]

Fiscal policy

Adam Smith's pervasive concern for economic growth also dominated his discussions of taxation and public debt. In the "Introduction and Plan" to *The Wealth of Nations*, Smith laid down two major determinants of the aggregate supply of output: (1) "the skill, dexterity and judgement with which its labour is generally applied," and (2) "the proportion between the number of those who are employed in useful labor and those who are not so employed." Smith argued that high taxes on wages would hurt these determinants. He wrote:

> If direct taxes upon the wages of labour have not always occasioned a proportionable rise in those wages, it is because they have generally occasioned a considerable fall in the demand for labour. The declension of industry, the decrease in employment for the poor, the diminution of the annual produce of the land and labour of the country, have generally been the effects of such taxes. In consequence of them, however, the price of

labour must always be higher than it otherwise would have been in the actual state of the demand; and the enhancement of price, together with the profit of those who advance it, must always be finally paid by the landlords and the consumers. . . . *Absurd* and *destructive* as such taxes are, however, they take place in many countries.[23]

Smith stressed that taxes on capital and profits would hurt savings and investment and that high import duties would encourage smuggling. He wrote:

High taxes, sometimes by diminishing the consumption of the taxed commodities, and sometimes by encouraging smuggling, *frequently afford a smaller revenue to government than what might be drawn from more moderate taxes*. When the diminution of the revenue is the effect of the diminution of consumption, *there can be but one remedy, and that is the lowering of the tax*. When the diminution of the revenue is the effect of the encouragement given to smuggling, it may perhaps be remedied in two ways; either by diminishing the temptation to smuggle, or by increasing the difficulty of smuggling.[24]

As observed by Robert E. Keleher,[25] the inverse relationship between high tax rates and tax revenue stated by Adam Smith in the preceding passage clearly anticipated the "Laffer curve" of our time. However, arguing that high taxes on a particular commodity might reduce tax revenue associated with the taxed commodity is quite different from arguing that marginal tax rates on income are sufficiently high that greater revenue could be drawn with a lower tax rate.

Adam Smith and his successors generally opposed deficit spending and advocated paying off the national debt. Smith wrote:

In the payment of the interest of the public debt, it has been said, it is the right hand which pays the left. The money does not go out of the country. It is only a part of the revenue of one set of the inhabitants which is transferred to another; and the nation is not a farthing the poorer. This apology is founded altogether in the sophistry of the mercantile system. . . .[26]

Smith further pointed out that the existence of a huge public debt required higher taxes to pay the interest on the debt. Is it safe to presume that Smith would endorse the major elements of today's supply-side economics? Contemporary "supply-siders" would like to think so.

Perspective

The promises of classical economics were to a large extent realized, especially for Great Britain. The United Kingdom was able to monopolize the Industrial Revolution for one hundred years. What is the explanation for this phenomenal success? The answer lies partially in the institutional environment of the time. James T. Laney perceptively observes that the moral basis of capitalism depends upon disciplined, public-spirited citizens who are willing to postpone immediate reward for the sake of future productivity. He writes: "It is important for us to recognize that the basic condition for the emergence of capitalism was the postponement of gratification for the sake of investment and enterprise, in other words, for the sake of future productivity."[27] That these virtues were widely upheld during the classical period is documented by Richard H. Tawney in his *Religion and the Rise of Capitalism* and by Max Weber in his *Protestant Ethic and the Spirit of Capitalism.*[28]

CHAPTER 2

The "Supply-Side" Economics of David Ricardo

Ricardo and a theory of secular distribution

In the preface of *The Principles of Political Economy and Taxation*, David Ricardo states his main theme:

> The produce of the earth—all that is derived from its surface by the united application of labour, machinery and capital, is divided among three classes of the community, namely the proprietor of the land, the owner of the stock or capital necessary for its cultivation, and the labourers by whose industry it is cultivated.
>
> But in different stages of society, the proportions of the whole produce of the earth which will be allotted to each of these classes, under the names of rent, profit, and wages will be essentially different. . . .To determine the laws which regulate this distribution is the principal problem of Political Economy: much as the science has been improved by the writings of Turgot, Stuart, Smith, Say, Sismondi, and others, they afford very little satisfactory information respecting the natural courses of rent, profit, and wages.[1]

The reason for Smith's neglect in developing a rigorous theory of distribution was that his interest was focused on the two main factors responsible for increasing the wealth of nations, i.e., (a) technology; and (b) the employment of productive labor. In developing his arguments, Smith, as Hla Myint points out, adopted the "labor commanded" measure of value as a "cast-iron argument to show that the economic welfare of society could invariably be increased by increasing the amount of savings."*

*Hla Myint explains the Smithian "labor commanded" measure of value by the following arithmetic example: "Let us say that the current social output is made up of 1000 units of wage goods and that out of this 1000 units, 600 units are paid out as

Smith thought that the distribution of income could be explained through the theory of production prices. He maintained that the production prices of every commodity, including the supply price of the means of production, could be reduced to wages, profits, and rent. Thus Maurice Dobb refers to the Smithian distribution doctrine as an "adding up theory,"[2] which Harry G. Johnson considers to be "no theory of distribution at all."[3] In the opinion of Alessandro Roncaglia, total decomposition of price into wages, profits, and rent is impossible. He says:

> In fact, whenever there is at least one commodity directly or indirectly necessary for the production of all commodities in the economy [a "basic product" in Sraffa's terminology], the cost of production of each commodity will include a residual, and no matter how many times the process of reduction is repeated this residual cannot be eliminated, even as the process of reduction tends to infinity.[4]

Ricardo criticized Smith for mixing up production price with the problem of distribution. He also objected to the Smithian treatment of wages, profits, and rents in the "total decomposibility theorem" as being independent of one another. Since Ricardo's objective was to examine the laws which regulate the distribution of net product (surplus) among the three classes of society, and since he considered the capitalist class to be the engine of growth, it was important to him to be able to determine whether the capitalists would receive additional resources when distribution changed. Thus Smith's "labor commanded" measure of value was not suitable for Ricardo's purpose, for the quantities expressed by the "labor commanded" measure were not independent of relative prices and the money wage rate. What Ricardo

---

wages and 200 units each are paid out as rents and profits. Then according to Smith this state of affairs means that: (i) the current social output of 1000 wage units is the product of only 600 units of labor 'embodied' in its production. (Given the money wage rate of one unit per man, the 1000 units divided by the given money wage rate can command 1000 units of labor); (ii) if the entire amount of the 1000 units have been saved and reinvested or 'embodied' in the next year's production, the social output of that year would be raised very appreciably. Thus, assuming labor yields a constant return, if 600 units of labor can produce 1000 units of wage goods, then 1000 units of labour can produce 1666 units. Assuming the supply of labour remains elastic at the wage of one wage unit per man, then this would give society a command over 1666 units of labour" (Hla Myint, *Theories of Welfare Economics* [New York: Augustus M. Kelley, 1948], p. 21).

sought was an invariant measure of value which would be independent of distribution.

The main thrust of the Ricardian theory can be summarized in the flow diagram in Figure 2.1. This chapter considers each component in the diagram and then discusses some of the lasting influences of the Ricardian analysis.

Ricardo expounded the "labor embodied" theory both as an invariable measure and as the source of value. He asserted:

> The value of a commodity, or the quantity of any commodity for which it will exchange, depends on the relative quantity of labour which is necessary for its production, and not on the greater or lesser compensation which is paid for that labour.[5]

The introduction of capital does not invalidate the "embodied labor" theory in Ricardo's view. He maintained that the same principle would still hold true.

> Not only [does] labour applied immediately to commodities affect their value, but the labour also which is bestowed on the implements, tools, and buildings with which such labour is assisted.[6]

In other words, Ricardo treated capital as "labor embodied" in the capital goods produced in the previous periods. However, Ricardo was not a diehard "labor embodied" theorist. As observed by George J. Stigler, Ricardo's emphasis on the quantitative importance of labor was an empirical, rather than an analytical, proposition. "An analytical statement concerns functional relations; an empirical statement takes account of the quantitative significance of the relationships."[7] Stigler further points out:

> McCulloch, Bailey, and Malthus correctly understood Ricardo's theory to be a cost-production theory excluding rent, and De Quincey should probably be added to this group. The theory was understood as a simple labor-quantity theory by Say and Mill, and also by Torrens. It is worth repeating that Ricardo accepted Malthus' analysis and rejected Mill's. The theory was more widely understood in its correct sense in Ricardo's time than later times.[8]

The same view was expressed by John M. Cassels in his article "A Re-Interpretation of Ricardo on Value." Cassels emphasized that

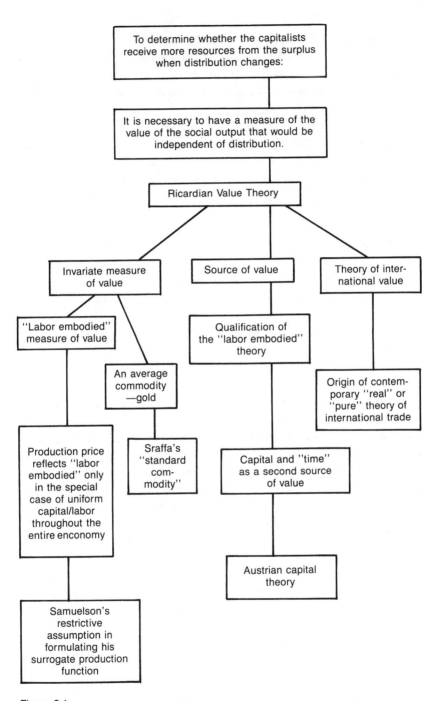

Figure 2.1

The main thrust of Ricardian theory

"Ricardo's famous chapter on value was never intended as an exposition of any theory of value in the accepted sense of the term but was written for the special purpose of providing him a particular logical link that was required in his elaborate chain of reasoning about the dynamics of distribution."[9]

The special purpose Ricardo envisioned was to use the "labor embodied" theory to clinch his arguments against the corn laws.* In order to simplify the analysis, Ricardo formulated a simple corn model to present his case. Its policy orientation and Ricardo's non-Walrasian methodology prompted Joseph A. Schumpeter to call it "the Ricardian vice."[10]

The Ricardian corn model

The Ricardian corn model consists of four building blocks: (i) the West–Malthus–Ricardo theory of differential rent; (ii) the wages fund doctrine; (iii) the subsistence theory of wages; and (iv) the "embodied labor" theory of value. Ricardo describes the first two building blocks in *Essay on the Influence of a Low Price of Corn on the Profit of Stock* (1815) and the last two in *The Principles of Political Economy and Taxation* (1817).

Ricardo's wages fund theory is similar to that of Adam Smith. The subsistence wage theory is derived from the Malthusian theory of population. The main idea of the theory of differential rent is that land is variable in quality and fixed in supply. Therefore, when a country is sparsely populated, only the best quality land is cultivated. As the population grows, it becomes necessary to cultivate land of inferior quality. Thus, there are diminishing returns in agriculture. Ricardo's argument is that, should the corn laws be enacted, England would be condemned to raise her required food from her fixed supply of land. As the population grew and the margin of cultivation was extended, the owners of better quality land would receive rent. Rent per acre thus represents the difference between the net profit per acre on the better quality land and that on the inferior land. If no rent were charged on the better quality land, there would be no incentive for farmers to extend the margin of cultivation to inferior land. At the extensive margin of cultivation, there would be zero rent. The better quality land would be

---

*The term "corn" was used sometimes to mean not only grain but all agricultural wage goods. The purpose of the "corn laws" was to protect British wheat farmers by prohibiting foreign wheat import.

intensively cultivated. However, the principle of diminishing marginal returns would also apply to the intramarginal land, with the intensive margin of cultivation reached when the net profit per acre disappears.[11]

As a master model builder, Ricardo demonstrated his superior skill by eliminating rent as a component of the production costs of the homogeneous wage-good, corn. He pointed out that rent "is never a new creation of value but always a part of the revenue already created." Ricardo wrote:

> The value of corn is regulated by the quantity of labour bestowed on its production on that quality of land, or with that portion of capital, which pays no rent. Corn is not high because a rent is paid, but a rent is paid because corn is high; and it has been justly observed that no reduction would take place in the price of corn although landlords should forego the whole of their rent.[12]

The reasoning behind this famous passage was perceptively explained by Mark Blaug as follows: "In the Ricardian system, resources are viewed as shifting between land and industry, never between different uses of land. Since land has no alternative uses, rental payments do not affect the supply price of agricultural produce. 'Pure rents' are transfer costs and involve no using up of resources."[13]

Ricardo further asserted that the interests of the landlords are always opposed to the interest of every other class in the community. When the price of corn increases owing to increased difficulty in production, "the landlord is doubly benefited. . . . First, he obtains a greater share, and, secondly, the commodity in which he is paid is of greater value."[14]

The Ricardian corn model can be described by two alternative graphical presentations. We shall consider the Kaldorian formulation first[15] and then summarize Baumol's formulation.[16] The agricultural sector of the economy may be depicted by the Kaldorian diagram in Figure 2.2.

The vertical axis of Figure 2.2 measures the quantity of the homogeneous wage-good, corn, while the horizontal axis measures the amount of labor employed in agriculture. The curve Ap represents the average product of labor and the curve Mp denotes labor's marginal product. The downward slope of the two curves reflects the assumption of diminishing marginal returns in agriculture. Given the demand for food, the quantity of labor employed is determined by the distance $0M$

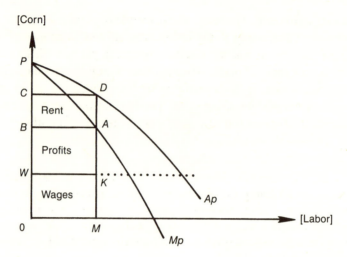

Figure 2.2

Kaldor's rendition of the Ricardian corn model

Source: Nicholas Kaldor, ''Alternative Theories of Distribution,'' *Review of Economic Studies,* *23* (2), 1955–56.

on the horizontal axis in Figure 2.2. Given $0M$ units of labor, total output of corn is represented by the rectangle $0CDM$. Rent is the difference between the average and marginal products of labor. The average product of labor is indicated by the vertical distance DM (= $C0$) and the marginal product of labor is denoted by the vertical distance AM (= $B0$). Total rent is represented by the rectangle $BCDA$. Note that the marginal product of labor is not equal to the wage rate. It is the sum of wages and profits. Here $0W$ (= KM) depicts the long-run subsistence wage rate which is assumed to be constant over time and is determined by the Malthusian theory of population. In modern parlance, the Ricardian hypothesis implies an infinitely elastic supply curve of labor indicated by the horizontal line WK. What is the demand for labor in this model? It is the agricultural wages fund indicated by the rectangle $0WKM$, which shows the total quantity of labor employed at the subsistence-wage rate $0W$.

What about the rate of profit? It is represented by the ratio r = profits/wages. In Figure 2.2, $r = ((AK - KM)/KM) \times 100\% = ((AK/KM) - 1) \times 100\%$. Inasmuch as KM is assumed to be constant, it follows that the rate of profit varies with AK. As capital accumulates, the quantity of labor employed will grow, so that any addition to the total wages fund will tend to be a horizontal addition pushing the vertical line *KM* to the right.

Ricardo was able to draw precise predictions about the secular changes in the distributive shares from his corn model. These predictions are demonstrated by Figure 2.3. The initial equilibrium situation is represented by the rectangle 0*CDM*. The distributive shares are: rent (*BCDA*), profits (*WBAK*), and wages (0*WKM*). Over the course of capital accumulation and population growth, the margin of cultivation is extended. As a result of diminishing marginal productivity of labor at the margin, the secular distributive share of the landlords will rise at the expense of the capitalists' share. This tendency of increasing rent and a failing rate of profit is represented in Figure 2.3 by the rectangle 0*FEN*, which is the total corn output resulting from the employment of 0*N* units of labor. Total rent is now *GFEH*, which is greater than the original rectangle *BCDA*. Total profits are indicated by the rectangle *WGHL*, which is smaller than the original rectangle *WBAK*. Total wages also rise from 0*WKM* to 0*WLN*. Since the subsistence-wage rate remains unchanged at 0*W*, the rate of profit consequently falls.

However, the "stationary state" eventually will arrive. The "doomsday" is indicated by the point *U* where total corn output is represented by the rectangle 0*TSR*; total rent is denoted by the rectangle *WTSU*; and the total subsistence-wage bill is the rectangle 0*WUR*. Thus, the total output of corn is entirely eaten up by rent and wages. Profits are entirely wiped out. This is Ricardo's indictment of the corn laws.

The model implies that, should England follow the law of comparative labor costs and acquire additional corn through free trade, the "doomsday" would be postponed. Alternatively, technical progress in agriculture could put off the "doomsday" for some time. Free trade or technical progress would be reflected in an upward shift of the *Ap* and *Mp* curves in Figure 2.3. However, unless the two curves could be shifted up continuously, the inevitability of the "doomsday" would not be eliminated.

An alternative description of Ricardo's predictions has been suggested by William J. Baumol (Figure 2.4). The horizontal axis measures the size of the working population, while the vertical axis measures total product and total wage payments after deducting rent. Since the subsistence-wage rate is constant, total wage payments are given by the straight line 0*S* through the origin. The slope of 0*S* indicates the

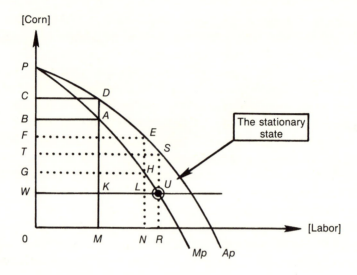

Figure 2.3

Ricardo and the stationary state

Source: Nicholas Kaldor, ''Alternative Theories of Distribution,'' *Review of Economic Studies*, 23 (2), 1955–56.

subsistence-wage rate; $0P$ represents the total product of corn after deducting rent. The shape of the production function reflects the assumption of diminishing returns in agriculture and conveys the idea that rent payments will grow simultaneously with the increase in the working population.

The prediction of a falling rate of profit and the arrival of the ''stationary state'' are explained as follows: Suppose that we start with a working population of $0R_1$. Total subsistence-wage payments will be $R_1 S_1$ and an amount $S_1 P_1$ will be left over for profits. This will induce capital accumulation, which, in turn, will drive market-wage payments up to $R_1 P_1$. Once the disparity between the market-wage payments and the subsistence-wage payments takes place, capital accumulation will cease. In the meantime, following the Malthusian theory, population will increase. As the resulting supply of labor exceeds the demand for labor, competition among laborers for employment will drive the market-wage rate down to the subsistence level again. Consequently, population growth will be checked at the point $0R_2$. Once more a profit

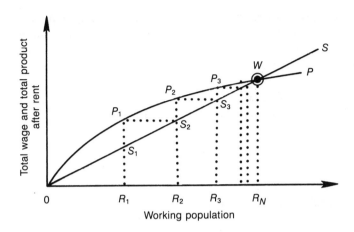

Figure 2.4

Baumol's rendition of Ricardo's corn model

Source: William J. Baumol, *Economic Dynamics, An Introduction* (New York: The Macmillan Co., 1951), p. 18. Reprinted with permission of Macmillan Publishing Company from *Economic Dynamics, An Introduction* by William J. Baumol. Copyright © 1951 by William J. Baumol.

margin will appear (the distance S_2P_2), and capital accumulation will again take place. Market-wage payments are soon driven up to R_2P_2, population grows to $0R_3$, and so on, in a series of steps represented by the stepped line $S_1P_1 S_2P_2 S_3P_3 \ldots$, gradually approaching the point W, where the two curves intersect. At W, total output is completely exhausted by rent and subsistence-wage payments. The rate of profit is zero and the "stationary state" has arrived.

Ricardo's standard commodity

To generalize the simple corn model, Ricardo sought to find the link between distribution in the agricultural sector and distribution in the community as a whole. He found the introduction of fixed capital to greatly complicate the problem, for an element of "time" was thus introduced into the production process. The ratio of fixed capital to the circulating capital paid to labor (the capital–labor ratio) may differ among occupations, fixed capital may differ in durability, and the rates of turnover of circulating capital may differ. Ricardo wrote:

It appears, then, that the division of capital into different proportions of fixed and circulating capital, employed in different trades, introduces a considerable modification to the rule, which is of universal application when labour is almost exclusively employed in production. . . .[17]

In section 4 of Chapter 1 "On Value," Ricardo gave two arithmetic examples to illustrate the necessary qualifications to the "labor embodied" theory.

CASE I: The introduction of fixed capital into the production of the more expensive commodity. Suppose that two men each employ 100 laborers each year, but in the second year one uses machines produced in the first year. In the second year, the machine-user must make not only the regular return on the circulating capital used to employ labor, but a rate of profit on the circulating capital invested must be included in the production price of the commodity.

Year (1)—One man employs 100 laborers at the wage rate of £50 per man to construct a machine. So the total wage bill is £5,000. The other man also employs 100 laborers at the wage rate of £50 per man to grow corn. His total wage bill is £5,000. At the end of the year, the value of the machine = the value of the corn = £5,000 plus 10 percent profit = £5,500.

Year (2)—One employs 100 men = £5,000 to grow corn, as before; the value of the corn = £5,000 plus £500 = £5,500. The other employs 100 = £5,000 plus capital worth £5,500 to produce cloth; the value of the cloth = £5,000 plus £500 plus 10 percent of £5,500 = £6,050.

Ricardo points out:

> Here, then, are capitalists employing precisely the same quantity of labour annually on the production of their commodities, and yet the goods they produce differ in value on account of the different quantities of fixed capital.[18]

CASE II: Variations in the period of production. Suppose that two commodities each require 40 man-years to produce; in one case, 20 men are employed for two years, and in the other 40 men for one year.

Commodity (1)—In the first year 20 laborers are employed to produce the commodity at the wage rate of £50 per man. The total wage bill equals £1,000. The value of the output is £1,000 plus 0.1 (£1,000) or £1,100. In the second year, the same number of men are employed at the same wage rate. The total wage bill is £1,000. But 10 percent must be earned also on the investment made in the first year. The total value of output for the two years is £1,100 plus £1,100 plus 0.1(£1,100) = £2,310.

Commodity (2)—To produce the second good, the capitalist employs the entire 40 men in one year at the wate rate of £50 per man. His total wage bill = £2,000; the value of his output = £2,000 plus 0.1(£2,000) = £2,200.

Ricardo observes:

> This case appears to differ from the last, but is, in fact, the same. In both cases the superior price of one commodity is owing to the greater length of time which must elapse before it can be brought to market.[19]

Ricardo thus included the remuneration of capital in production costs and admitted that "waiting" (or time) was also a source of value. This implies that any change in money wage rates or in the rate of profit will alter the structure of relative prices and therefore the valuation of the output to be distributed. Since Ricardo's theory of value is subsidiary to his theory of distribution, another invariant measure had to be found. Ricardo believed that a "standard commodity" would provide an "invariable measure of value." He wrote:

> Neither gold, then, nor any other commodity, can ever be a perfect measure of value for all things; but I have already remarked that the effect on the relative prices of things, from a variation in profits, is comparatively slight; that by far the most important effects are produced by the varying quantities of labour required for production; and, therefore, if we suppose this important cause of variation removed from the production of gold, we shall probably possess as near an approximation to the standard measure of value as can be theoretically conceived. May not gold be considered as a commodity produced with such proportions of the two kinds of capital as approach nearest to the average quantity employed in the production of most commodities? May not these proportions be so nearly equally distant from the two extremes, the one where little fixed

capital is used, the other where little labour is employed, as to form a just mean between them?*

Ricardo then pointed out:

> If, then, I may suppose myself to be possessed of a standard so nearly approaching to an invariable one, the advantage is that I shall be able to speak of the variations of other things without embarrassing myself on every occasion with the consideration of the possible alteration in the value of the medium in which price and value are estimated.[20]

Although the choice of metallic money as the invariable measure was just a hypothesis, Ricardo intended to show that a rise in wages would raise the price of all commodities produced largely with embodied labor or with capital of less than average durability and that a rise in wages would lower the relative prices of goods produced with fixed capital of more than average durability. Ricardo's idea of using a "standard commodity" as the invariable measure of value has been demonstrated by Piero Sraffa. Sraffa showed how such a commodity might be formed as a composite good. His analysis will be discussed in the following section.

The lasting influences of Ricardo: the "Sraffian Revolution"

The "Ricardian problem" was solved by Piero Sraffa† in his *Production of Commodities by Means of Commodities* in 1960.[21] The main

---

*David Ricardo, *The Principles of Political Economy and Taxation* (London: J. M. Dent & Sons Ltd., 1955) pp. 28–29. It is interesting to note that Ricardo considered that the effect on relative prices of a change in the total wage bill and in the rate of profit "could not exceed 6 or 7 percent" (p. 22). Hence George J. Stigler refers to the Ricardian theory as the "93 percent labor theory of value." Stigler observes: "I can find no basis for the belief that Ricardo had an analytical labor theory of value, for quantities of labor are not the only determinants of relative values. Such a theory would have to reduce all obstacles of production to expenditures of labor or assert the irrelevance or non-existence of non-labor obstacles, and Ricardo does not embrace that view. On the other hand, there is no doubt that he held what may be called an empirical labor theory of value, that is, a theory that the relative quantities of labor required in production are the dominant determinants of relative values" (George C. Stigler, "Ricardo and the 93 Per Cent Labor Theory of Value," reprinted from the *American Economic Review*, 47, June 1958, in his *Essays in the History of Economics* [Chicago: University of Chicago Press, 1965], p. 333).

†The label "Sraffian Revolution" was given by Alessandro Roncaglia. See his essay "The Sraffian Revolution" in *Modern Economic Thought*, edited by Sidney

objective of his book was to provide an alternative to the modern marginal theory of relative prices. An integral part of the Sraffian analysis is the "standard commodity," which serves as the invariable measure of value to distinguish changes in relative prices caused by changes in distribution from those relative price changes resulting from changes in the technique of production. There are several by-products of the terse Sraffian theory. One of these is the possibility of capital reversal and reswitching which caused the Post-Keynesians to question neoclassical capital theory. The so-called "Cambridge controversies in the theory of capital" will be considered in Part 3 of this book. Another important by-product of the Sraffian theory is the purging of Say's law from the classical concepts. As observed by Alessandro Roncaglia:

> In the conception of the economy implicit in Sraffa's analysis, the decisions of the entrepreneurs are independent because they are assumed to be logically antecedent to, and not concomitant with, the decisions of the consumers. The elements of uncertainty that characterize entrepreneurial decision making are thus placed in the forefront of the analysis. This uncertainty should be considered as "structural" in nature, for it stems directly from the very organization of the economic system around several diversified decision-making centres.[22]

In this respect, Roncaglia asserts that "Sraffa's research on relative prices also provides the opportunity to purify the Keynesian theory of any marginal residuals.[23]

The chain of reasoning leading to Sraffa's solution to the "Ricardian problem" may be depicted as in Figure 2.5. In the preface of his book, Sraffa emphasizes:

> This investigation is concerned exclusively with such properties of an economic system as do not depend on changes in the scale of production or in the proportions of "factors". . . . The marginal approach requires

---

Weintraub (University of Pennsylvania Press, 1977), pp. 163–177. In his examination of the Marxian "transformation problem," Paul A. Samuelson made passing reference to what he called "this age of Leontief and Sraffa." See Samuelson's essay, "Understanding the Marxian Notion of Exploitation: A Summary of the So-Called Transformation Problem Between Marxian Values and Competitive Prices" in the *Journal of Economic Literature*, 9 (2), June 1971. Subsequently, A. L. Levine wrote an article entitled "This Age of Leontief . . . And Who? An Interpretation" in the same journal, *12* (3), September, 1974.

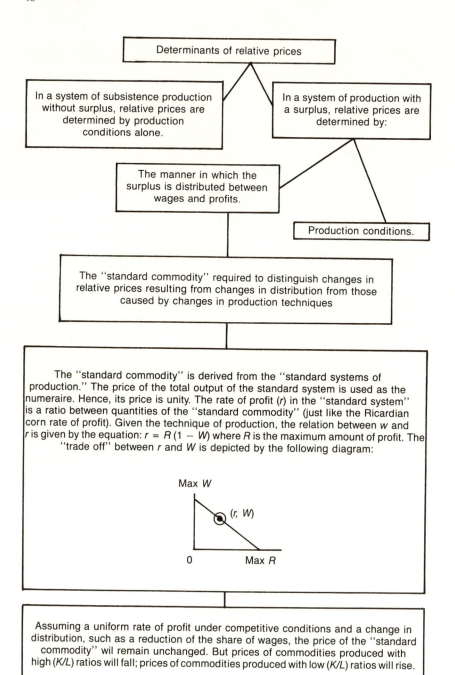

Figure 2.5

Sraffa's "invariable measure of value"

attention to be focused on change, for without change either in the scale of an industry or in the "proportions of the factors of production" there can be neither marginal product nor marginal cost.[24]

Since Sraffa considers the case where there are no changes in output and no changes in the proportions in which different means of production are used, the question of variation or constancy of returns simply does not arise.

The main theme of the book is the analysis of relative prices. Sraffa observes that, in the case of an extremely simple society which produces just enough to maintain itself (production for subsistence), relative prices are determined by production conditions alone. Sraffa writes:

> There is a unique set of exchange-values which if adopted by the market restores the original distribution of the products and makes it possible for the process to be repeated; such values spring directly from the methods of production.[25]

In other words, this is the Sraffian version of the classical natural prices considered in Chapter 1 of this book.

On the other hand, if the economy's production system generates a surplus (over and above the minimum necessary for replacement and subsistence), the problem of distributing the surplus appears. In this case, the determinants of relative prices are: (a) conditions of production and (b) the manner in which the surplus is distributed between wages and profits. Surplus may be considered the national income which will be exhausted by the payments of wages and profits. It follows that variations in the distribution between wages and profits will cause relative prices to change. In the extreme case where the whole national income goes to wages, the relative prices of the commodities produced would conform to the "labor embodied" theory of value. The other extreme case would be where profits exhaust the entire surplus. What concerns Sraffa is the problem of determining changes in relative prices caused by changes in the wage share between the two limiting cases. It should be noted that, in adopting variable wages, Sraffa departs from the classical subsistence-wage model of Ricardo. In doing so, Sraffa points out: "The quantity of labour employed in each industry has now been represented explicitly, taking the place of the corresponding quantities of subsistence."[26]

An arithmetic illustration of the actual system with surplus is given by Sraffa in the accompanying tabulation.[27]

T. iron		T. coal		Qr. wheat		Labour		
90	+	120	+	60	+	3/16	=	180 t. iron
50	+	125	+	150	+	5/16	=	450 t. coal
40	+	40	+	200	+	8/16	=	480 qr. wheat
180		285		410		1		

Here, "since iron happens to be produced in a quantity just sufficient for replacement (180 t.), the national income (surplus) includes only coal and wheat and consists of 165 t. of the former and 70 qr. of the latter."[28] All three industries are defined to be basic industries. A basic good (in a system without joint products) is defined as one which enters as an input in the production of all commodities directly or indirectly. A nonbasic good is one that does not enter as an input into a basic good. Nonbasic goods have no part in the determination of the system of prices.

Sraffa takes the value of the national income as a numeraire. Its price, therefore, is unity. "It thus becomes the standard in terms of which the wages and prices are expressed."[29] Once a numeraire is arbitrarily chosen, Sraffa points out that the study of price movements following a change in distribution becomes complicated:

It is impossible to tell [for] any particular price fluctuation whether it arises from the peculiarities of the commodity which is being measured or from those of the measuring standard. The relative peculiarities . . . can only consist in the inequality in the proportions of labour to means of production in the successive "layers" in to which a commodity and the aggregate of its means of production can be analysed; for it is such an inequality that makes it necessary for the commodity to change in value relative to its means of production as the wage changes.[30]

To obtain an "invariable measure of value," Sraffa sought a "standard commodity" which would be invariate in price with respect to the aggregate means of production. This condition is met only by an industry that produces a "standard commodity" using inputs (means of production) which are physically homogeneous with the output produced. The derivation of the "standard commodity" is illustrated by Sraffa as follows:[31]

First, the "standard system" is obtained by reducing the production equations for iron and coal in the actual system by a certain percentage. A fraction of 3/5 is extracted from the means of production and the output of the coal industry. The reduced production equation for the coal industry is:

30 iron + 75 coal + 90 wheat + 3/16 labour = 270 t. coal*

A fraction of 3/4 is extracted uniformly from the means of production and the output of the wheat industry. The reduced production equation for the wheat industry is:

30 iron + 30 coal + 150 wheat + 6/16 labour = 360 qr. wheat

The reduced-scale system is the "standard system," which consists of the following three equations in the accompanying tabulation.

90 iron +	120 coal +	60 wheat +	3/16 labour =	180 t. iron
30 iron +	75 coal +	90 wheat +	3/16 labour =	270 t. coal
30 iron +	30 coal +	150 wheat +	6/16 labour =	360 qr. wheat
150	225	300	12/16	

In Sraffa's words, "the proportions in which the three commodities are produced in the new system (180 : 270 : 360) are equal to those in which they enter its aggregate means of production (150 : 225 : 300)."[32] The "standard commodity" sought is accordingly made up in the proportions: (150/150 : 225/150 : 300/150) = (180/180 : 270/180 : 360/180) = (1 t. iron: 1.5 t. coal: 2 qr. wheat).

Next, Sraffa derives the "standard ratio" from the "standard system." Since in the "standard system" the three commodities are produced in the same proportion as they enter the aggregate means of production, the implication is that the rate by which the quantity produced exceeds the quantity used up in production is the same for each of them. In the above example the rate of surplus for each commodity is 20 percent:

*3/5(50) = 30; 3/5(125) = 75; 3/5(150) = 90; 3/5(5/16) = 3/16; and 3/5(450) = 270.

$(90 + 30 + 30) (1 + 0.20) = 180$ t. iron
$(120 + 75 + 30) (1 + 0.20) = 270$ t. coal
$(60 + 90 + 150) (1 + 0.20) = 360$ qr. wheat

The 20/100 ratio is what Sraffa calls the "standard ratio."

The "standard ratio," R, is the maximum technically determined rate of surplus for the "standard system." J. A. Kregel observes:

> As the rate of surplus is the same for all processes there is no problem of aggregation. Thus the standard ratio may be determined irrespective of the prices of the goods and the ratio is invariant even when all the commodites are multiplied by their prices. Because of the nature of the standard system, the proportions of the component commodities in the ratio of aggregate net product to the aggregate means of production will be unchanged when the net product is divided in any proportions between wages and profits (despite the necessary concomitant changes in prices). Thus the rate of surplus is the same in both physical and value terms when the division of the surplus between wages and profits changes.[33]

With the aid of the "standard commodity," Sraffa makes a general statement about the relationship between the proportion of the surplus paid as wages and the rate of profit, r, in the "standard system." This relationship is depicted by the straight line wage–profit frontier in Figure 2.6.

The equation for Sraffa's wage–profit frontier is: $r = R(1 - W)$ where W is the proportion of the surplus (net product) of the "standard system" that goes to wages and R is the maximum rate of profit. The actual rate of profit is represented by the symbol r. The derivation of the wage–profit equation is as follows:

(1) r = profits/means of production = P/M
(2) R = surplus/means of production = S/M
(3) $r/R = P/S$
(4) $S = 1 = W + P$, or $P = 1 - W$
(5) $r/R = 1 - W$, or $r = R(1 - W)$.

One of the most important by-products of Sraffian theory is that it provided a stepping stone in the "Cambridge controversies" in capital theory. In the opinion of J. A. Kregel:

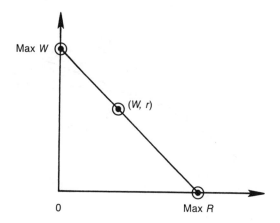

Figure 2.6

The wage–profit frontier

Sraffa reaches his most forceful conclusions concerning the effect of the rate of profits and distribution on the valuation problem by extending the results of the dated labour and fixed capital approaches to the problem of the choice of techniques of production. It is in this exposition that Sraffa's "critique" of existing economic theory (as suggested by the subtitle of his book) is most explicit.[34]

The neoclassical theory of the choice of techniques assumes that the cost of each of the existing techniques is known and invariant to different wage rates and profit rates. The orthodox neoclassical proposition is that high capital intensity (a high capital–labor ratio) is always associated with a low rate of profit and a high wage rate. Behind this neoclassical theorem is the principle of factor substitution. A low rate of profit means capital is the abundant factor; the high wage rate indicates that labor is the scarce factor. In order to maximize profits and minimize costs, entrepreneurs will choose the technique of production that uses the cheaper factor more than the expensive factor. The neoclassical capital deepening theorem may be represented by the familiar diagram in Figure 2.7.

If the assumption of invariant costs is replaced by the assertion that the costs of constructing different techniques vary when the rates of wages and profit change, then the neoclassical theorem is invalidated.

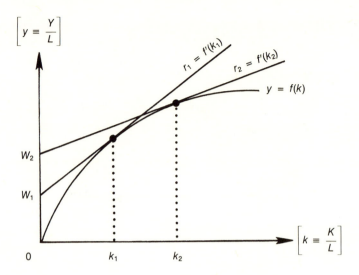

Figure 2.7

The neoclassical capital deepening theorem

This is what Sraffa does in employing an operation of "reduction to dated quantities of labour." This operation is one "by which, in the equation of a commodity, the different means of production used are replaced with a series of quantities of labour, each with its appropriate date."[35]

Following Sraffa, take the equation which represents the production of a commodity "*a*," where the wage rate, the input prices, and also the output price, P_a, are expressed in terms of the "standard commodity":

$$(A_a p_a + B_a p_b + \ldots + K_a p_k)(1 + r) + L_a w = A p_a$$

where "*a*," "*b*," . . . ,"*k*" represent commodities, each produced by a separate industry. Sraffa calls A the quantity annually produced of "*a*"; B the similar quantity of "*b*"; and so on. A_a, B_a, . . . , K_a represent the quantities of "*a*," "*b*," . . . ,"*k*" annually used by the industry which produces the output A.

By "reduction to dated quantities of labour," Sraffa asserts that the means of production of output A (i.e., $A_a + B_a + \ldots + K_a$) can be replaced by their own means of production and quantities of labor, each with appropriate "date." Thus Sraffa is able to express prices in a series composed of terms containing wages and rates of profit with a finite upper limit, the maximum rate of profit, R.

Using an example of J. A. Kregel,[36] suppose there are two techniques, each requiring 25 periods for construction and each requiring 20 units of labor but applied in different time patterns. Technique A requires that all of the 20 units of labor be applied during period 8; technique B spreads the application of labor, requiring 19 units at the beginning of construction and then applying one unit during the last period before completion. Thus, the construction costs of A and B will be:

$$\text{Cost of A} = w0(1 + r)^1 + \ldots + w20L(1 + r)^8 + \ldots + w0(1 + r)^{25}$$

$$\text{Cost of B} = w19L(1 + r)^1 + \ldots + w0(1 + r)^8 + \ldots + wL(1 + r)^{25}$$

If the real wage rate is equal to one, then the rate of profit is equal to zero (the maximum W on the wage–profit frontier). As the rate of profit rises, the real wage falls. Thus there will be a real wage value associated with each rate of profit above zero; R is reached when the real wage falls to zero. Kregel gives a numerical illustration of this phenomenon in the accompanying tabulation.

Rate of profit (r)	Real wage (w)
0	1
5	4/5
10	3/5
15	1/5
20	1/5
25	0

Source: J. A. Kregel, The Reconstruction of Political Economy: An Introduction to Post-Keynesian Economics (New York: John Wiley and Sons, 1973), p. 95. Reprinted by permission of Macmillan, London and Basingstoke.

Thus for a rate of profit of 0.05 and a real wage of 4/5 the costs of the two techniques will be:

Cost of A $= 4/5w \times 20L(1 + 0.05)^8$

Cost of B $= 4/5w \times 19L(1 + 0.05)^1 + 4/5w \times 1L(1 + 0.05)^{25}$

The above illustration shows clearly that the relative costs of the two techniques change at different rates of profit. Technique B is cheaper at low rates of profit and becomes more expensive at high rates of profit. Hence, there exists the possibility of "capital reversal" and "double switching." These phenomena are documented by G. C. Harcourt in his 1972 book, *Some Cambridge Controversies in the Theory of Capital*.[37]

Ricardo and Post-Keynesian economics

It may sound paradoxical that the classicist, Ricardo, should be embraced by the Post-Keynesians. However, Post-Keynesians have repeatedly stated that their work is a more or less conscious return to the method, if not the exact theorems, of Ricardo. Luigi L. Pasinetti observes:

> In spite of Keynes' own understandable enthusiasm for Malthus (in view of the latter's treatment of effective demand), and in spite of Keynes' frequent harsh remarks on Ricardo, it is basically the Ricardian method of analysis that Keynes has revived. The most typical indication of this is to be found in the directness with which Keynes proceeds to state his assumptions. Like Ricardo, he is always looking for fundamentals. He singles out for consideration the variables he believes to be the most important.*

Joan Robinson thinks that "Ricardo can help Keynes out in the concepts of the normal rate of profit and the value of capital." She points out:

*Luigi L. Pasinetti, *Growth and Income Distribution: Essays in Economic Theory* (London: Cambridge University Press, 1974), p. 43. Pasinetti also points out that Schumpeter perceived this very clearly when he wrote: "The similarities between the aims and methods of those two eminent men, Keynes and Ricardo, is indeed striking, though it will not impress those who look primarily for the advice a writer tenders. Of course, there is a world between Keynes and Ricardo in this respect, and Keynes' views on economic policy bear much more resemblance to Malthus'. But I am speaking of Ricardo's and Keynes' methods of securing the clear-cut result. On this point they were brothers in spirit" (Schumpeter, *History of Economic Analysis*, p. 473n).

Sraffa's revival of the classical theory of the rate of profit provides the normal long-period analysis that the post-Keynesian theory requires. It was wrong to class Ricardo with Pigou. Keynes knocked out neoclassical equilibrium and set his argument in historical time. Here he and Ricardo are on the same side.[38]

Turning to the theory of distribution and growth, the Post-Keynesians frame their theory in the tradition of Ricardo and Marx. Nicholas Kaldor's "widow's cruse" theory of distribution is an illustration of this tradition. As pointed out by Pasinetti:

If Harrod-Domar hypotheses are inserted into Ricardo's theoretical scheme and proper account is taken of Keynes' effective demand requirements for full employment, we are led back to the old Ricardian problem of income distribution, but with an entirely new answer. Nicholas Kaldor was the first to see this clearly.*

The Post-Keynesians also embrace the classical concept of competition in the tradition of Smith, Ricardo, and Marx. Peter Kenyon observes:

Competition in classical economic thought from Adam Smith to Karl Marx is . . . a process, not an end-state. As reflected in investment and growth policies, competition involves the process by which resources are allocated—and, ultimately, income distribution—between social classes over time rather than just their allocation among individuals at a point in time. This emphasis reflects the preoccupation of the classical economists (particularly Ricardo and Marx) with the concept of capital and the process of capital accumulation.[39]

Along with the rejection of the Walrasian concept of competition, the Post-Keynesians' approach to the theory of prices is more or less in the classical tradition. Alfred S. Eichner points out that a distinctive Post-Keynesian price theory is now emerging.[40] Essentially, it consists of two types of studies: (a) the study of long-period steady-state prices building on the work of Sraffa, Leontief, and von Neumann, and (b) the study of historically observed changes in price levels, based on the works of M. Kalecki, J. Steindl, A. S. Eichner, and D. Levine. The Post-Keynesians emphasize that the essential role of prices is to assure

---

*Pasinetti, *Growth and Income Distribution*, p. 97. The Kaldorian theory will be considered in Part 3 of this book.

the viability and expansion of the system. "This new theory diverges sharply from the models of pricing behavior found in economics textbooks. Since the price level depends, via the need for funds to finance investment, on the rate of economic expansion, the Post-Keynesian theory of price formation is a dynamic one."*

Ricardo and the "new classical macroeconomics"

Economics, like politics, sometimes makes for strange bed fellows. While the Post-Keynesians in their critique of the "neoclassical synthesis" have some affinity to Ricardo's framework, so do the theorists of the "new classical macroeconomics" (exponents of the "rational expectations" hypothesis)† embrace some of the Ricardian propositions in their revision of the same orthodoxy. In this regard, an important controversy over the effectiveness of deficit financed compensatory fiscal policy has arisen between the "revisionists" and the Keynesians.

The controversy was highlighted by Robert J. Barro's essay, "Are Government Bonds Net Wealth?"[41] While Barro did not mention Ricardo in his essay, James M. Buchanan points out that "the thrust of Barro's argument supports the Ricardian theorem to the effect that taxation and public debt issue exert basically equivalent effects."[42] Buchanan refers to this proposition as the "Ricardian equivalence theorem."

The implications of Barro's analysis for macroeconomic theory and policy are succinctly summarized by James Tobin as follows:[43]

(a) The "Ricardian equivalence theorem" denies the potency of deficit financed compensatory fiscal policy.

(b) If deficit finance is ineffective in the short run, it is also innocuous in the long run for (i) it "crowds out" neither private capital formation nor foreign investment and (ii) it does not add fuel to the flames of inflation.

(c) It denies the "Pigou effect."

(d) It denies that Social Security benefits stimulate consumption. The expansionary effect of such payments is viewed as completely offset by the "rational expectations" of the public, who interpret

*Alfred S. Eichner, "Introduction to the Symposium: Price Formation Theory," *Journal of Post Keynesian Economics, 4* (1), Fall 1981, p. 81. The Post-Keynesian price theory will also be considered in Part 3 of this book.

†The "new classical macroeconomics" combines the assumptions of "rational expectations" and continuous market clearing. Some of the chief exponents are Robert Lucas, Thomas Sargent, Neil Wallace, Robert Barro, and E. Malinvaud.

benefits as suggesting a higher stream of future social insurance taxes and restrain present consumption accordingly.

(e) It denies the effectiveness of open-market purchases of government securities.

(f) It denies the long-run burden of public debt, since the revived Ricardian theorem asserts that private capital formation will not be "crowded out" by government deficit finance.

Thus, Tobin observes: "The 'Ricardian equivalence theorem' is fundamental, perhaps indispensable, to monetarism."[44]

Ricardo did convey the "equivalence theorem" in the following passages from *Principles*:

> When, for the expenses of a year's war, twenty millions are raised by means of a loan, it is the twenty millions which are withdrawn from the productive capital of the nation. The million per annum which is raised by taxes to pay the interest of this loan is merely transferred from those who pay it to those who receive it, from the contributor to the tax to the national creditor. The real expense is the twenty millions, and not the interest which must be paid for it. Whether the interest be or be not paid, the country will neither be richer nor poorer.[45]

> A man who has 10,000, paying him an income of 500, out of which he has to pay 100 per annum towards the interest of the debt, is really worth only 8000, and would be equally rich, whether he continued to pay 100 per annum, or at once, and for only once, sacrificed 2000.[46]

Gerald P. O'Driscoll, Jr., points out that Ricardo wrote an article after *Principles* concerning the "Funding System."* In that article, Ricardo made more explicit statements on the "equivalence theorem," as O'Driscoll points out.[47] Both Tobin and O'Driscoll comment that Ricardo added important qualifications to the "equivalence theorem." In the view of the latter, O'Driscoll states, "Ricardo continued his analysis in a manner that not merely modified it but completely changed it from "equivalence theorem" to a "non-equivalence theorem."[48]

Ricardo's defense of taxation as opposed to borrowing as a method of financing a war is conveyed by the following passages from his *Principles*.

*The article appeared in the fourth, fifth, and sixth editions of the *Encyclopedia Britannica*.

It is error and delusion to suppose that a real national difficulty can be removed by shifting it from the shoulders of one class of the community, who justly ought to bear it, to the shoulders of another class, who, upon every principle of equity, ought to bear no more than their share. From what I have said, it must not be inferred that I consider the system of borrowing as the best calculated to defray the extraordinary expenses of the state. It is a system that tends to make us less thrifty—to blind us to our real situation.[49]

A country which has accumulated a large debt is placed in a most artificial situation; . . . it becomes the interest of every contributor to withdraw his shoulder from the burden, and shift this payment from himself to another; and the temptation to remove himself and his capital to another country, where he will be exempted from such burdens, becomes at last irresistible.[50]

Ricardo and contemporary "supply-side" economics

While contemporary "supply-siders" often cite Adam Smith and tend to neglect Ricardo, Ricardo's policy recommendations are not out of step with contemporary "supply-side" economics. In the first place, Ricardo was a firm believer in the efficacy of the market mechanism. His attacks on the "corn laws" and his formulation of the comparative cost doctrine of international trade provide ample evidence of this contention.

Secondly, he was opposed to excessive government spending and high burdens of taxation. On the destructive effects of taxation, Ricardo wrote:

There are no taxes which have not a tendency to lessen the power to accumulate. All taxes must either fall on capital or revenue. If they encroach on capital, they must proportionately diminish that fund by whose extent the extent of the productive industry of the country must always be regulated; and if they fall on revenue, they must either lessen accumulation, or force the contributors to save the amount of the tax, by making a corresponding diminution of their former unproductive consumption of the necessaries and luxuries of life. Some taxes will produce these effects in a much greater degree than others; but the great evil of taxation is to be found, not so much in any selection of its objects, as in the general amount of its effects collectively.[51]

This passage certainly has a modern ring. It could well be a contemporary "supply-sider" arguing for tax reduction.

Ricardo, like Smith, opposed deficit spending. As observed by Thomas Sowell, "Like Smith, he was concerned that the political advantages of deficit spending would increase the total amount spent, and increase the danger of 'wantonly' (both men used the same word) becoming engaged in war." He (Ricardo) added: "There cannot be any greater security for the continuance of peace than the imposing on the ministers the necessity of applying to the people for taxes to support a war."[52]

Turning to Ricardo's monetary policy prescriptions, recall that during the "Bullionist controversy" in the inflationary phase of the Napoleonic war* Ricardo led the "Bullionists" who argued that the main culprit of the currency depreciation was the overissue of bank notes by the Bank of England. According to Jacob Viner,

> Their conclusions rested on the following reasoning: The rate of exchange between two currencies depended solely or mainly on their relative purchasing power over identical transportable commodities in the two countries; on quantity theory of money grounds, prices in the two countries depended on the quantities of money circulating therein; the price of bullion in paper currency was governed by the exchange rates with metallic standard currencies; therefore, if the exchanges were below metallic parity, and if there was a premium on bullion over paper, this was evidence that prices were higher in England, and the quantity of currency in circulation greater, than would have been possible under the metallic standard prevailing to the suspension of convertibility.†

The policy prescription of Ricardo for this economic ill was a tight rein on the note issue of the Bank of England. Should he be transported to our time, Ricardo would recommend a slow and steady growth in the money supply.

---

*For a lucid and detailed account of the "Bullionist controversy," see Jacob Viner, *Studies in the Theory of International Trade* (New York: Harper & Brothers Publishers, 1937), Chapters 3 and 4. The "Bullionists" were Walter Boyd, Lord King, Henry Thornton, John Whaeately, Francis Horner, and Ricardo. The "Anti-Bullionists" were Nicholas Vansittart, George Ross, Henry Boase, Bosanquet, Coutts Trotter, and J. C. Herries.

†Viner, *Studies*, p. 126. England suspended specie payments in 1797 following a general panic which was induced by rumors of a French landing on English soil and which, accentuated by failures and suspensions on the part of the country's banks, led to a general clamor for gold.

CHAPTER 3

The "Demand-Side" Economics of Thomas Robert Malthus

David Ricardo argued that capital accumulation would lead to economic growth until the "stationary state" was reached. This argument was
supported by Say's law, which in essence denied the possibility of
prolonged insufficiency of effective demand.* Ricardo employed the
method of comparative statics in his analysis of secular growth and
consequently ignored disturbances in the transition process. Ricardo
wrote: "I put these immediate and temporary effects quite aside, and
fixed my whole attention on the permanent state of things which will
result from them."[1] This orthodox classical thesis was criticized by

---

*For an in-depth discussion of Say's law, see Thomas Sowell, *Say's Law* (Princeton, New Jersey: Princeton University Press, 1972). Thomas Sowell points out:
"Say's Law as it appeared in classical economics involved seven major propositions: (1) Production necessarily generates purchasing power of equal value, in the
form of factor payments, so that it is always objectively possible to sell any given
level of output at cost-covering prices (James Mill). (2) People's behavior patterns
are such that they will not desire to save more than they desire to invest, nor do
they generally desire to hold money balances beyond that needed for transactions in
the immediate period (Adam Smith). (3) Investment does not reduce aggregate demand, but merely transfers it from one group of potential consumers (capitalists) to
another (workers in the investment goods sector) (Adam Smith). (4) As output increases, increased quantities of some goods exchange against increased quantities of
other goods; increased supply creates correspondingly increased demand (J. B.
Say). (5) Each individual works only in anticipation of consumption equal to his
own output, so that aggregate quantity supplied equals the aggregate quantity demanded ex ante as well as ex post (James Mill). (6) Increased savings (quantity or
function not distinguished) increase the rate of growth (Adam Smith). (7) Periods of
unsold goods are due to internally disproportionate production, which can be eliminated by increasing the output of some other goods which will be traded for the
goods currently in excess (J. B. Say)" (pp. 32–33).

writers on both sides of the English channel.* The leading critic of Ricardian economics in England was Thomas Robert Malthus.

Mark Blaug observes that "from the moment of their first meeting in 1811 Malthus and Ricardo disagreed on almost all the fundamental topics of political economy."[2] During the post–Napoleonic War depression, Malthus took issue with Ricardo on the efficacy of capital accumulation in his *Principles of Political Economy* (1820). The polemics has been referred to as "the glut controversy" by students of the history of economic thought. In Book I of his *Principles*, Malthus attacked the Ricardian embodied labor theory of value by refining and extending the Smithian labor-commanded theory. The purpose of this tortuous presentation was to bring out the pivotal role of effective demand. While the Malthusian attack is most unpalatable, his major point is clear and concise. As Blaug pointed out, "The unsatisfactory character of Malthus' value theory, however, is of no great moment to his basic theme. Though designed to serve as a theoretic warrant for the contention that general gluts were possible, the entire analysis of Book I of Malthus' *Principles* is strictly speaking irrelevant to that proposition."[3]

Malthus—a Keynesian?

Malthus's basic theme was the examination of optimum saving in a growth context. This was explored in Book II of his *Principles*. He never really considered the determination of the static equilibrium level of income in the short run. Thus his notion of insufficient effective demand takes on a non-Keynesian meaning.† The reasons that Malthus failed to formulate a precise theory of income determination of the Keynesian type may best be explained with the aid of the familiar textbook model in the accompanying tabulation.[4]

*The well-known critics were Sismondi, Malthus, William Spence, Lauderdale, and Chalmers. M. F. Bleaney observes: "Two main strands of underconsumptionism are identified, whose main propositions are somewhat different. One strand—the Malthusian heritage—emphasizes the absolute level of saving, while the other—stemming from Sismondi—emphasizes the distribution of income per se as the cause of crises." See his *Underconsumption Theories: A History and Critical Analysis* (New York: International Publishers, 1976), p. 3.

†In his *Essays in Biography* (London: Macmillan and Co., Ltd., 1933, pp. 144–145), Keynes wrote: "If only Malthus, instead of Ricardo, had been the parent stem from which nineteenth-century economics proceeded, what a much wiser and richer place the world would be today! I have long claimed Robert Malthus as the first of the Cambridge economists. . . ." Again in *The General Theory of Employment,*

The classical system	The Keynesian system
(1) $y = y(N)$.	(1') $y = y(N)$.
(2) $N_d = D\dfrac{W}{P}$.	(2') $N_d = D\dfrac{W}{P}$.
(3) $N_s = S\dfrac{W}{P}$.	(3') $W = W_0$.
(4) $M = kPy$.	(4') $M = kPy + L(r), \dfrac{\partial L}{\partial r} = \infty$.
(5) $S = S(r)$.	(5') $S = S(Y)$.
(6) $I = I(r)$.	(6') $I = I(r)$.
(7) $S = I$.	(7') $S = I$.

The classical system as expressed in the tabulation is a composite model constructed by contemporary macrotheorists to sharpen our understanding of the differences between Keynesian theory and pre-Keynesian ideas. Equation (1) is the short-run aggregate production function with fixed capital stock and one variable factor, labor. The symbol y stands for real output and N denotes employment of labor. Equation (2) is the demand for labor function where N_d denotes labor demanded and the real wage rate is symbolized by W/P. Equation (3) is the supply of labor function which is also dependent on the real wage rate.

Interest and Money (London: Macmillan and Co., Ltd., 1936, p. 362), Keynes praised Malthus's notion of insufficiency of effective demand as "a scientific explanation of unemployment." Closer examinations of Malthus's theory by contemporary writers, however, show that Keynes's praise was overly generous. See Mark Blaug, *Ricardian Economics: A Historical Study* (New Haven: Yale University Press, 1958), p. 87; Thomas Sowell, *Say's Law*, Chapter 3; B. A. Corry, *Money, Saving, and Investment in English Economics 1800–1850* (London: St. Martin's Press, 1962), Chapter 7; Michael Bleaney, *Underconsumption Theories*, Chapter 2; and Lionel Robbins, *The Theory of Economic Development in the History of Economic Thought* (New York: St. Martin's Press, 1968), p. 59.

The money market equilibrium condition is represented by Equation (4) where M is the supply of nominal money, determined exogeneously by the monetary system. The demand for nominal money balances is represented by kPy.

Equation (5) is the savings function and Equation (6) is the investment function. Both savings and investment are functions of the rate of interest, r. Equation (7) is the output market equilibrium condition.

The spirit of Say's law is inherent in the system. Under the assumptions of certainty and perfect competition, the model shows that price flexibility automatically assures full employment equilibrium. The employment level is determined by the interaction of supply and demand functions in the labor market. With equilibrium employment determined, the output level is determined through the equation for the short-run aggregate production function. The system is essentially supply-side determined. The demand forces represented in Equations 4 through 7 exercise no influence in the determination of the output level. The nature of the system of equations virtually rules out the possibility of underemployment equilibrium due to insufficiency of effective demand.

The above Keynesian model reveals the fundamental theoretical innovations employed by Keynes to break Say's law. There are several possible approaches to finding the Achilles' heel of Say's law. One way is through the assumption of wage rigidity as represented by Equation (3'). If for some reason the labor market is unable to determine a unique equilibrium level of employment, demand forces become an ingredient in income determination. Alternatively, it would be sufficient to demonstrate the possibility of shortage of effective demand, by invoking the concept of the "liquidity trap" $\partial L/\partial r = \infty$. Another route to reach the same destination would be to highlight the fact that saving and investment are made by different groups of peoople with different motives. Recognizing such, we see that there is no guarantee that ex ante saving and investment will always be equal. This idea is conveyed by Equations (5') and (6') where savings is shown as a function of income while investment is treated as depending upon interest rates. Any one of these alternative routes is sufficient to break Say's law. To have all of them in one model might be deemed "over-kill."

Did Malthus follow any of these alternative routes in his attack on

Say's law? He did not. Not only did he not consider wage rigidity; Malthus also ruled out monetary causes of underemployment equilibrium. In his arguments there was no place for hoarding, let alone a 'liquidity trap.'' Furthermore, he subscribed to the Smithian saving-is-spending theorem, which is one of the building blocks of Say's law. Thus, he failed to consider any divergence between ex ante saving and investment. In addition, Malthus recognized only the "capacity-creating effect" of investment and neglected the demand generating effects of investment (the familiar Keynesian investment multiplier). Malthus had no notion of the Keynesian investment multiplier effect. Should he have grasped the dual effect of investment, viz., the demand-generating and capacity-creating effects, he could have developed a growth theory in the spirit of Domar and R. Harrod.* Malthus also neglected the role of technical progress. Thus he had no concept of autonomous investment. These analytical weaknesses explain why Malthus failed to break Say's law. In spite of these limitations, we "cannot," as Luigi L. Pasinetti says, "take away from him the merit of having been aware precisely of the problem of lack of effective demand, which Keynes was able to deal with, in a theoretically better and successful way, a century later."[5]

The Malthusian theory of optimal savings

Let us now consider the main theme of Thomas Malthus. The stumbling block of Malthus's dynamic analysis appears to be the saving-is-spending theorem. Like Ricardo, Malthus assumed that only the propertied class had the capacity to save. But he differed from Ricardo by assuming that an act of saving by the propertied class had a dual effect, namely: (i) it decreased the demand for consumer goods by the savers and (ii) it simultaneously led to an increase in the productive capacity

---

*See E. D. Domar, "Capital Expansion, Rate of Growth and Employment," *Econometrica*, 1964, pp. 137–147, and his "Expansion and Employment," *American Economic Review*, 1947, pp. 34–35. Also see R. F. Harrod, *Towards A Dynamic Economics* (London: Macmillan, 1948). The Keynesian concern for insufficiency of investment is clearly stated by Domar as follows: (i) $\Delta Y_d = (1/\alpha)\Delta I$ where the subscript d indicates aggregate demand. This equation states the Keynesian investment multiplier. Malthus failed to consider this aspect. (ii) $\Delta Y_s = \sigma I$ where the subscript s denotes potential productive capacity and $\sigma = 1/\beta = Y/K$. This equation represents the Keynesian "capacity-creating effect" of investment which Malthus recognized. (iii) Equation $\Delta Y_d = \Delta Y_s$ states the equilibrium condition. By substitution, the following equation is derived: (iv) $\Delta I/I = \alpha\sigma$, which states the required rate of increase in investment in order to maintain equality between aggregate demand and aggregate supply continuously over time. Malthus did not understand this implication of Keynesian growth theory.

through the capacity-creating effect of investment. Although Malthus recognized that the demand for productive labor was a function of capital accumulation, he assumed that the additional demand for consumer goods following the increased employment of productive labor could offset the reduced demand by savers. The overall result would be a state of "general glut." The falling rate of profit would check capital accumulation prior to the arrival of the "stationary state." Malthus's general conclusion was that there should be an optimal level of savings in order to keep the economy on the steady-state path. Oversaving and too much investment would lead to underconsumption and stagnation.[6]

It is interesting to note that Malthus's optimum saving theory bears formal resemblance to Edmund Phelps's "golden rule of accumulation."[7] We emphasize the term "formal," for the two theories are different in their analytical content. The "golden rule of accumulation" is one of the theorems of neoclassical growth theory which is the antithesis of the Malthusian analysis. Yet both theories emphasize the desirability of optimum saving. The "golden rule of accumulation" is illustrated by Figure 3.1.

Figure 3.1 is the familiar diagram depicting a simple neoclassical growth model without technical progress such as that discussed by R. M. Solow in his seminal article "A Contribution to the Theory of Economic Growth" (1956).[8] The vertical axis measures per capita output, y; the horizontal axis measures the per capita capital/labor ratio, k. The curve $y = f(k)$ is the linearly homogeneous neoclassical production function in per capita terms. The slope at any point on the production function measures the marginal productivity of capital (in per capita terms) which, in equilibrium under conditions of perfect competition, is equal to the rate of profit; viz., $f'(k) = r$. The curve $sf(k)$ is the saving function, where s denotes the constant saving ratio. The curve nk may be called the "golden age line," for it is the locus of all possible "golden age" or "steady state" growth paths. The "golden age" growth path is characterized by output, capital, and labor all growing at the same constant rate:

(a)
$$\frac{\Delta Y}{Y} = \frac{\Delta K}{K} = \frac{\Delta L}{L} = n.$$

where n is the constant demographically determined labor force growth rate. It follows that along any "golden age" or "balanced growth" path, $k = 0$. The nk line is derived as follows: Rewrite Equation (a)

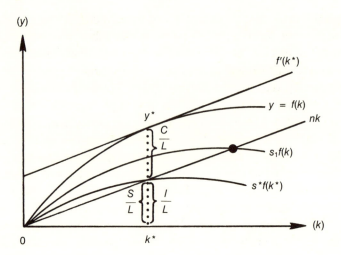

Figure 3.1

The "golden rule of accumulation"

Source: Adapted from Edmund S. Phelps, *Golden Rules of Economic Growth* (New York: Norton, 1966).

and transform it into per capita terms:

(b) $$\frac{S}{L} = \frac{I}{L} = nk.$$

Since, in the neoclassical analysis, it is assumed that saving always equals investment, equation (b) may be stated as

(c) $$sf(k) = nk.$$

This equation is the necessary condition for the "golden age" growth path. It states the condition necessary for investment (saving) per man to keep the capital/labor ratio constant ($\dot{k} = 0$). In Figure 3.1 the "golden age output" is indicated by y^* and the corresponding "golden age capital/labor ratio" by k^*.

The "golden rule of accumulation" requires choice of a per capita consumption maximizing k^* along a "golden age growth path." It is really a central planning problem. Suppose one could choose among different "golden age growth paths," each characterized by a different k^* and corresponding saving ratio, s^*, required to keep $\dot{k} = 0$. To find the optimum s^*, first locate k^*. We begin by writing an expression for per capita consumption:

(d)
$$c \equiv \frac{C}{L} = \frac{Y}{L} - \frac{I}{L} = f(k) - \frac{\dot{K}}{L},$$

which simply states that consumption per man equals output per man minus investment per man. Multiplying the term K/L by K/K we obtain:

(e)
$$c = f(k) - \frac{\dot{K}}{L}\frac{K}{K} = f(k) - \frac{\dot{K}}{K}\frac{K}{L}.$$

Since the constrained optimization problem under consideration here refers to the "golden age growth path" and since along this growth path $\dot{K}/K = n$, Equation (e) may be rewritten as:

(f)
$$c = f(k) - nk.$$

Differentiating this equation with respect to k and setting it equal to zero yields:

(g)
$$\frac{dc}{dk} = f'(k) - n = 0.$$

The "golden age" k^* is found when the slope of the production function, $f'(k)$, parallels the slope of the nk line, which is n. This is shown in Figure 3.1. It is interesting to note that the condition stated in Equation (g) is formally identical to the static profit maximization condition of the theory of the firm.

Having located k^*, now try to find the corresponding s^*. First define the saving ratio:

(h)
$$s \equiv \frac{S}{Y} = \frac{I}{Y} = \frac{\dot{K}}{Y}.$$

Multiplying Equation (h) by K/K yields:

(i)
$$s = \frac{\dot{K}}{Y} \frac{K}{K} = \frac{\dot{K}}{K} \frac{K}{Y}$$

Along the "golden age growth path," $\dot{K}/K = n$ and $n = f'(k)$, so one obtains Equation (j):

(j)
$$s^* = f'(k) \frac{K}{Y} = \frac{rK}{Y} .$$

Equation (j) states that the optimum saving ratio, s^*, is equal to capital's share of total output, rK/Y. It is at this optimum saving rate that c^* is at the maximum. Oversaving as depicted by the $s_1 f(k)$ curve in Figure 3.1 would cause c^* to fall.

The neoclassical view of saving and investment is somewhat similar to the Malthusian saving-is-spending theorem. Both theories assume perfect competition, but the broad similarities end here in that Malthus had no notion of the so-called "neoclassical parables."* Likewise he had no clear conception of the price mechanism which eliminates the "Harrodian knife-edge problem" in the neoclassical growth model. Malthus's general policy recommendation for avoiding underconsumption was to do everything possible to encourage "unproductive consumption" by the propertied class. Here his view was colored by his conservative ideology. As pointed out by Mark Blaug: "Since the landlord is the principal unproductive consumer, the prosperity of the community depends on the wealth and spending power of landlords. Indeed, Malthus' defense of the corn laws and his theory of gluts are cut out of the same cloth."[9]

*See Charles E. Ferguson, *The Neoclassical Theory of Production and Distribution* (London: Cambridge University Press, 1969), pp. 252–254. The label "neoclassical parables" was coined by G. C. Harcourt in *Some Cambridge Controversies in the Theory of Capital* (London: Cambridge University Press, 1972). For more discussions of the "neoclassical parables," see Part 2 of this book.

CHAPTER 4

Causality in Classical Economics

The Newtonian heritage

The intellectual heritage of classical economics is that of Newtonian mechanics. Sir Isaac Newton (1642–1727) taught the philosophers of the Enlightenment to think in terms of gravity reaching out from the sun millions of miles away and keeping the planets in their orbits. This concept gave rise to the view that nature was rational and orderly. Consequently, the universe could be conceived as a "world machine," invariant in time. Accurate prediction of the future was therefore considered possible. "It follows," observed Sir James Jeans, "that changes of the world at any instant depend only on the state of the world at that instant, the state being defined by positions and velocities of the particles; changes in position are determined by the velocities, and changes in velocities by the forces, which in turn are determined by the positions."[1] The Newtonian world view was epitomized by the assertion of the French mathematician Pierre Simon, Marquis de Laplace (1749–1827), in his *Essay on Probability* (1812):

> if the state of the world at its creation were specified in its minutest details to an infinitely capable and infinitely industrious mathematician, such a being would be able to deduce the whole of its subsequent history.[2]

The aspiration of Laplace is still apparent in contemporary economic theory. The opening paragraph of Edwin Burmeister and A. Rodney Dobell's *Mathematical Theories of Economic Growth* (1970) provides ample evidence to this point:

The mathematician Laplace is reputed to have said, "Give me only the equations of motion, and I will show you the future of the Universe." Likewise, economists studying the evolution of a large general equilibrium system ask only for the equations of motion in order to bring their work to completion.[3]

John Hicks and causality in economics

The Newtonian world view gave birth to a new interpretation of causality. According to John Hicks, the "Old Causality" in which "causes are always thought of as actions of either a human agent or a supernatural agent" was replaced in Newtonian physics by a system of thought which Hicks calls the "New Causality." The Aristotelian grip on intellectual thought was completely broken by this new concept.* Hicks writes:

> Causation can only be asserted, in terms of the New Causality, if we have some theory, or generalization, into which observed events can be fitted; to suppose that we have theories into which all events can be fitted, is to make a large claim indeed. It was nevertheless a claim that thinkers of the eighteenth century, dazzled by the prestige of Newtonian mechanics, were tempted to make.[4]

Economists today are still attempting to fit observed events into some theory.

Sir Arthur Eddington has stated, "Causality is closely bound up with time's arrow; the cause must precede the effect. The relativity of time has not obliterated this order."[5] Nevertheless, Hicks points out that there is one basic difference between economics and experimental science with respect to time: "Experimental science, in its nature, is out of historical time; it has to be irrelevant, for the significance of an experiment, at what date it is made, or repeated."[6] Economics, conversely, is always in historical time. Hicks writes:

> The economist is concerned with the future as well as with the past; but it is from the past that he has to begin. It is the past that provides him with

*The Aristotelian "final cause" gave nature its teleology or purpose. The goal of medieval science was to explain the teleology of natural phenomena. "The secret of the success of modern science was the selection of a new goal for scientific activity. This new goal, set by Galileo and pursued by his successors, is that of obtaining quantitative descriptions of scientific phenomena independently of any physical explanations" (Morris Kline, *Mathematics in Western Culture* [(New York: Oxford University Press, 1964] p. 184).

his facts, the facts which he uses to make his generalizations; he then uses these generalizations as bases for predictions and for advice on planning.[7]

Hicks would give timely warning to economists who try to ape the experimental sciences:

> It is just that economics is in time, in a way that the natural sciences are not. All economic data are dated; so the inductive evidence can never do more than establish a relation which appears to hold within the period to which the data refer. If a relation has held, with no more than intelligible exceptions, over (say) the last fifty years, we may reasonably guess that it will continue to hold this year, and perhaps next year, and perhaps for the year after that. But we cannot even reasonably guess that it will continue to hold for the next fifty years. In the sciences such guesses are reasonable; in economics they are not.[8]

Hicks distinguishes three kinds of causality in relation to time: (1) sequential causality, in which cause precedes effect; (2) contemporaneous causality, in which both cause and effect relate to the same time period; and (3) static causality, in which both cause and effect are permanencies.

Static causality in classical economics

Adam Smith was among the circle of eighteenth-century intellectuals influenced by the Newtonian world view. His thinking was in terms of both ''Newtonian mechanics'' and the ''New Causality.'' Mark Blaug calls attention to the fact that Smith, in his posthumously published essay, ''The Principles Which Lead and Direct Philosophical Enquiries: Illustrated by the History of Astronomy'' (written only sixty years after Newton's *Principia*), described the Newtonian method as one in which we lay down ''certain principles, primary or proved, in the beginning, from whence we account for the several phenomena, connecting all together by the same chain.''[9] Adam Smith's commitment to the ''New Causality'' is evidenced by his search for ''laws,'' or generalizations on which he tried to fit various events.

The causality in Smith's writing is ''static'' in the Hicksian sense. Smith regarded the causes and effects of capital accumulation as permanencies. To him they were the invariant and universally applicable principles governing the increase in the wealth of nations. As pointed out by Hicks, the theories of Adam Smith did have direct reference to facts during Smith's time. For instance, in discussing his famous dictum that the division of labor is limited by the extent of the market, Smith wrote:

> As by means of water-carriage a more extensive market is opened to every sort of industry than what land-carriage alone can afford it, so it is upon the sea-coast, and along the banks of navigable rivers, that industry of every kind naturally begins to subdivide and improve itself, and it is frequently not till a long time after that those improvements extend themselves to the inland parts of the country.[10]

The relation between the costs of water and land transport was a fact which appeared in Smith's time to be quite permanent. Likewise the techniques of production did not appear to be rapidly changing. Hence it seemed reasonable to Smith that the technical coefficient of production was fixed, that the natural prices of commodities were determined by technical conditions, and that relative prices would remain constant over time.

It should be noted that "static causality" is not limited to the writings of Smith. Many of the theorems of neoclassical economics (to be considered in Part 2) belong to the same category. The so-called "neoclassical parables" assert the following to be permanencies in the Hicksian sense: (a) that higher values of capital per man employed are associated with lower rates of profit; (b) that lower rates of profit are associated with higher capital–output ratios; and so forth. We may also include C. W. J. Granger's causality test and that of Christopher A. Sims[11] as examples of Hicksian "static causality." In both tests, the time series are assumed to be "permanencies" or "stationary," in that the means and variances of the information sets are invariant with respect to time.

The institutional and factual elements which figured so prominently in the *Wealth of Nations* fade into the background in the writings of Ricardo. Ricardo and his followers consciously emulated Newtonian mechanics. Like Greek tragedies, the Ricardian theorems seem to be inescapable. Mark Blaug observes: "On the one hand, Ricardo wrote to Malthus that his object was to elucidate principles and, therefore, he 'imagined strong cases . . . that might show the operation of these principles'; on the other hand, he was forever telling Parliament that some of the conclusions of economics were as certain as the principle of gravitation."[12] The Ricardian "stationary state" implies static causality, for, once established, all the variables and their values in the model remain unchanged. Thus Hicks does not exclude Ricardo from the category of "static causality."

What about Malthus? In spite of the "glut controversy," Malthus's methodology was not substantially different from that of Ricardo. Malthus seemed to be groping for some sort of "correspondence principle" to supplement the Ricardian comparative static analysis. This point is made clear by the following passage from Samuelson's *Foundations of Economic Analysis*:[13]

> The equations of comparative statics are . . . a special case of the general dynamic analysis. [Most likely that was Ricardo's methodology.] They can indeed be discussed by abstracting completely from dynamical analysis. In the history of mechanics, the theory of statics was developed before the dynamic problems were even formulated. [Recall that both Smith and Ricardo emulated Newtonian mechanics.] But the problem of stability of equilibrium cannot be discussed except with reference to dynamical considerations, however implicit and rudimentary. [Malthus was aiming, though unsuccessfully, at the same thing.] We find ourselves confronted with the paradox: in order for the comparative-statics analysis to yield fruitful results, we must first develop a theory of dynamics.

Malthus never questioned the possibility of the Ricardian "stationary state." What he wanted to point out was the possibility that, prior to the arrival of the "stationary state," oversaving on the part of the propertied class would reduce effective demand, which, in turn, would cause the rate of profit to fall. Consequently, capital accumulation would be choked off.[14] Thus, it seems safe to suggest that Malthus never succeeded in escaping from the grips of "static causality."

Part II

Contemporary Reinterpretations of the Neoclassical Synthesis

CHAPTER 5

The ''Golden Age'' of the ''Neoclassical Synthesis''

Early expositions of the Keynesian revolution conceived of the economy in terms of homogeneous flows of total expenditures, thereby paying little attention to the microfoundations of macroeconomics. Alan Coddington has referred to this trend in analysis as ''hydraulic Keynesianism.'' Coddington states:

> It is the belief that there are indeed stable relations among the various overall flows in the economy that provides a basis for ''the government'' to pursue its policy goals regarding the overall level of economic activity and hence, relatedly, of the level of employment.[1]

After the initial conquest of ''hydraulic Keynesianism,'' the economics profession began to look inward to consider the microfoundations of Keynesian macroeconomics. Long before the popularization of the ''neoclassical synthesis,'' John Hicks (1939) made what he considered to be a ''breakthrough.'' This is reflected in the following remarks:

> I believe I have had the fortune to come upon a method of analysis which is applicable to a wide variety of economic problems. . . . It turns out, on investigation, that most of the problems of several variables, with which economic theory has to concern itself, are problems of the interrelation of markets. Thus, the more complex problems of wage-theory involve the interrelations of the market for labour, the market for consumption goods, and (perhaps) the capital market. . . . *What we mainly need is a technique for studying the interrelations of markets.*[2]

The technique developed by Hicks was essentially a Walrasian general equilibrium analysis without the auctioneer. "So viewed," noted E. Roy Weintraub, "general equilibrium theory is coextensive with the theory of the microfoundations of macroeconomics."[3]

The perception of economic problems as involving the interrelationships of markets, and the need for a technique to study such interactions, opened a floodgate of advance in economic analysis. During the period from 1939 to 1956, the economics profession witnessed rapid progress in the clearing of conceptual underbrush and the sharpening of analytical tools. Samuelson (1947) introduced "stability analysis" and clarified ambiguities in comparative statics with his "correspondence principle."[*] In the early 1950s, Kenneth J. Arrow, Gerard Debreu, and other distinguished mathematical economists completed rigorous proofs of the existence of competitive equilibria.[4] This was a productive and exciting period in the development of economic analysis. As E. Roy Weintraub stated, "Henceforth study of models could proceed mechanically from existence proofs through uniqueness of equilibrium arguments to stability analysis of equilibrium states."[5] The stability analysis of the standard IS-LM model as well as the causal determinacy and stability of dynamic equilibrium in the two-sector neoclassical growth model are two familiar illustrations of this procedure.[†]

In 1956 Don Patinkin integrated monetary and value theory within the neo-Walrasian general equilibrium framework.[6] E. Roy Weintraub states:

*Paul A. Samuelson, *Foundations of Economic Analysis* (Cambridge, Mass: Harvard University Press, 1948). Samuelson wrote: " . . . the problem of stability of equilibrium is intimately tied up with the problem of deriving fruitful theorems in comparative statics. This duality constitutes what I have called the correspondence principle" (p. 258). He added: "We find ourselves confronted with this paradox: in order for the comparative-static analysis to yield fruitful results, we must first develop a theory of dynamics" (pp. 262–263).

† Obviously the increasing sophistication of "hydraulic Keynesianism" and its eventual exposition as the "neoclassical synthesis" did not rest well with those who envisioned the Keynesian Revolution to imply a more radical departure from the existing state of economic analysis than simple cases of rigid prices and slow adjusting markets. The perceptions of these interpreters of Keynes, the so-called "fundamentalist Keynesians," will be explored in Part 3 of this volume. Indeed, it may be these differing views of what Keynes meant to say, and the resulting differences in models and implications, that prompted Hicks, reflecting upon the development of the IS-LM model, to express the concern that he might have done a disservice to the profession by oversimplifying the important contributions of Keynes and giving fuel to his detractors.

In any event, by say 1960, the microfoundations problem appeared, on the surface, to be settled. There existed a detailed model of a competitive private ownership economy for which a stable equilibrium was known to exist. Patinkin had shown that money could be introduced into that system in a "natural" way respecting the stability of that equilibrium.[7]

The joint efforts of these writers made the grand "neoclassical synthesis" the reigning paradigm in economics, putting the "Keynes vs. Classics" debate to rest. The period from the 1950s to the end of the 1960s was indeed the "golden age" of the "neoclassical synthesis." In the following section, we consider a "standard" macroeconomic model in the spirit of the "neoclassical synthesis."

A "standard" macroeconomic model of the "neoclassical synthesis"

The "standard" macroeconomic model of the "neoclassical synthesis" paradigm presented here is a simplified version of a model presented by Don Patinkin.[8] This general equilibrium model consists of four markets: the market for labor services, the market for commodities, the market for bonds, and the market for money. Each market is described by three equations: a demand equation, a supply equation, and an equilibrium condition. Walras' law holds at each moment, in that if any three equilibrium equations are satisfied, the remaining one must also be satisfied. Money in this model is "outside" money. Perfect competition, absence of "money illusion," and absence of "distribution effects" are assumed for the supply and demand equations.*

The market for labor services

(1) $$Y = \phi(N, K_0).$$

(2) $$N^d = Q\left(\frac{W}{P}, K_0\right).$$

*Patinkin writes: "Each of the foregoing aggregate functions is assumed to reflect absence of money illusion. Each is also assumed to remain unaffected by any change in the distribution of real income or financial assests (bonds and money)" (Don Patinkin, *Money, Interest and Prices*, 2nd ed. [New York: Harper and Row, 1965], p. 200).

(3)
$$N^s = R\left(\frac{W}{P}\right).$$

(4)
$$N^d = N^s.$$

Equation (1) is a linearly homogeneous production function with fixed capital stock, K_0. Equation (2) is the demand function for labor stating that the demand for labor, N^d, is inversely related to the real wage rate, W/P. Equation (3) is the supply-of-labor function and indicates that the supply of labor, N^s, is positively related to the real wage rate. Equation (4) is the equilibrium condition for the labor market. The determination of the full-employment output, Y_0, by the above-mentioned equations is depicted graphically in Figure 5.1.

The market for commodities

(5)
$$C = g\left(Y, r, \frac{M_0^H}{P}\right).$$

(6)
$$I = h\left(Y, r, \frac{M_0^F}{P}\right).$$

(7)
$$G = G_0$$

(8)
$$E = F\left(Y, r, \frac{M_0}{P}\right).$$

(9)
$$F\left(Y, r, \frac{M_0}{P}\right) \equiv g\left(Y, r, \frac{M_0^H}{P}\right) + h\left(Y, r, \frac{M_0^F}{P}\right) + G_0.$$

(10)
$$Y = S\left(\frac{W}{P}, K_0\right).$$

(11)
$$E = Y.$$

Equation (5) is the aggregate consumption function, which states that aggregate consumption expenditure C is a function of real income

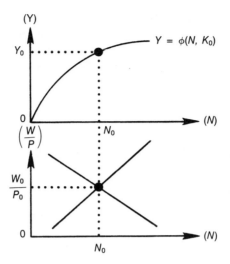

Figure 5.1

The determination of full employment output

Y, the rate of interest r, and real money balances held by households, M_0^H/P. Equation (6) is the aggregate investment function, which pinpoints the three major determinants of investment expenditures; namely, Y, r, and the real money balances held by firms, M_0^F/P. Equation (7) states that government spending is determined exogeneous to the model. Equation (8) is the aggregate demand function. "Real balances" (M_0/P) is listed as one of the three major determinants. The inclusion of real balances makes aggregate demand sensitive to price changes. Equation (9) is an identity equation ($E = C + I + G$). Aggregate supply is depicted by Equation (10), while Equation (11) is the equilibrium condition for the commodity market. The full employment equilibrium situation is explained graphically in Figure 5.2.

The market for bonds

$$(12) \qquad \frac{B^d}{rP} = H\left(Y, \frac{1}{r}, \frac{M_0^H}{P}\right).$$

$$(13) \qquad \frac{B^s}{rP} = J\left(Y, \frac{1}{r}, \frac{M_0^F}{P}\right).$$

$$(14) \qquad B^d = B^s.$$

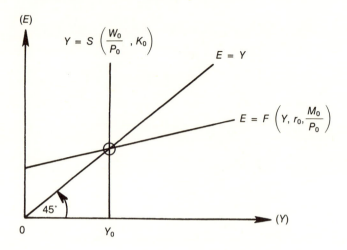

Figure 5.2

Full employment equilibrium in the commodities market

Equation (12) is the demand function for bonds in real terms. It depicts the behavior of lenders. The symbol B^d represents the number of bonds demanded. The expression $1/r$ represents per unit bond price in dollars. The real value of bond holdings demanded is given by the expression B^d/rP, where P is the absolute price level and depends on Y, r, and M_0^H/P. Patinkin states:

> The demand curve B^d also depicts Keynes' basic proposition that there is a minimum positive rate of interest on which individuals insist in order to compensate themselves for the loss of liquidity involved in holding bonds instead of money. . . . For the given real income Y_0, the initial money balances $M^H{}_0$ and the price level P_0, the r at which the desired amount of bond holdings become zero is r_2. This is the economic meaning of the fact that above the price $1/r_2$, the demand curve for bonds is identical with the vertical axis.[9]

Equation (13) is the supply-of-bonds function which explains the behavior of borrowers. The expression B^s/rP represents the real value of bond offerings. The "real balance effect" is again incorporated into

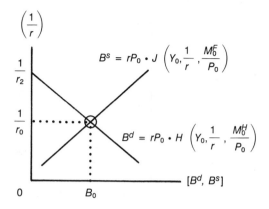

Figure 5.3

Equilibrium in the bond market

this function in the form of M_0^F/P. Equation (14) is the equilibrium condition in the bond market. Figure 5.3 depicts the determination of the equilibrium bond price.

The market for money

(15)
$$\frac{M^d}{P} = L\left(Y, r, \frac{M_0}{P}\right).$$

(16)
$$M^s = M_0.$$

(17)
$$M^d = M^s.$$

Equation (15) is the demand function for real money holdings M^d/P, where M^d represents the amount of nominal money holdings demanded by both households and firms. In nominal terms, the demand function for money may be written as: $M^d = P \cdot L (Y, r, M_0/P)$. Equation (16) states that the nominal supply of money is determined exogenously and is treated as a datum, M_0. Equation (17) is the equilibrium condition for the money market. The determination of the equilibrium rate of interest is graphically depicted in Figure 5.4.

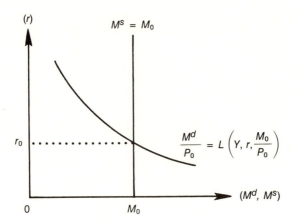

Figure 5.4

Equilibrium in the money market

The initial full employment equilibrium situation is presented in Figure 5.5, which consists of four panels. Panel (a) shows the full-employment magnitude of labor N_0; the corresponding real wage rate W_0/P_0; and the full employment level of output Y_0. Panel (b) shows that at the equilibrium price level, P_0, with corresponding equilibrium rate of interest, r_0, and given money supply, M_0, aggregate effective demand, E, is just sufficient to clear the market for output Y_0. Panel (c) of Figure 5.5 describes the determination of the equilibrium bond price, $1/r_0$, which is consistent with the full-employment values of P_0, W_0, Y_0, and M_0. Panel (d) depicts the determination of the equilibrium rate of interest in the money market.

Following Patinkin's discussion, the workings of the model are graphically described in Figure 5.6. Starting with Panel (b): suppose, for some reason, aggregate effective demand falls from E_0 to E_1. Consequently, producers reduce both prices and output in order to avoid unintended accumulation of inventories. Thus, the output level temporarily falls from Y_0 to Y_1 and the price level declines from P_0 to P_1. The disturbance in the commodity market will have immediate repercussions in the other three markets. First look at the labor market—Panel (a). Suppose, as a first approximation, the nominal price level and wage rate fall proportionately and simultaneously. In this case, the real wage rate remains unchanged ($W_0/P_0 = W_1/P_1$). However, there will be an involuntary departure of firms from their labor

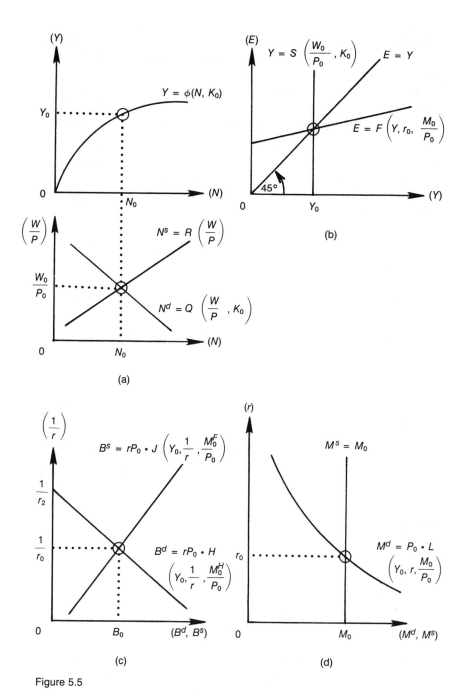

Figure 5.5

The "standard" neoclassical macroeconomic model

demand curve as revealed by point A, "which," in Patinkin's words, "is the simple counterpart of their involuntary departure from their commodity supply curve as revealed by point G" in Panel (b).[10] Patinkin further states: "Not being able to sell all they want, they cannot employ all they want. This is the neglected obverse side of involuntary unemployment."[11] As long as the demand conditions in the commodity market continue to be described by the curve E_1, the corresponding demand conditions in the labor market are described by the kinked curve $RTAN_1$ in Panel (a). Involuntary unemployment is measured by the distance $N_0 - N_1$, and (given the aggregate production function) output falls correspondingly from Y_0 to Y_1.

Turning to Panel (d), we see that the demand for money curve shifts downward from the original M^d to M_1^d due to the "real-balance effect." The determinants of the demand for money as described by Equation 15 are Y, r, and M/P. With money supply remaining unchanged at M_0, the decline in the price level from P_0 to P_1 increases the real value of the given money balances held by wealth holders in the economy. Hence, they wish to hold less money balances; liquidity preference declines, and consequently the rate of interest falls from r_0 to r_1.

The fall in the rate of interest in the money market causes the price of bonds to rise from the original $1/r_0$ to $1/r_1$. The "real-balance effect" is the equilibrating force behind the new and higher bond price. It should be noted that the price level, P, appears in the demand for bonds equation $B^d = rP \cdot H(Y, 1/r, M_0^H/P)$ twice. The P outside of the parentheses indicates that an increase (decrease) in the price level will result in a proportional increase (decrease) in B^d. The second P appears inside the parentheses in the denominator of real balances, M_0/P. Therefore, when the price level increases (decreases), real balances fall (rise). In the present case, the fall in the price level causes M_0/P_1 to rise. Since the demand for bonds is equivalent to lending, the "real-balance effect" in this case will increase B^d, attenuating the force exerted by the P outside the parentheses to cause a proportionate decrease in B^d. The combined effect is that the demand for bonds falls, but less than proportionately.

On the supply side of the bond market, Equation 13 states that the supply of bonds, B^s, in nominal terms may be stated as: $B^s = rP \cdot J(Y, 1/r, M_0^F/P)$. The price level again appears twice in this equation. The first P, outside of the parentheses, indicates that a fall in the price level will lead to a proportionate fall in B^s. The second P, inside the parentheses, will cause B^s to decline further since B^s is the same as the firms' borrowing, and a rise in their real balances will certainly decrease their need for borrowing. Thus, the combined effect implies that B^s declines with P, but more than proportionately.

The combined effects of the lower P and r cause the aggregate demand curve in Panel (b) to be restored to its original full employment position. Simultaneously, full employment is also restored in the labor market as revealed by the disappearance of the kinked demand for labor curve in Panel (a). The involuntary departures from the firms' demand curve for labor and supply curve for commodities are entirely removed, as price flexibility finally restores full employment equilibrium. This is the "tâtonnement" process which not only, in Patinkin's words, "states that the free market itself acts like a vast computer,"[12] but that it also assures the stability of the system.*

Walrasian general equilibrium analysis forms the microfoundation of this "standard" static model. The following important features of the model have been pointed out by E. Roy Weintraub:

1. The system is firmly choice-theoretic, all agents being supposed to make simultaneous (but nonbinding) decisions to optimize, taking prices as given;

2. an equilibrium is characterized by agents not modifying their decisions, so that the prices taken as parameters for each agent, who optimizes subject to these prices, are, in equilibrium, precisely those prices that result (in the market) from such optimizing behavior;

3. all transactions are, in consequence, co-terminal and subsequent to the decision process. Put briefly, the salient feature of the system is that it is *timeless* and, since stable, always in equilibrium.[13]

In such a static world with a constant money stock, price flexibility assures full employment. But the question then arises as to how this model can be reconciled with Keynesian macroeconomics, which permits an extended period of underemployment equilibrium. "The [neoclassical] assumption that the agents all face the same price system," observes Jean Michel Grandmont, " . . . means that they have a common and perfect foresight of future prices and interest rates. While this theory is a very useful framework of reference, its extreme assumptions make it an inadequate tool for representing the world we live in."[14] Patinkin was probably the first to call attention to the important point that "the attempt to interpret Keynes' analysis of unemployment within

*Patinkin pointed out: " . . . a stable system is one in which the process of tâtonnement will succeed in establishing equilibrium prices; an unstable system is one in which it will not" (ibid., p. 39).

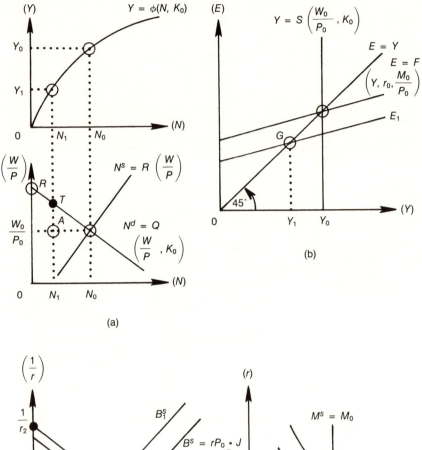

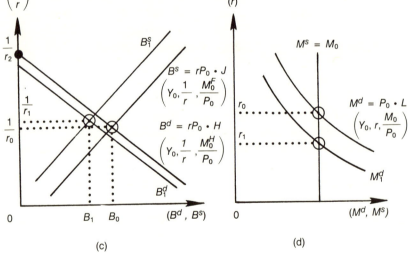

Figure 5.6

The workings of the "standard" neoclassical macroeconomic model

a static equilibrium framework makes it mandatory, by definition, to assume the existence of wage rigidities."[15] This is the negative conclusion of the "neoclassical synthesis" on Keynes's contribution to economic theory. The conclusion is that the *General Theory*, in the realm of static general equilibrium analysis, is but a special case of classical theory, obtained by imposing a restrictive assumption on the latter. As Axel Leijonhufvud wrote, "This broad proposition gives a thumbnail description of the so-called 'Neoclassical Synthesis.' It embodies a concept of the state of art which is perhaps better described in Professor Clowers's term, as 'the Keynesian Counterrevolution' for it represents the final rejection of Keynes' every claim to being a major theoretical innovator."[16] "But," Patinkin wrote, in 1965, "this narrowing of the analytical distance between Keynesian and Classical economics does not generate a corresponding narrowing of the policy distance. It still leaves Keynes insisting that the inefficacy of the automatic adjusting process is so great as to be remediable only by a direct government investment in public works."[17]

The theoretical heritage of the "neoclassical synthesis"

Subjective utility theory, stemming from the so-called "marginal revolution" in the 1870s, forms the theoretical heritage of the "neoclassical synthesis." The "revolution" was a revolt against the Ricardian theory of value and distribution, considered in Chapter 2. Ricardo's preoccupation with the growth process prompted him to make a sharp distinction between those commodities that could not be reproduced by the application of labor and raw materials, such as old masters' paintings, and those that were reproducible. Clearly the first category of goods has nothing to do with economic growth while the second does. Since he had no interest in the first category of goods, Ricardo focused his full attention on the exchange value of the second category of commodities.

The marginalists recognized the dichotomy of the Ricardian analysis and attempted to achieve a more unifying theory of value and distribution. In doing so they replaced the classical objective real cost theory of value with the more elegant subjective value theory which culminated in a unified general theory of economic choice. As Hicks pointed out in 1939:

What begins as an analysis of the consumer's choice among consumption goods ends as a theory of economic choice in general. We are in sight of a unifying principle for the whole economy.[18]

The foundation for this unifying principle was first laid by Carl Menger (1840–1921), who applied the theory of subjective value directly to the evaluation of productive services. Menger pointed out that factors of production exhibit the character of goods because they derive their want-satisfying power from the consumer goods which they help to create. In the parlance of the Austrian school, consumer goods are "first order" ("lower order") goods, while resources are second, or higher order goods, depending on the number of processes they are removed from the final products. George J. Stigler observed: "This is the germ of the theory of distribution through 'imputation'—i.e., the derivation of the value of productive agents from the value of their products."* Stigler added: "Menger does make one specific contribution to production theory, a contribution the importance of which literally cannot be exaggerated. That contribution consists in the realization that the proportions in which productive agents may be combined to secure the same product are variable—later known as the law of 'proportionality' or 'substitution.'"[19] This law leads directly to the marginal productivity theory of distribution.

The precise link between the factor and good markets was finally provided by Philip Wicksteed (1844–1927) and A. W. Flux (1867–1942), who introduced the linearly homogeneous production function into the neoclassical theory of production. Once the Euler Theorem was invoked, the marginal productivity theory of distribution was born. The aesthetic sense of symmetry of this new approach is best described by C. E. Ferguson:

> There is basically one neoclassical theory embracing production, distribution, capital, and growth. . . . [it] is a beautiful edifice erected upon the foundations of microeconomic production functions (and input-output pricing processes). If these production functions, and the aggregate production function derived from them, possess certain characteristics [linearly homogeneous], the central results of neoclassical theory are ob-

---

*George J. Stigler, *Production and Distribution Theories: The Formative Period* (New York: Macmillan, 1946), p. 139. Stigler wrote: "The greatest contribution of the theory of subjective value to theoretical economic analysis lies in the development of a sound theory of distribution. This means the view of distribution as the allocation of the total product among the resources which combine to produce it, through valuation by imputation" (pp. 151–152).

tained and the theory of production and distribution is validated. That is, if certain production relations hold, one may prove that the permanently sustainable consumption stream varies inversely with the rate of interest and that the maximum sustainable consumption per capita is attained when the rate of growth equals the rate of interest (or capital rent).*

Based on the work of Ferguson, the central theorems of the neoclassical system may be stated as follows:

(a) $\qquad\qquad y = f(k) \quad f'(k) > 0, \quad f''(k) < 0.$

Equation (a) is the aggregate linearly homogeneous production function in per capita terms. The symbol y stands for per capita output, Y/L, and k represents capital per man, K/L. This neoclassical production function is the foundation of production theory. It stands or falls with the validity of the homogeneous k inserted in the parentheses. There are basically two strands of neoclassical thought in neoclassical capital theory: (i) the Austrian theory of capital and interest expounded by Eugene von Böhm-Bawerk (1851–1914), who adopted the concept of the "average period of production" to avoid the thorny problem of capital measurement; and (ii) the real homogeneous capital model of the American economist John Bates Clark (1847–1938).[20] The homogeneous k in Equation (a) follows the Clarkian concept.

Further, we have

(b) $\qquad\qquad\qquad\qquad f'(k) = r$

where $f'(k)$ stands for the marginal product of capital and r denotes the rate of profit. And

(c) $\qquad\qquad\qquad w = f(k) - f'(k)k.$

where w represents the real wage rate per man. Equation (c) may be

---

*C. E. Ferguson, *The Neoclassical Theory of Production and Distribution* (Cambridge: Cambridge University, 1969), pp. 11–12. It is interesting to note that Professor Ferguson in replying to the "Cambridge Criticism" of neoclassical theory said: "Until the econometricians have answers for us, placing reliance upon neoclassical economic theory is a matter of faith. I personally have the faith; but at present the best I can do to convince others is to invoke the weight of Samuelson's authority as represented, for example, by the flyleaf quotation." In the flyleaf of Ferguson's book, a quotation from Samuelson reads: "Until the laws of thermodynamics are repealed, I shall continue to relate outputs to inputs—i.e., to believe in production functions. . . ."

used to illustrate the marginal productivity theory of distribution. We can rewrite Equation (c) as:

(d) $$f(k) = w + f'(k)k, \text{ or } y = w + rk.$$

If we multiply both sides of the preceding equation by L, we obtain:

(e) $$Y = wL + rK.$$

Equation (e) is the familiar "production exhaustion" theorem stating that under perfect competition, if each factor is paid according to its marginal product, then total output will be exhausted by factor payments, no more or less. Figure 5.7(a) is a graphical representation of the marginal productivity theory of distribution in per capita terms.

(f) $$dr/dk = f''(k) \quad f''(k) < 0.$$

Equation (f), one of G. C. Harcourt's "Neoclassical Parables,"[21] states that there is an association between a lower rate of profit and higher values of capital per man. This particular relation is depicted by Figures 5.7(b) and 5.7(c).

(g) $$\frac{dw}{dk} = \frac{d}{dk}\left[f(k) - f'(k)k\right] = f'(k) - \left[kf''(k) + f'(k)\right]$$
$$= -kf''(k).$$

Equation (g) describes still another "Neoclassical Parable," linking a rising real wage per man to an increasing value of capital per man. This is another way of stating the traditional belief that capital accumulation is the best way to raise the standard of living—Figure 5.7(d).

(h) $$\eta = \frac{-\dfrac{dw}{w}}{\dfrac{dr}{r}} = -\left(\frac{dw}{dr}\right)\frac{r}{w} = -(-k)\frac{r}{w}$$

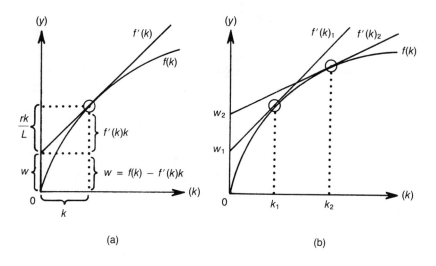

(a)

(b)

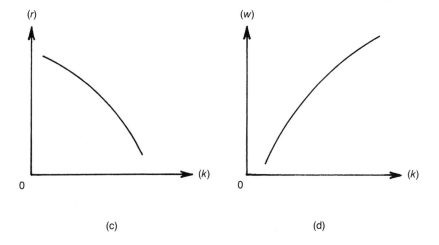

(c)

(d)

Figure 5.7

The neoclassical theorems

$$= \left(\frac{K}{L} \right) \frac{r}{w} = \frac{rK}{wL} \ .$$

The Marshallian elasticity of the factor-price frontier is the ratio of aggregate factor shares, which is the meaning of Equation (h). We thus arrive at the marginal productivity theory of distribution once again.

Since the neoclassical theorems are derived from the per capita production function, all relevant variables are dependent functions of k. Equations (a) through (h) are forceful testimonies of this essential feature. In addition, savings per man, capital widening, and capital deepening can also be stated as functions of k. These relations are described by the following equations:

(i) $\qquad\qquad S/L = I/L = sf(k),$

where s denotes the constant saving ratio;

(j) $\dot{K}/K = \dot{L}/L = n,$ or $\dot{K} = nk,$ or $I/L = nk = sf(k),$

where n represents the exogenously determined constant growth rate of the labor force. Equation (j) depicts the "golden age" rate of capital accumulation, or capital widening. In other words, the "golden age" rate means $\dot{k} = 0$. Then,

(k) $\qquad\qquad \dot{k} = sf(k) - nk,$ or $\dot{k} = \psi(k).$

Equation (k) describes capital deepening, or the increasing value of the capital–labor ratio, k. It will be recalled that this equation is the fundamental equation of Solow's one-sector growth model referred to in Chapter 3.[22]

The general equilibrium analysis of the "standard" macro model, considered in the preceding section, stems from the pioneering work of Leon Walras (1834–1910).* It is interesting to note that both Walras and Marx were great post-Ricardians. Michio Morishima observes:

---

*Recent studies of Walrasian general equilibrium theory have been mainly devoted to his pure economics, which was expounded in *Elements of Pure Economics or Theory of Social Wealth* (1874). It should be noted that Walras also made intensive studies of practical issues. His contributions in this area were incorporated in two collections of essays: *Etudes d'economic social* (1896) and *Etudes d'economie politique appliquee* (1898). Ben B. Seligman in his *Main Currents in Modern Econom-*

Both Walras and Marx founded their respective scientific socialisms on their economics—in the case of Walras, on his pure economics and, in the case of Marx, on his scientific economics. We may say, therefore, that Marx would have held Walras in as much respect as he did Ricardo. It is not right to assume that Marx and Walras would have been completely antagonistic towards each other, as many contemporary economists believe. They were the two greatest disciples—or critics—of Ricardo. [23]

Post-Keynesian developments in general equilibrium analysis have focused on the problem of proving, re-proving, or generalizing the theorems of Walras. The following statement, from one essay of Kenneth J. Arrow and Gerard Debreu (1954), [24] provides ample evidence of this development:

L. Walras first formulated the state of the economic system at any point of time as the solution of a system of simultaneous equations representing the demand for goods by consumers, the supply of goods by producers and the equilibrium condition that supply equal demand in every market. It was assumed that each consumer acts so as to maximize his utility, each producer acts so as to maximize his profit, and perfect competition prevails, in the sense that each producer and consumer regards the price paid and received as independent of his own choices. Walras did not, however, give any conclusive arguments to show that the equations, as given, have a solution. The investigation of the existence of solutions is of interest both for descriptive and normative economics. [25]

The Arrow-Debreu general equilibrium theory was a major intellectual achievement. Unfortunately, it evidenced a significant gap between itself and the macroeconomics of Keynes. Frank Hahn voiced this concern as follows:

---

ics (New York: The Free Press of Glencoe, 1962) wrote: "In the main, the general outlook expressed in his less technical writings was a reflection of the spirit of 1848. Society, he knew, was an association of all men, not merely a device to facilitate the exploitation of some by others. He also knew of the intense disparities that had accompanied economic development. Wages then were as depressed in France as they had been in Britain during the industrial revolution; the distress of the working class was plain for all to see; . . . the socialists had ample reason to grumble. The outcome of this exacerbating situation had been the inevitable explosion of 1848. Although the irrepressible faith in progress which overthrew Louis Philippe appeared perfectly sound to Walras, he abhorred revolution. Change, he thought, should be slow and scientific. Men ought to search carefully for the correct social ideal and, when this was discovered, should advance toward it steadily and without fear. Science at all times, said Walras, would have to be the guide to practice" (pp. 369–370).

General Equilibrium Theory is an abstract answer to an abstract and important question: Can a decentralized economy relying only on price signals for market information be orderly? The answer of General Equilibrium Theory is clear and definitive: One can describe such an economy with these properties. But this does not mean that any actual economy has been described. An important and interesting theoretical question has been answered and in the first instance that is all that has been done. This is a considerable intellectual achievement, but it is clear that for praxis a great deal more argument is required.[26]

Some of the additional arguments required are considered in the following chapter.

CHAPTER 6

The Revisionists of the "Neoclassical Synthesis"

The "standard" macro model described in the preceding chapter reflects the attempts of writers within the camp of the "neoclassical synthesis" to force the economics of Keynes into a market equilibrium framework. As Robert J. Barro and Herschel I. Grossman point out, "The result has been to leave conventional macroeconomics with an embarrassingly weak choice-theoretic basis, and to associate with it important implications which are difficult to reconcile with observed phenomena."[1] Critics of the "neoclassical synthesis" usually attribute these attempts to the writings of Hicks (1937), Reddaway (1936), Meade (1937), and Patinkin (1956).[2]

Don Patinkin's disequilibrium macroeconomics

Ironically, Patinkin was one of the earliest revisionists of the "neoclassical synthesis." In Chapter 13 of *Money, Interest and Prices* (1965), Patinkin reinterprets Keynesian macroeconomics in the context of "temporary equilibrium with quantity rationing."* By denying that

*Jean Michael Grandmont observes: "Systematic efforts have been made recently by general equilibrium theorists . . . to move closer to economic reality. The idea underlying these works is not new and can be found in the writings of J. Hicks, under the label temporary equilibrium. The method was also adopted by Patinkin. . . . According to this viewpoint, at each date every agent has to make decisions in the light of his expectations about his future environment, which depends upon his information on the state of the economy in the current and past periods. One can then study the state of the market in the current period either by postulating that adjustments are made only by price movements (temporary competitive equilibrium), or by assuming that prices are temporarily fixed during the period and that adjustments are made by quantity rationing (temporary equilibrium with quantity rationing)" ("Temporary General Equilibrium Theory," *Econometrica*, 45 (3), April 1977, p. 536).

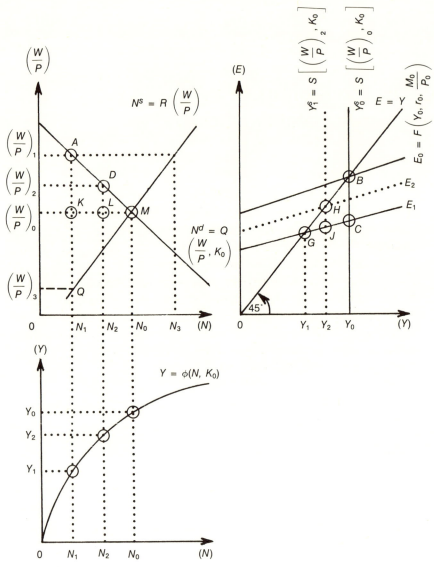

Figure 6.1

Patinkin's disequilibrium analysis

Keynesian involuntary unemployment has its origin in wage rigidities,
Patinkin claims that his analysis is "more Keynesian that Keynes."[3]
Patinkin considers involuntary unemployment of labor to be a direct
consequence of disequilibrium in the commodity market. This analysis
that supposedly "out-Keyneses" Keynes may be summarized.

The labor market and the commodity market are depicted by Figure 6.1. The initial equilibrium in the commodity market is indicated by point B and in the labor market by point M. The equilibrium values of the variables are Y_0, N_0, K_0, r_0, P_0, W_0, and M_0.

Suppose aggregate demand decreases from E_0 to E_1 creating a "glut" in the commodity market, measured by the distance BC. The pressure of this excess output causes firms to bid down the prices of commodities and also decreases the demand for labor. At the real wage rate $(W/P)_0$ less labor input is now demanded. According to Patinkin, "At an unchanged real wage rate their labor input consists of N_2 units instead of N_0." But the downward pressure will continue, for at Y_2 the firms' output will still exceed their sales by HJ units. "Only when this input has been reduced to N_1 with a corresponding reduction in output to Y_1 will these pressures cease; for only then will firms finally succeed in selling all that they produce."

Through this process the economy is brought to a position described by point K in the labor market and its corresponding point, G, in the commodities market. Patinkin emphasizes: " . . . this position is not one of equilibrium; for at point K there is an excess supply of labor, $N_0 - N_1$, which continues to press down on the money wage rate, and at point G there is an excess supply of commodities, $Y_0 - Y_1$, which continues to press down on the price level."[4] Patinkin further stresses:

> In particular, the involuntary departure of firms from their demand curve as revealed by point K is the simple counterpart of their involuntary departure from their commodity supply curve as revealed by point G. Not being able to sell all they want, they cannot employ all they want. This is the neglected obverse side of involuntary unemployment.[5]

> [Involuntary unemployment] can have no meaning within the confines of static equilibrium analysis. Conversely, the essence of dynamic analysis is involuntariness: its domain consists only of positions off the demand or supply curves. Indeed, it is this very departure from these curves, and the resulting striving of individuals to return to the optimum behavior which they represent, which provides the motive power of the dynamic process itself. Thus our first task in studying involuntary unemployment is to *free ourselves of the mental habit—long ingrained by the method of static analysis—of seeing only the points on the demand or supply curve.*[6]

Patinkin's arguments have been further clarified by Robert J. Barro and Herschel I. Grossman.[7] They point out that if the real wage rate should decline to $(W/P)_3$ in Figure 6.1, the supply and effective demand for labor will be equilibrated at point Q. "At point Q, involuntary unemployment has vanished, but clearly this situation is not optimal. The reduced real wage has induced MK man-hours of labor to leave the labor force. Employment remains MK man-hours below the level associated with general equilibrium. Involuntary, i.e. excess supply, unemployment has been replaced by voluntary unemployment."[8] Barro and Grossman further emphasize:

> The conclusion is that too high a real wage was not the cause of the lower employment, and a reduction in the real wage is only a superficial cure. The real cause of the problem was the fall in commodity demand, and only a reflation of commodity demand can restore employment to the proper level. . . . Thus disequilibrium analysis of the labor market suggests that real wages may move procyclically. This result differs from the conventional view that employment and real wages must be inversely related.[9]

Inasmuch as point K in the labor market and point G in the commodity market are not optimal positions, excess supply in the two markets reinforces one another, exerting downward pressure on both wages and prices. Assume for the moment that these decline in the same proportion. What will be the equilibrating mechanism? Again, it is the old reliable "real-balance effect." The "real-balance effect" gradually pushes the aggregate demand curve upward and eventually restores it to its original position. Full employment general equilibrium is again attained.

Patinkin points out that the essential nature of this equilibrating process is not changed if wages and prices do not initially fall in the same proportion. We shall not describe the equilibrating process since the main thrust of the Patinkin arguments has already been stated. To conclude, we quote the following perceptive statements of Patinkin:

> First we see that involuntary unemployment can exist even in a system of perfect competition and wage and price flexibility.[10]

> [Although involuntary unemployment need not have its origin in wage rigidities,] our theory does depend on rigidities. For, by definition, any system which fails to respond quickly and smoothly to equilibrating market forces is suffering from rigidities. But the offending rigidities are not those of extraneous monopolistic elements . . . . They are the rigidities of sovereign consumers and investors unwilling to modify their expenditure habits on short notice.[11]

Disequilibrium macroeconomics and
Robert W. Clower

Robert Clower's revision of the "neoclassical synthesis" and Don Patinkin's disequilibrium analysis may be considered complements. As Barro and Grossman point out, "Patinkin's model involves utility maximization subject to an employment constraint."[12] Clower's revision concentrates on the distinction between effective and notional demand for labor; Patinkin's emphasizes the difference between effective and notional demand for output.

Clower (1965) demonstrates that the Keynesian consumption function and the associated "income-constrained" multiplier process can be explained in a general equilibrium framework without removing relative prices.[13] In Clower's words, "Keynesian economics is price theory without Walras' law, and price theory with Walras' law is just a special case of Keynesian economics."[14] To understand Clower's statement, consider the derivation of Walras' law within conventional general equilibrium theory.

Assume that there are 100 goods being exchanged in a closed economy under conditions of perfect competition. If the tenth good is selected as the numeraire, then the price of the tenth good is determined, $P_{10}=1$. This means that there will be 99 equilibrium prices yet to be determined. To determine the equilibrium prices of each of the 99 goods, three notional equations are required:

A demand equation: $Q_{12} = D_{12} (P_{12}, P_2, \ldots , P_{99})$

A supply equation: $Q_{12} = S_{12} (P_{12}, P_2, \ldots , P_{99})$

An equilibrium condition: $D_{12} = S_{12}$, or $D_{12} - S_{12} = 0$.

The three equations are notional in that they are based on the implicit assumption that all transactors can buy and sell all they want at market clearing prices. In the demand equation, one of the prices, say P_{14}, is the market clearing wage rate, which provides the desired labor income for the household. Thus, the actual (current) variable is not included in the demand function.

General equilibrium requires that all 100 excess demand equations be equal to zero. If money is only a unit of account, then the following identities hold:

Demand for goods $\equiv$ Supply of money.

$$\sum_{i=1}^{99} P_iD_i \equiv S_{10}.$$

Supply of goods $\equiv$ Demand for money.

$$\sum_{i=1}^{99} P_iS_i \equiv D_{10}.$$

The total demand as measured in money value for the 100 goods is:

$$\sum_{i=1}^{100} P_iD_i \equiv \sum_{i=1}^{99} P_iD_i + D_{10} \equiv S_{10} + D_{10}, \, i = (1, 2,..., 100).$$

The total supply as measured in money value for the 100 goods is:

$$\sum_{i=1}^{100} P_iS_i \equiv \sum_{i=1}^{99} P_iS_i + S_{10} \equiv D_{10} + S_{10}, \, i = (1, 2,..., 100).$$

It follows that the total money value of all items demanded must equal the total money value of all items supplied. In algebraic notation, this means that:

$$\sum_{i=1}^{100} P_iD_i \equiv \sum_{i=1}^{100} P_iS_i.$$

This identity is called "Walras' law." However, it is relevant only under full employment conditions. As pointed out by Clower:

> Clearly, orthodox analysis does not provide a general theory of disequilibrium states: firstly, because it yields no direct information about the magnitude of realized as distinct from planned transactions; secondly, because it tacitly assumes that the forces at any instant to change prevailing market prices are independent of realized transactions at the same moment (this includes as a special case the assumption, made explicitly in all "tâtonnement," "recontract" and "auction" models, that no disequilibrium transactions occur.[15]

As shown by Barro and Grossman, Clower's price theory without Walras' law may be succinctly stated as follows:
(a) Maximize

$$U = U\left(N^s, y^d, \frac{M}{P} + m^d\right).$$

Equation (a) is the household's utility function. The choice variables are all notional in nature. The symbol N^s represents the notional supply of labor time; y^d denotes notional demand for output; M/P represents real money balances; and m^d is the notional demand for additional money balances. Utility maximization implies that N^s, y^d, and m^d are all functions of the real wage rate, w, real money balances, M/P, and non-labor income, π.

(b) Subject to the budget constraint:

$$wN^s + \pi = y^d + m^d.$$

As Barro and Grossman state, "The important point is that the notional demand functions for commodities and additional money balances do not have the forms of the usual consumption and saving functions with income as an argument, because the household simultaneously chooses the quantity of labor to sell."[16] In other words, effective demands for commodities and money balances arising from realized income are indistinguishable from notional demands assuming full employment. All household decisions are accomplished simultaneously and instantaneously. This is what Clower termed the "unified decision hypothesis."[17]

In contrasting the above notional process to a situation in which labor services are in excess supply, Clower points out that the utility function in the latter case would be written as follows:

(c) $$U = U \left(N, y^{d'}, \frac{M}{P} + m^{d'} \right),$$

where N represents the realized employment which is smaller than the notional labor supply, N^s. The representative household is unable to sell its notional labor supply and obtain its notional labor income. Thus, actual income differs from full employment income and the disappointed household is forced to revise its consumption and savings plans. This is what Clower calls the "dual decision hypothesis."[18] The consumption function (savings function) effective in the market is the one which is obtained after this reexamination and is the foundation of the Keynesian consumption function. In this situation, "labor income," as observed by Barro and Grossman, "is no longer a choice variable which is maximized out, but is instead exogenously given."[19]

As a result, the utility maximization problem amounts to the optimal disposition of the realized income, $wN + \pi$, which is smaller than the notional income $wN^s + \pi$. The effective budget constraint is therefore:

(d) $$wN + \pi = y^{d'} + m^{d'},$$

where $y^{d'}$ and $m^{d'}$ denote the effective demands for commodities and money. Utility maximization now implies:

(e) $$y^{d'} = y^{d'}\left(wN + \pi, \frac{M}{P}\right),$$

and

(f) $$m^{d'} = m^{d'}\left(wN + \pi, \frac{M}{P}\right).$$

This type of analysis leads Clower to the following conclusions:

First, orthodox price theory may be regarded as a special case of Keynesian economics, valid only in conditions of full employment.

Second, an essential difference between Keynesian and orthodox economics is that market excess demands are in general assumed to depend on current market transactions in the former and to be independent of current market transactions in the latter. This difference depends, in turn, on Keynes's tacit use of a dual-decision theory of household behavior and his consequent rejection of Walras' law as a relevant principle of economic analysis.

Third, chronic factor unemployment at substantially unchanging levels of real income and output may be consistent with Keynesian economics even if all prices are flexible.[20]

The disequilibrium macroeconomics of Axel Leijonhufvud

Building upon the analysis of Robert Clower, Axel Leijonhufvud suggested that "the 'Keynes and the Classics' issues are better approached from a dynamic rather than comparative static perspective."[21] Considering the model of Keynes to be static, while its theory is dynamic, Leijonhufvud states that "the subject of his [Keynes's] work is not 'unemployment equilibrium' but the nature of the macroeconomic process of adjustment to a disequilibrating disturbance."[22] In sharp contrast, the macroeconomic process of adjustment in the Walrasian general equilibrium model relies on the "tâtonnement" process* among transactors who are price takers. As noted by Kenneth J. Arrow (1959):[23]

> The standard development of the theory of behavior under competitive conditions has made both sides of any market take price as given by some outside agency. Thus, for a single market,
>
> $$D = f(p), \; S = g(p) \tag{1}$$
>
> where D is the demand for the commodity, S its supply, and p its price. The functions $f(p)$ and $g(p)$ represent the behavior of consumers and producers respectively. But relation (1) constitutes only two equations with the three unknowns D, S and p.
>
> The theoretical structure is usually completed by adding the condition of equality of supply and demand,
>
> $$S = D \tag{2}$$
>
> What is the rationale of relation (2)? . . . it is regarded as the limit of a trial-and-error process [tâtonnement] describable by an equation of the general type:
>
> $$dp/dt = h \; (S - D) \tag{3}$$
>
> where
>
> $$h' < 0, \; h(0) = 0.$$

*Axel Leijonhufvud writes: "Tâtonnement (literally 'groping') was Walras' term for the hypothetical trial-and-error auction process which he sketched as a simulation suggesting how an actual economic system might arrive at the equilibrium vector of prices. His sketch assumed that actual economic activities were suspended during the 'groping' process and only resumed when the right solution was found" (*Two Lectures on Keynes' Contribution to Economic Theory* [London: Institute of Economic Affairs, 1969], p. 30, note 1).

. . . It is not explained whose decision it is to change prices in accordance with equation (3).

Each individual participant is supposed to take prices as given . . . there is no one left over whose job is to make a decision on price.[24]

Arrow's question was no doubt recognized by Walras. That is probably why Walras entrusted the "job of making a decision on price" to a deus ex machina—the "auctioneer," who was supposed to supply price takers with the "true" market-clearing prices at zero cost. Just like Maxwell's demon in the theory of thermodynamics, the Walrasian "demon" was to perform the sorting process during the tatonnement process and ensure that the system could hop blithely from one equilibrium vector of prices to another. "False trading" at "false prices" was eliminated and the stability of the system was assured.[25]

To make the transition from Walras' world to that of Keynes, the Walrasian "demon" has to be exorcised. Leijonhufvud views Keynes, the exorcist, as reversing the Marshallian ranking of price and quantity-adjustment speeds.* As observed by Leijonhufvud, "Keynes' long struggle to escape seems primarily to have been a struggle with the dynamics of the Marshallian period-analysis."[26] If prices do not adjust instantly, transactions will be concluded at disequilibrium prices. Hicks (1939) called this type of transaction "false trading."[27] Leijonhufvud points out:

Clower's contribution forces a drastic revision of this view [Hicksian] of false trading. Here the attention is focused not on the distribution effects caused by transactions that do in fact take place at false prices, but on the aggregative income effects caused by the transactions which do not take place because of the false prices. Clower considers the specific instance of a disequilibrium price pertaining to the market for factor services supplied by households, thus staying close to the theoretical structure of the *General Theory* ["wages are rigid"]. Current household receipts ["income"] are determined not by the quantity of services a household would want to supply at the price at which such services are currently bought, but by how much it will actually succeed in selling. Its effective demand in other markets will be constrained by the income actually achieved. This is

*In the Marshallian analysis, price can be altered more easily than the rate of output, which in turn can be altered faster than the size of the plant. "In the Marshallian short run . . . the speed of price adjustment is regarded as infinite, that of capital stock as zero" (Leijonhufvud, *Two Lectures on Keynes*, p. 52).

the crucial point. Realized transaction quantities enter as arguments of the excess demand functions in addition to prices.[28]

The Keynesian multiplier analysis is characteristic of Keynesian quantity-adjustment models. In the opinion of Leijonhufvud, the quantity-adjustment model "implies an information process which, like the Walrasian tatonnement, functions apart from the trading process itself, but relates to quantities, not to prices. Households are informed of their real income 'before any trade takes place' . . . The two 'pure' models differ in terms of the kind of information which they assume will be available to transactors in the short run when a previous equilibrium has been disturbed. Both types of models confine attention to information that is available at zero cost."[29]

To complete the exorcism, information cost must be taken into consideration. In the nontatonnement world of Keynes, ignorance and uncertainty abound.[30] Here Leijonhufvud invokes the analysis of Armen A. Alchian, who observes:

A large and costly portion of so-called marketing activity is information-dissemination activity. Advertisement, window displays, sales clerks, specialist agents, brokers, catalogs, correspondence, phone calls, market research agencies, employment agencies, licensing . . . facilitate the spread and acquisition of knowledge about potential demanders and suppliers and their goods and about prices they can expect to see prevail.[31]

Building upon Alchian's analysis, Leijonhufvud (1969) emphasizes: "When 'in the real world' the market situation is changing, it is not possible to have all transactors making decisions just on quantities but never on prices. They must decide what prices to charge or to accept."[32] Thus, when excess supply develops in the output market, sellers must decide on their "reservation-price"; when excess supply develops in the labor market, the worker in the process of searching for a new job must set himself a "reservation-wage." Leijonhufvud writes:

As the sampling of job openings progresses, his knowledge of the current state of the market improves and his reservation-wage will be adjusted accordingly—downwards or upwards, depending upon whether the market is found worse or better than initially anticipated. At some point, the rate at which the best offer known improves will appear to no longer warrant the costs of further research and he will accept a job.[33]

A similar situation will confront sellers. At some point in the transitional process, sellers will realize that their reservation prices have to be lowered due to increasing search costs. Hence, the final outcome will be consistent with the predictions of the "standard" model of the "neoclassical synthesis." However, the nature of the macroeconomic process of adjustment is entirely different. Leijonhufvud's reinterpretation of Keynes's *General Theory* makes the "standard" model a special case of Keynes's more general theory, for it relies on the tatonnement process to restore full employment equilibrium. In Leijonhufvud's own words:

> The only thing which Keynes removed from the foundations of classical theory was the deus ex machina—the auctioneer which is assumed to furnish, without charge, all the information needed to obtain the perfect coordination of the activities of all traders in the present and through the future. Which, then, is the more general theory and which the special case? Must one not grant Keynes his claim to having tackled the more general problem?[34]

The revisionism of the Monetarists

Monetarists' criticisms of the "neoclassical synthesis" focus on three areas: (a) macroeconomic theory, (b) economic stabilization policy, and (c) economic research methodology. Our emphasis here is on macroeconomic theory with some implications for stabilization policy.

The Monetarists criticize the Keynesians of the "neoclassical synthesis" persuasion for failure to (i) make a clear distinction between nominal and real quantities of money and (ii) differentiate between the phenomenon of high interest rates and that of rising interest rates. The Monetarists emphasize that the nominal quantity of money is an exogenous policy variable. The real quantity of money is an endogenous variable, the equilibrium solution of which is determined by the general equilibrium of the real and monetary sectors of the economy. Hence, real money balances are not under the direct control of the monetary authority. This important distinction is made more clear with the aid of the Patinkin diagram[35] reproduced in Figure 6.2.

The vertical axis of Figure 6.2 measures the value of money, which is the reciprocal of the price level $(1/P)$; and the horizontal axis measures the quantity of nominal money demanded and supplied. The initial equilibrium situation is point R where the supply of nominal

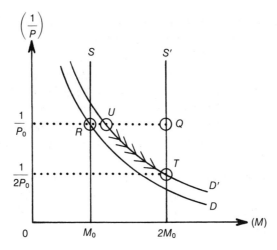

Figure 6.2

Real money balances and money market adjustment

Source: Figure III-2 from *Money, Interest and Prices*, Second Edition by Dr. Don Patinkin. Copyright © 1965 by Tmira Patinkin. Reprinted by permission of Harper & Row, Publishers, Inc.

money M_0 intersects the demand for money D. The equilibrium value of the real quantity of money is depicted by the rectangle $0 \, (1/P_0) \, R \, M_0$. The equilibrium price level associated with M_0, the exogenously given money supply, is P_0.

Suppose the monetary authority increases the supply of nominal money from M_0 to $2M_0$. This will cause a rightward shift of the supply curve to S'. The increased quantity of nominal money disturbs the original optimal portfolio balance of wealth holders. The original optimal money holding is M_0/P_0. If the price level remains at P_0, the increased nominal quantity of money would be in excess supply. As pointed out by Patinkin, "Not all of the increased endowment is expended in the commodity markets. That is, there is also a real-balance effect in the money market. This is reflected diagrammatically as a rightward shift from D to D': at the same level of absolute prices, individuals—because of their increased wealth—feel themselves able to indulge in a higher level of liquidity."[36]

The dynamic process by which the money market moves from R to T is described as follows. At the price level P_0 the amount of excess supply of nominal money is measured by the distance UQ. Wealth holders will dispose of the excess money directly (Cantillon–Hume mechanism), or indirectly via the bond market (Thornton–Wicksell mechanism), raising aggregate demand in the commodities market. Thus, pressures exist in the commodity markets to drive P up and $1/P$ down. Both the money market and the commodity market will be simultaneously in equilbrium again when the price level is bid up to $2P_0$. Equilibrium in the money market is depicted by point T, at which the excess supply of nominal money is eliminated and the equilibrium solution of the real quantity of money is represented by the rectangle, $0(1/2P_0)T\,2M_0$.

Several important points follow from this dynamic process:

(1) The demand-for-money function is the logical link between the real and monetary sectors. This is the reason Milton Friedman calls attention to the fact that

> The quantity theory is in the first instance a theory of demand for money
> . . . and the theory of the demand for money is a special topic in the theory
> of capital. [37]

(2) The real quantity of money is an endogenous variable beyond the control of the monetary authority.

(3) Monetarists have a monetary theory of the price level.

(4) The monetary dynamics illustrates the renowed theorems of the quantity theory of money: short-run nonneutrality and long-run neutrality of money.

(5) The Monetarists' emphasis on the close relation between nominal money and the price level is the basis for their rejection of the liquidity preference theory as a general theory of money and interest rates. As observed by David I. Fand:

> Monetarists, following the Quantity Theory, do not accept . . . the liquidity preference theory of interest rates for several reasons: First, they suggest that an increase in money may directly affect expenditures, prices and a wide variety of implicit yields on physical assets, and need not be restricted to a small set of conventional yields on assets. Second, they view the demand for money as determining the desired quantity of real balances, and not the level of interest rates. Third, and most fundamentally, they reject the notion that the authorities can change the stock of real balances—an endogenous variable—and thereby bring about a permanent change in interest rates, except for very special circumstances. [38]

With regard to the distinction between high and rising interest rates, the Monetarists, following Irving Fisher, relate monetary growth to market interest rates via changes in the price level.[39] They argue that in a fully anticipated inflation, market interest rates will be high, reflecting the rate of inflation, even though real rates (the interest rates implied by the rate of exchange between present and future goods) remain unchanged. Rising market interest rates (the rate represents an exchange between money now and money in the future) is a phenomenon reflecting "adaptive expectations of the rate of inflation." The market rates will continue to rise until the rate of inflation is fully anticipated.

The Monetarists' emphasis on the role of price expectations has important policy implications since it provides the rationale for two paradoxical statements made by Milton Friedman:[40]

(1) Monetary policy "cannot peg interest rates for more than very limited periods" and

(2) Monetary policy "cannot peg the rate of unemployment for more than very limited periods."[41]

It has been generally recognized that the first paradoxical statement is designed to show "why interest rates are such misleading indicators of whether monetary policy is 'tight' or 'easy.' For that, it is far better to look at the rate of change of the quantity of money.[42] Figure 6.3 depicts the arguments made by Friedman against using the level of market interest rates as an indicator of monetary policy.

The diagram is the familiar IS-LM model. The nominal rate of interest is represented by i, and r represents the real rate. The initial full-employment equilibrium is indicated by the intersection of the $(IS)_0$ and $(LM)_0$ curves. With $P/P = 0$, $i = r$. Suppose the monetary authority increases the nominal quantity of money. Consequently, $(LM)_0$ shifts downward to $(LM)_1$; the "liquidity effect" drives i down to i_1 which is below the real rate. The lower nominal rate of interest not only induces an increase of aggregate demand but also causes the demand for assets or speculative money balances to increase. The "income effect" generated by the increase in aggregate demand forces the transactions demand for nominal money balances to increase. Since the economy is already at full employment, the increase in aggregate demand will lead to an increase in prices. The joint force of increases in both the demand for money and rising prices pushes the $(LM)_1$ curve back to $(LM)_0$. Simultaneously, the nominal rate of interest rises. However, this is not the end of the dynamic movements. As the price

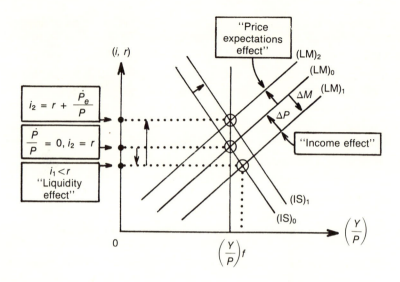

Figure 6.3

The interest rate as an indicator of monetary policy

level continues to rise, a "price expectations effect" is invoked. The LM curve is pushed further back to $(LM)_2$. Simultaneously, the high money cost of investment projects (at the same real rate) pushes the IS curve to the right—from $(IS)_0$ to $(IS)_1$. The dynamic adjustment process comes to an end when $(IS)_1$ intersects $(LM)_2$ and the new equilibrium market interest rate is $i_2 = r + \dot{P}_e/P$, which is higher than the initial equilibrium rate. Thus Friedman observes:

> These subsequent effects explain why every attempt to keep interest rates at a low level has forced the monetary authority to engage in successively larger and larger open market purchases. They explain why, historically, high and rising nominal interest rates have been associated with rapid growth in the quantity of money, as in Brazil or Chile or in the United States in recent years, and why low and falling interest rates have been associated with slow growth in the quantity of money, as in Switzerland now [1969] or in the United States from 1929 to 1933.[43]

Turning to the second paradoxical statement made by Milton Friedman, many economists believe that monetary policy cannot peg the rate of unemployment for more than very limited periods. This is another way of stating the hypothesis of the natural rate of unemployment. The argument is that Phillips curve trade-offs disappear as the expectations of workers adapt to actual inflation experience, yielding a vertical long-run Phillips curve at the natural rate of unemployment. The natural rate of unemployment is the rate at which the expected rate of inflation equals the actual rate of inflation and the real wage rate is at its equilibrium level. The adaptive expectations hypothesis and the vertical Phillips curve are graphically explained by Figure 6.4.

Suppose the economy is initially at point U_0 where both the actual and expected rates of inflation are equal to zero and the rate of unemployment is at its natural level. Assume that the monetary authority implements an expansionary monetary policy with the objective of moving the unemployment rate to a lower level, say U_1. In the diagram, the trade-off for this lower unemployment rate is represented as 4 percent inflation. This is shown by the movement from U_0 to point A on the short-run Phillips curve S_1. The trade-off is made possible by the fact that workers at first do not fully anticipate the 4 percent inflation. Sooner or later, however, their expectations will adapt to the actual rate of inflation and workers will incorporate the fully anticipated inflation rate into their wage bargains. The real wage rate will rise, which, in turn, will cause employers to cut back on employment. Consequently, the economy will move from A to B on the long-run Phillips curve. In the next round, the short-run Phillips curve will be S_2. If the monetary authority still wishes to maintain the target rate U_1, it can do so only by accelerating the increase in the rate of inflation. Thus, Friedman asserts:

> There is always a temporary trade-off between inflation and unemployment; there is no permanent trade-off. The temporary trade-off comes not from inflation per se, but from unanticipated inflation, which generally means, from a rising rate of inflation . . . The monetary authority controls nominal quantities—directly, the quantity of its own liabilities . . . It cannot use its control over nominal quantities to peg real quantities—the real rate of interest, the rate of unemployment, the level of real national income, the real quantity of money, the rate of growth of real national income, or the rate of growth of the real quantity of money.[44]

Turning to fiscal policy, Monetarists generally assert that government spending, financed either by taxing or borrowing from the public, "crowds out" private spending. This view had long been popularized by macroeconomics textbooks before 1972.[45] The monetarist position

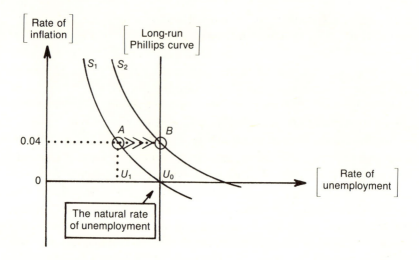

Figure 6.4

The long-run Phillips curve

was usually depicted by a vertical LM curve reflecting the asssumption that the interest elasticities of the demand for and supply of money are zero. Milton Friedman (1972) argued, however, that the slope of the LM curve was irrelevant to the "crowding out" phenomenon. Instead, Friedman based the monetarist position on the "wealth effect." He wrote:

> One way to characterize the Keynesian approach is that it gives almost exclusive importance to the first-round effect. This leads it to attach importance primarily to flows of spending rather than to stocks of assets. Similarly, one way to characterize the quantity-theory approach is to say that it gives almost no importance to first-round effects . . . The empirical question is how important the first-round effects are compared to the ultimate effects. Theory cannot answer the question. (p. 922)*

*Milton Friedman, "Comments on the Critics," *Journal of Political Economy, 80,* September-October 1972, pp. 906–950. Similar views were advanced by Karl Brunner and Allan H. Meltzer in their essay, "Money, Debt and Economic Activity," *Journal of Political Economy, 80,* September-October 1972, p. 951–977. As observed by Roger W. Spencer and William P. Yohe, the "crowding out" hypothesis is not a new one. They write: "It was, in fact, the dominant view before the Keynesian Revolution of the 1930s. Classical economists including Adam Smith and David Ricardo, and neo-classicists including F. A. Hayek and R. G. Hawtrey, found little use for fiscal stabilization efforts" (*Review,* Federal Reserve Bank of St. Louis, October 1970, p. 14). The more recent renewal of the "crowding out" controversy, as observed by Keith M. Carlson and Roger W. Spencer (*Review,*

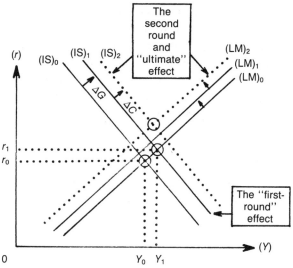

Figure 6.5

Fiscal policy, crowding out, and the wealth effect

Source: Adapted from Milton Friedman, "Comments on the Critics," *Journal of Political Economy, 80,* September-October 1972.

Friedman's "first-round" and "ultimate" effects are explained graphically by Figure 6.5.

Figure 6.5 presents the familiar IS-LM diagram in which the initial equilibrium levels, r_0 and Y_0, are given by the intersection of (IS)$_0$ and (LM)$_0$. An increase in government spending is indicated by the outward shift of the IS curve to (IS)$_1$. Consequently, income rises from Y_0 to Y_1. If the increased spending is financed by borrowing, the "wealth effect" of the increased bond holdings by the public, together with the income increase, will lead to higher consumption and lower saving. Hence, the IS curve will shift further outward to (IS)$_2$. This is what Friedman refers to as the "first-round" effects. The "second-round" effects refer to the leftward shifts of the (LM) curve, since the "wealth effect" will affect the financial markets also. As household wealth increases, the demand for both money and bonds will also increase. As a result, (LM)$_0$ will shift leftward to (LM)$_1$. But the shift will not stop at

Federal Reserve Bank of St. Louis, December 1975), "is traceable primarily to the empirical results published by Anderson and Jordan in 1968 and supporting studies by Keran in 1969 and 1970" (p. 3).

$(LM)_1$, for as long as government's deficits persist, the LM curve will continue to shift leftward. Such shifts have a deflationary impact on the level of national income. They may potentially swamp the "first-round" stimulative effects of deficit spending.

An answer to Friedman was provided by Alan S. Blinder and Robert M. Solow in 1973.[46] They demonstrated that "certain theoretical arguments can be adduced in support of the conventional view that fiscal policy works."[47]

The main purpose of the Blinder-Solow analysis was to determine whether the effects of financing a government deficit by issuing bonds differ from those produced when the deficit is financed by money creation. The Blinder-Solow model consists of the following nine equations:*

(1) (goods market equilibrium) $Y = C + I + G$

(2) (consumption function) $C = C (Y + i_B - T, W)$

(3) (net investment function) $I = I (r)$

(4) (tax function) $T = T (Y + i_B)$

(5) (demand for real balances) $\dfrac{M^d}{P} = L (r, Y, W)$

(6) (exogenous money supply) $M^s = \bar{M}$

(7) (money market equilibrium) $M^s = M^d$

(8) (definition of wealth) $W = K + \dfrac{M}{P} - \dfrac{B}{rP}$

(9) (government budget constraint)

$$G + i_B + Tr = T_x + \frac{\dot{B}}{rP} + \frac{\dot{M}}{P}$$

*The notation follows that of Blinder and Solow with some minor alterations. A dot over a variable denotes a time derivative.

In the wealth equation, B/rP is the real value of the stock of government bonds. The symbol i_B represent interest payments by the government on bonds. While interest payments represents an expenditure to the government, they are also income to the recipients, income on which taxes are paid. Hence, such interest payments are included in both the consumption function and the tax function. The government budget constraint requires that, in each period, total government expenditure $(G + i_B + T_r)$ must equal the total flow of financing from all sources $(T_x + B/rP + M/P)$. The symbol T represents net taxes $(T \equiv T_x - T_r)$.

Blinder and Solow point out: "The IS-LM model usually treats the price level as exogenously fixed, and we shall adhere to this convention. However, it should be noted that we do this strictly for simplicity. There are no real difficulties in adding a production function and a labor market and allowing the price level to be endogenously determined."[48] If P is set equal to 1, the symbol P drops out of equations (5), (8), and (9). The equation for the government budget constraint becomes:

(10)
$$G + i_B = T + \frac{\dot{B}}{r} + \dot{M}.$$

Blinder and Solow further point out: "Suppose that we ignore the dynamics of the model and look only at the long-run steady-state solution [in addition, interest payments are abstracted]. This means $\dot{M} = \dot{B}/r = 0$, so that (10) implies $G = T(Y)$, that is the government budget must be balanced in the long run."[49] It follows that

(11) $$dG = T'dY \quad \text{or} \quad dY/dG = 1/T'.$$

As Blinder and Solow state: "Observe that this long-run multiplier expression holds regardless of how the deficit is financed, and is independent of all functional relations in the model except the tax function. In a word, if the model is stable under each mode of financing [so that it actually approaches its steady state], the long-run multipliers for bond and money-financed deficit spending are identical."[50]

A different result is obtained, however, when interest payments are not abstracted from the long-run steady-state solution. In this case the "steady-state" equation for the government budget constraint is

(12) $$G + i_B - T(Y + i_B) = 0$$

so that

(13) $$dY/dG = \frac{1 + (1 - T') \, dB/dG}{T'} .$$

If the deficits are financed by money creation, then $dB/dG = 0$ and, as before, $dY/dG = 1/T'$. On the other hand, if the deficits are bond financed, the long-run "steady-state" multiplier is greater under bond financing than under money creation, since

$$\frac{1 + (1 - T') \, dB/dG}{T'} > \frac{1}{T'} ,$$

assuming $(1\ T') > 0$ and $dB/dG > 0$.

According to James Barth,

> The interpretation of the difference between the two multipliers given by Blinder and Solow is based upon "second round" effects. Starting from equilibrium with a balanced government budget, an increase in government spending financed by money creation will cause a shift in the IS curve which produces an increase in the equilibrium level of income. This is the explanation offered in "traditional" IS-LM analysis; that is, the "first round" effect. If the deficit is financed by bonds, however, "second round" effects will also occur due to wealth effects and the fact that interest payments on bonds must be made. There are two reasons that a deficit financed by bond sales will be larger than that financed by money creation: (1) income rises less so that the induced tax receipts are smaller and (2) the increased debt will require increased interest payments. The increase in the number of bonds outstanding requires a greater rise in income to induce an increase in tax receipts sufficient to cover the additional interest payments and to cover the deficit in order to achieve long-run steady-state equilibrium.[51]

Although Blinder and Solow have provided theoretical arguments in support of the conventional view that fiscal policy works, the "crowding out" controversy has yet to be put to rest. As observed by Keith M. Carlson and Roger W. Spencer,

> Apparently these issues will not approach solution until additional structural models are developed and tested. The Keynesians [of the "neoclassical synthesis" persuasion] have developed many models, but these models have not been tested as interdependent units. Monetarists, on the other hand, have not offered structural models to go along with their reduced form results.[52]

The counterrevolution of the rational expectations school

The advocates of rational expectations are purists. In their view, the "Keynesian counterrevolution" accomplished by the architects of the "neoclassical synthesis" is not thorough enough. To them, too many irrational elements and inconsistencies of Keynesian economics are retained in the analysis.* Thus, the main objective of the rational expectations school is to apply neoclassical utility optimization principles to all economic problems, specifically to the problems of expectations formation and macroeconomic policy. Neil Wallace raises the pertinent question:

> Perhaps the main problem confronting macroeconomics is the explanation of observed positive correlations between aggregate demand variables, on one hand, and output and employment, on the other hand. More directly, why do not shifts in aggregate demand impact only on prices as is

---

*Mark H. Willes succinctly summarized the shortcomings of Keynesian models as follows: (1) Irrational expectations: "Macro-model builders have generally given their agents 'adaptive expectations.' Agents who have adaptive expectations expect the future to be essentially a continuation of the past . . . The model consequently has no way of formulating expectations for a future that is substantially different from the past." (2) Inconsistencies: "Conventional modeling is inconsistent because its premises about aggregate behavior are based on conflicting assumptions about individual behavior . . . Conventional models often treat consumption and labor as unrelated variables, which implies that agents are inconsistent or even schizoid. . . . The things Keynes has thrown away have made macro models impotent for evaluating policies." (3) Arbitrary measures of success: "In Keynesian models the success of a policy cannot be clearly determined. Because these models replace individual decisions with aggregate actions, they say nothing about individual welfare. . . . Policies designed to reduce employment fluctuations, even if they succeed, can reduce people's economic welfare over the course of the business cycle." See his essay, "Rational Expectations as a Counterrevolution," in Daniel Bell and Irving Kristol, eds., *The Crisis in Economic Theory* (New York: Basic Books, Inc., 1981), pp. 85–90.

implied by what might be called the "classical" full employment flexible wage and price macroeconomic model?[53]

The "classical" model referred to by Wallace has nothing to do with the Smithian or Ricardian models. The term "classical," in essence, is neoclassical theory and refers to a series of composite models constructed by contemporary writers with the sole purpose of sharpening understanding of the differences between Keynesian economics and the pre-Keynesian views. Only in the money market equations can one detect the heritage of Richard Cantillon, David Hume, Henry Thornton, and other monetary theorists of the classical period.

To highlight the relationship between the "classical" macroeconomic model and the macroeconomics of the rational expectations school, we attempt to trace the roots of rational expectations modeling by presenting Branson's "classical model" as background (Figure 6.6).[54]

Demand-side equilibrium:

(1) Output market equilibrium:

$$y - c[y - t(y)] = i(r) + g; \text{ (the IS curve)}$$

(2) Money market equilibrium

$$\frac{\bar{M}}{P} = l(r) + k(y); \text{ (the LM curve)}$$

Supply-side equilibrium

(3) Aggregate production function:

$$y = y(N, \bar{K})$$

(4) Labor market equilibrium:

$$Pf'(N) = P^e g(N)$$

Equation (1) is the output (goods) market equilibrium condition. The symbol y stands for real income; the expression $y - c[y - t(y)]$

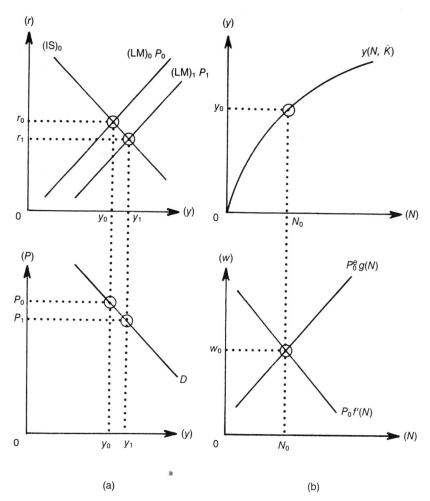

Figure 6.6

Branson's "classical" macroeconomic model

Source: Adapted from William H. Branson, *Macroeconomic Theory and Policy*, 2nd ed. (New York: Harper and Row, 1979), pp. 129–131.

represents real consumption; the symbol t denotes net tax revenue in real terms: $t = t(y); t' > 0$. The symbol i is investment expenditure in real terms, and g is government spending in real terms.

In Equation (2) the two components of the demand for real money balances are $l(r)$ and $k(y)$. The first stands for speculative and asset demand and the second for transactions demand. The supply of money is represented by the symbol M, which is assumed to be determined exogenously.

The intersection of the IS and LM curves determines the equilibrium levels of r and y simultaneously. The aggregate demand curve is derived by asking "what happens to equilbruim output demanded as the price level, P, changes, allowing other variables, such as the interest rate, also to adjust to their equilibrium levels."[55]

The aggregate supply curve is derived from Equations (3) and (4). The left-hand side of Equation (4) symbolizes the demand for labor and the right-hand side, the supply of labor. The demand-for-labor function is:

$$w = \frac{W}{P} = f'(N) = \frac{\partial y}{\partial N},$$

or

$$W = P \cdot f'(N).$$

The supply side-of-labor function is:

(i) $$N_s = N_s(w_e),$$

where w^e is expected real wage rate; or

(ii) $$w^e \equiv \frac{W}{P^e} = g(N),$$

where P^e is expected price level; or

(iii) $$W = P^e g(N).$$

(iv) $$W = \frac{W}{P^e} \cdot \frac{P^e}{P}.$$

By substitution, we obtain:

(v) $$W = P^e g(N).$$

In the "classical" case, perfect foresight is assumed. This assumption implies that $P^e = P$ and that the full-employment output y_0 is determined independent of aggregate demand.[56] The aggregate supply curve in the "classical" case is vertical as depicted in Figure 6.7(a). Figure 6.7(b) shows that under these assumptions an autonomous shift of aggregate demand only leads to an increase in prices without any impact on y_0.

With the "classical" macroeconomic model as background, consider the following simple macroeconomic model illustrative of the rational expectations school.

(1) *The aggregate supply function.* Here,

$$y_t - \bar{y} = a(P_t - P_t^e) + U_t,$$

where y_t is the current supply of output and $\bar{y}$ stands for the full employment output (same as y_0 in the "classical" model) corresponding to the "natural rate of unemployment." The symbols P_t, P_t^e, and U_t represent the price level of the current period, the expected price level of the current period, and deviations of output from the full employment level, $\bar{y}$. The equation states that expectational errors will cause y_t to deviate from $\bar{y}$ and that the deviations will disappear when expectational errors vanish. Expectations in this simple model refer mainly to price expectations. The microfoundation of this assertion, in the words of James Barth, is based on the assumption:

> . . . that a firm will supply output based on relative prices. The market price is not known to the firm. This requires that the firm form an expectation about this price. With less than perfect knowledge, the firm's expectations will be correct only on average. Sometimes it will err on the high side, while other times it will err on the low side. It is assumed, however, that these errors cancel. This is what is meant by rational expectations: an individual or firm will on average be correct, so that any errors tend to cancel and these errors are the "smallest" given available information (that is, not only unbiased but also "best" forecasts are formed).[57]

Thus, it should be stressed that rational expectations do not imply "perfect foresight." In this respect, the rational expectations school parts company with the "classical" model. It also diverges from the

126

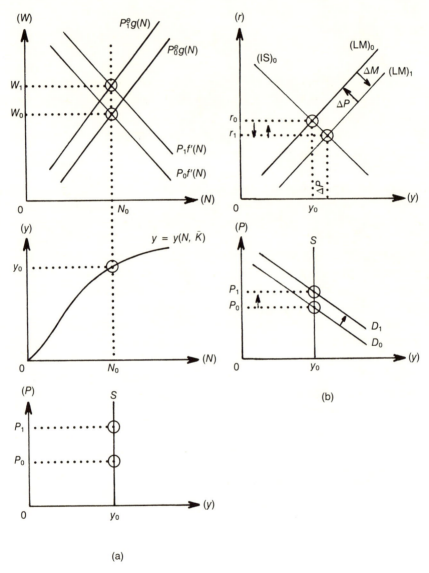

Figure 6.7

The ''classical'' case with $P = P^e$

Source: Adapted from William H. Branson, *Macroeconomic Theory and Policy*, 2nd ed. (New York: Harper & Row, 1979), pp. 125–126.

"adaptive expectations" hypothesis, for economic agents who have "adaptive expectations" always base their expectations on the past. Nothing is said about formulating expectations for a future that is not a continuation of the past. Thus, the rational expectations school considers "adaptive expectations" to be irrational expectations.

(2) *The demand-side price formation process.* Here,

$$P_t = \alpha\, M_t + V_t,$$

where M_t is the stock of money in existence at period t, and V_t is a proxy for all other variables that may affect the price level. This equation describes the inflation-generating process of the simple model and is essentially the quantity theory of money. It states that the price level is determined basically by the stock of money and by some transitory disturbances other than the growth of money stock. The monetary authority attempts to adjust money growth according to some sort of feedback control; that is to say, the current rate of money growth is treated as a function of last period's excess demand for money and some other random disturbances. Rational expectations of the movements of the price level should be the same as the price formation processes represented by Equation (2) of this simple model.

(3) *Rational price expectations.* Here,

$$P^e = \alpha\, M_t^e + V_t^e.$$

The information available to each agent frequently includes some unwanted "noise." Rational expectations imply that each agent will, through the process of trial and error, eventually purge these unwanted "noises." This procedure is often referred to as the "signal extraction problem." Consequently, V_t^e will be reduced to zero and $P_t^e = \alpha\, M_t^e$. This is the essence of the notion that expectations are "rational" in the Muthian sense and hence equal the predictions of the theory.*

*See John F. Muth, "Rational Expectations and the Theory of Price Movements," *Econometrica*, 29, July 1961, pp. 315–335. Muth defines rational expectations as the situation in which "expectations of firms (or more generally, the subjective probability distribution of outcomes) tend to be distributed, for the same information set, about the predictions of the theory (or the 'objective' probability distributions of outcomes)" (p. 316). More recently, P. A. V. B. Swamy, James R. Barth, and P. A. Tinsley in their paper "The Rational Expectations Approach to Economic Modeling," *Journal of Economic Dymamics and Control*, 4, 1982, pp. 125–147,

(4) *The reduced form of the simple model.* Here

$$y_t - \bar{y} = \alpha b(M_t - M_t^e) + bV_t + U_t.$$

Equation (4) is derived by substituting Equations (2) and (3) into (1) and indicates that any deviation from the full employment output is attributable to two causes: (a) the unwanted ''noises'' represented by V_t and U_t and (b) unanticipated changes in the money supply indicated by $(M_t - M_t^e)$. Rational expectations will render V_t^e and U_t equal to zero. Hence, only unanticipated changes in money supply matter. However, if rational people can correctly anticipate the systematic or predictable component of monetary policy, then $(M_t - M_t^e)$ will also equal zero. Under these conditions, $y_t - \bar{y}$ equals zero ($y_t = \bar{y}$), the ''classical'' perpendicular aggregate supply curve emerges, and the economy operates at the full employment rate of unemployment. Consequently, in this view, systematic monetary policy cannot affect real economic activity, not even short-run trade-offs between the rate of inflation and the rate of unemployment.

The general conclusions of the rational expectations hypothesis seem to present a dilemma. Thomas J. Sargent and Neil Wallace make the following observations:

> The conundrum facing the economist can be put as follows. In order for a model to have normative implications, it must contain some parameters whose values can be chosen by the policymaker. But if these can be chosen, rational agents will not view them as fixed and will make use of schemes for predicting their values. If the economist models the economy taking these schemes into account, then those parameters become endogenous variables and no longer appear in the reduced-form equations for the other endogenous variables. If he models the economy without taking the schemes into account, he is not imposing rationality.[58]

While many criticisms can be leveled at the rational expectations school (which is not our purpose here), one should not obscure its accomplishments. According to Rodney Maddock and Michael Carter:

---

pointed out ''that conventional formulations of the rational expectations postulate violate the axiomatic basis of modern statistical theory by confounding 'objective' and 'subjective' notions of probability. It is logically impossible to test the rationality of subjective expectations by comparison with observable frequencies. If a rational expectations conjecture is simply imposed on a model, conditions for identification of the model are more stringent than indicated in earlier literature'' (p. 125).

The development of rational expectations theory will make a more significant contribution to economics in the impetus it gives to research on the
vital areas of learning and expectations formation. It brings to the fore
questions about the availability and use of information. Instead of being
the finale of the monetarist's case against policy intervention, it should be
seen as the prologue for a revitalized theory of expectations, information
and policy.[59]

Criticisms from the Austrian school

Austrian economists are subjectivists. They are the true descendants of
the theory of Carl Menger. As pointed out by Israel M. Kirzner, the two
distinct insights of the Austrian school are:

> First, there is the insight that human action is purposeful, and Second,
> there is the insight that there is an indeterminancy and unpredictability
> inherent in human preferences, human expectations and human knowl-
> edge.[60]

The distinctive methodology of the Austrians is praxeology, which is
defined as the general theory of purposeful human action. The term
was first applied by Ludwig von Mises (1949).[61] Praxeology asserts
that individual agents adopt goals and believe, whether erroneously or
correctly, that they can achieve these by the employment of certain
means.

The common thread that ties the various specific Austrian doctrines
together is the notion of historical (calendar) time. Time is also the
central thrust of the Austrian critique of the "neoclassical synthesis."
Murray N. Rothbard observes:

> All action in the real world, furthermore, must take place through *time*;
> all action takes place in some *present* and is directed toward the *future*
> (immediate or remote) attainment of an end. If all of a person's desires
> could be instantaneously realized, there would be no reason for him to act
> at all. Furthermore, that a man acts implies that he believes action will
> make a difference. . . . Action therefore implies that man does not have
> omniscient knowledge of the future; for if he had such knowledge, no
> action of his would make any difference. Hence, action implies that we
> live in a world of an *uncertain*, or not fully certain, future.[62]

As did Mises, the Austrian economists consider purposeful human
action an unchanging phenomenon to be regarded as the "absolutism"
in economics. Mises wrote:

The philosophy of historical relativism—historicism—fails to see the fact that it is something unchanging that, on the one hand, constitutes the sphere of history or historical events . . . and, on the other hand, enables man to deal with these events. . . . This alone distinguishes human history from the history of changes going on outside the field of human action. . . . In human history we are dealing with the ends aimed at by the actors, that is, with final causes. In natural history, as in the other branches of the natural sciences, we do not know anything about final causes.[63]

The axioms of praxeology are valid a priori. They are not subject to verification or falsification on the ground of experiences and facts. Its statements and propositions are, like those of logic and mathematics, a priori. Friedrich A. Hayek stresses:

In fact most of the objects of social or human action are not "objective facts" in the special narrow sense in which this term is used by the [natural] sciences. . . . They cannot be defined in physical terms.[64]

The praxeology of the Austrian school emphasizes a much broader notion of purposeful human action than the Robbinsian concept (Figure 6.8 presents a comparison of Robbinsian and Austrian school concepts). Recall that Lionel Robbins (1932) defined the subject matter of economics as follows:

Economics is concerned with that aspect of behaviour which arises from the scarcity of means to achieve given ends. The economist is not concerned with ends as such. He is concerned with the way in which the attainment of ends is limited. The ends may be noble or they may be base. They may be "material" or "immaterial"—if ends can be so described. But if the attainment of one set of ends involves the sacrifice of others, then it has an economic aspect.[65]

Mises' concept of human action embodies an insight about man that is absent in the Robbinsian view. As observed by Kirzner,

This insight recognizes that men are not only calculating agents but are also alert to opportunities. Robbinsian theory only applies after a person is confronted with opportunities; for it does not explain how that person learns about opportunities in the first place. Misesian theory of human action conceives of the individual as having his eyes and ears open to opportunities that are "just around the corner." He is alert, waiting,

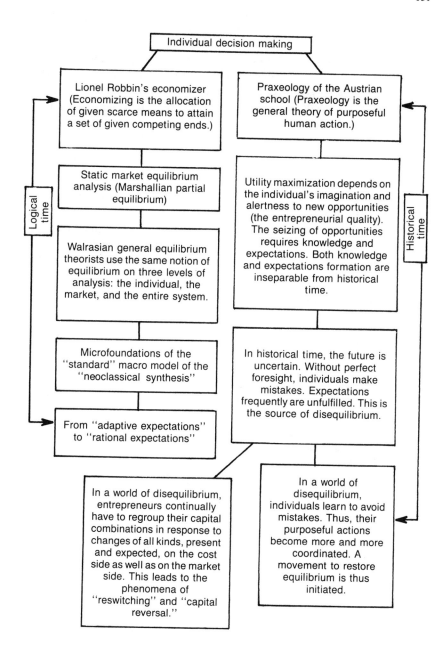

Figure 6.8

A Robbinsian–Austrian comparison

continually receptive to something that may turn up. . . . This alertness is the entrepreneurial element in human action, a concept lacking in analysis carried out in exclusively Robbinsian terms. At the same time that it transforms allocative decision making into a realistic view of human action, entrepreneurship converts the theory of market equilibrium into a theory of market process.[66]

It is interesting to note that the Austrian view of entrepreneurship is compatible with G. L. S. Shackle's emphasis on the role of imagination in the general theory of choice. According to Shackle, the very act of choice involves the imagination of the chooser. For ''choice must concern itself with time to come'' and ''the future is imagined by each man for himself, and this process of the imagination is a vital part of the process of decision.''[67] Expressing Shackle's ideas in the more familiar jargon of economics, one may say that utility maximization depends not only on the decision maker's preferences, budget contraint, and the objectively specified alternatives facing him, but also on the imagined future outcomes of his choice. Shackle says:

Reports from the field [of choosable entities] are labeled with the name of the present in which they are received. In that identified present, ''what is'' is not open to choice. It has already chosen itself. Choice must concern itself with *time-to-come*. The entities that are rivals for election by the chooser and are mutually exclusive for his choice, must, before his choice is made, be co-existent in his thought. They are not reports of ''what is'' but imaginations of what might be.[68]

A subset of man's imagination is what Shackle calls expectations. Imagination could be unconstrained, but expectations about the future outcomes of an individual's choices must be consistent with the individual and constraints. However, both imagination and expectations are essentially subjective in nature. S. C. Littlechild observes:

The concept of entrepreneurial alertness shares many of the properties of imagination: both provide a vehicle for moving outside the static neoclassical economizing problem, and thereby provide the basis for a dynamic market process taking place over *time*.[69]

The Austrian emphasis on a dynamic market process taking place in historical time leads to a second major point: The Austrian writers criticize the ''neoclassical synthesis'' for obscuring the element of unpredictability in human expectations and knowledge in the real world of uncertainty. They attribute these shortcomings to the microfoundations of the "neoclassical synthesis." Ludwig M. Lachmann argues that the Walrasian general equilibrium analysis should be abandoned, pointing out that:

> Walrasians, in using the same notion of equilibrium on three levels of analysis—the individual, the market, and the entire system—succumbed to the fallacy of unwarranted generalizations: They erroneously believed that the key that unlocks one door will also unlock a number of others. Action controlled by one mind is, as Mises showed, necessarily consistent. The actions of a number of minds in the same market lack such consistency, as the simultaneous presence of bulls and bears shows. Consistency of action in a number of markets within a system constitutes an even greater presumption.[70]

The Austrians' disenchantment with general equilibrium analysis is reiterated by Edwin G. Dolan:

> The theory of general equilibrium poses a number of attractive puzzles for neoclassical economists, particularly those wishing to display their virtuosity in mathematical analysis. . . .But from the point of view of an Austrian theorist bent on making the world intelligible in terms of human action the puzzles of general equilibrium are simply not the whole story. Far from being deterred by the fact that the decision-making process of the entrepreneur is not easily expressed in mathematical notation, a writer like Kirzner is able to exercise his own virtuosity at verbal-deductive analysis and produce a variety of useful insights.[71]

The dynamic market process, according to Hayek, is also an equilibrating mechanism. As observed by Mario J. Rizzo, the concept of equilibrium is not timeless, "for it involves the consistency of individual plans in the context of a near or remote future. The activity of planning necessarily implies a temporal framework or horizon."[72] Disequilibrium in the Hayekian sense implies lack of coordination of plans. In other words, in disequilibrium, man's knowledge is imperfect. A movement from disequilibrium to equilibrium must be one in which men gradually learn to avoid mistakes, so that their actions become more and more coordinated. The Austrian theorists do not reject the concept of equilibrium. As succinctly put by Kirzner, "If we reject this hypothesis, then we reject the basis for viewing the market process as an equilibrating mechanism—that is, rejecting the claim that economics can tell us anything definite about the unintended market consequences of human actions.''[73]

The central Austrian concept of a dynamic market process taking place over time is further reflected in Austrian capital theory. They reject the fundist–materialist dichotomy Hicks made in 1974. Hicks wrote:

> There are some for whom Real Capital is a Fund—I shall call them Fundists; and there are some for whom it consists of physical goods—I shall venture in this paper to call them Materialists. . . . Not only Adam Smith, but all (or nearly all) of the British Classical Economists were Fundists; so was Marx (how else should he have invented ''Capitalism''?); so was Jevons. It was after 1870 that there was a Materialist Revolution. It is not the same as the Marginalist Revolution; for some of the Marginalists such as Jevons and Böhm-Bawerk, kept the Fundist flag flying. But most economists, in England and America, went Materialist. Materialism, indeed, is characteristic of what nowadays is reckoned to be the ''neoclassical'' position. Not only Cannan, but Marshall and Pigou, and J. B. Clark, were clearly materialists. Anyone, indeed, who uses a Production Function, in which Product is shown as a function of labor, capital, and technology, supposed separable, confesses himself to be (at least while using it) a Materialist. . . . But the rethinking of capital theory and of growth theory, which followed from Keynes, and from Harrod on Keynes, led to a revival of Fundism. If the Production Function is a hallmark of Materialism, the capital-output ratio is a hallmark of modern Fundism.[74]

The Austrian economists occupy a position that is neither fundist nor materialist. As pointed out by Kirzner:

> Austrians reject the fundist–materialist dichotomy because of the special understanding of the role *individual plans* play in the *market process*. A capital good is not merely a produced factor of production. Rather it is a good produced as part of a multiperiod plan in which it has been assigned a specific function in a projected process of production. A capital good is thus a physical good with an assigned productive purpose.[75]

According to Kirzner, the Austrians vigorously reject the attempt to collapse the multidimensional collection of capital goods into a homogeneous quantity. ''They defy aggregation not only because of physical heterogeneity but also, more importantly, because of the diversity of the purposes to which these goods have been assigned."[76] Based on their fundamental tenets, the Austrian theorists provide an additional cause for the "reswitching" and "capital reversal" phenomena expounded by Post-Keynesian economists during the "Cambridge controversies in the theory of capital." Lachmann observes:

> In a world of *disequilibrium*, entrepreneurs continually have to regroup their capital combinations in response to changes of all kinds, present and *expected*, on the cost side as well as on the market side. A change in the mode of income distribution (the essential argument of the post-Keynesians) is merely one special case of a very large class of cases to which the entrepreneur has to give constant attention. No matter whether *switching* or *reswitching* is to be under-taken, or any other response to market change, *expectations* play a part, and the individuality of each firm finds its expression in its own way.[77]

It should be stressed that the only argument in Post-Keynesian economics (to be discussed in Part 3 of this book) acceptable to the Austrians is that of capital reswitching. They reject Post-Keynesian macroeconomics (or what they refer to as "neo-Ricardian theory") just as intensely as Carol Menger attacked Ricardian value theory. For the same reason, they even disown Böhm-Bawerk as a legitimate Austrian capital theorist. Lachmann stresses:

> Böhm-Bawerk never meant to be a capital theorist. He was essentially a Ricardian who asked a Ricardian question: "Why are the owners of impermanent resources able to enjoy a permanent income and what determines its magnitude?" The notion of temporal capital structure consisting of a sequence of stages of production was a mere by-product of an inquiry into the causes and the magnitude of the rate of return on capital and not the main subject. In pursuit of this Ricardian inquiry Böhm-Bawerk battled on and failed like a Ricardian.[78]

CHAPTER 7

Causality in the "Neoclassical Synthesis"

The workings of the "standard" macroeconomic model show both cause and effect taking place in the same time period. For instance, an exogenous decrease in aggregate demand (the cause) leads to changes in the price level, bond prices, and wage rate (the effects), leaving the real variables unchanged. The causality in the "standard" model is "contemporaneous" in the Hicksian sense.

In handling "contemporaneous causality," the modern economist has learned to think in terms of accounting periods. As pointed out by Hicks,

> An accounting period is not like the "period" of statics [static causality] which goes on indefinitely; it is a historical period, with a beginning and an end. A whole economy, like a firm, will begin its accounting period with inheritance from the past of a given stock of equipment. Though new equipment may be added during the period, the beginning-stock sets limits upon production possibilities; whatever is possible during the period must be consistent with it. The end-stock is not in the same way a limiting factor. It can be changed by current performance; it is nevertheless of great importance just how it is changed.[1]

Thus, "contemporary causality" has its advantages, but it also creates many thorny methodological problems for the modern economist, such as the length of the time period, the fitting together of stocks and flows, expectations, uncertainties, and so forth. This is a reason why students of economics face a bewildering variety of methodologies: the Marshallian "short period," the temporary equilibrium method of the Swedish school,* the Hicksian temporary equilibrium method of *Value*

*The architect of the temporary equilibrium method, as observed by Hicks, was Eric Lindahl (1891–1960), who was a student of Knut Wicksell. The methodological problem was discussed by Lindahl in his *Studies in the Theory of Money and*

and Capital, and Keynes's fixed-price static equilibrium method. They also have to grope their way out of the jungle of expectations elasticities: adaptive expectations, regressive expectations, rational expectations, and whatever other ways exist for dealing with those unquantifiables.

In dealing with "contemporaneous causality," one has to resort to the temporary equilibrium method. Hicks observes:

> [Suppose that] we are seeking to explain the level of income (which, at a given level of money wages, carries with it the level of employment) that was obtained in some particular past year, say 1975. We know the facts of that year, what investment (I) and income (Y) were in that year. We have to compare them with what they would have been if some cause, which in the present inquiry we are prepared to treat as exogenous, had been different. This is not on record; it can only be deduced with the aid of a theory. We have to construct a model, in which the exogenous element is allowed to vary, while other things, so far as possible, are to be kept unchanged.[2]

The deduced results of the "standard" model are by means of the tatonnement process. Implicit in the tatonnement process is the assumption of unitary elasticity of expectations. Both prices and price expectations are thus reciprocally determined in the adjustment process. Perfect competition in this case is a necessary condition. Hick's *Value and Capital* is a book of perfect competition throughout; so is Keynes's *General Theory*. As observed by Hicks, "Keynes was undoubtedly right in insisting that the model must be constructed consistently; so that the equality of saving and investment which is a pure accounting identity (at the beginning of the period), must hold in the model, as it does in fact."[3] In Keynes's formal model, the consistency problem is solved by use of the consumption function to establish the comparative-static multiplier. In this way, the temporary equilibrium method is validated. In the same vein, Keynes treated the difficult problem of expectations by making investment flows depend on long-run expectations, which would be so far in the future that any change in

---

Capital (New York: Farrar and Rinehart, Inc., 1939). Hicks, in his *Capital and Growth* (New York: Oxford University Press, 1965), observes: Lindahl "reduced the [Wicksellian cumulative process] of change to a sequence of single periods, such that, in the interior of each, change could be neglected. Within the single period, quantities and prices could thus be determined in what resembles a 'static' kind of analysis [which we have attributed to Smith and Marshall] save for one thing; the expectations are explicitly introduced as independent variables in the determination of the single-period equilibrium" (p. 60).

them would not matter much in the present. "So to this extent one could talk, and think, of unchanged expectations over the period."[4]

Although causality in Keynes's formal model is "contemporaneous," there is one essential part of Keynes's theory that is not at home under this methodological umbrella. This is his liquidity preference theory. It does not fit well with the other relations of the model. In the quantity theory of money, the bridge is provided by the velocity of circulation. Thus, Milton Friedman (1971) relied on the stable demand-for-money function to construct "A Monetary Theory of Nominal Income."[5] The "velocity bridge" is missing in Keynes's theory. To Keynes, money is not only the link between the past and the present; it is also the link between the present and the future. Thus the proper place for liquidity preference is in the realm of "sequential causality" (in which cause precedes effect) which will be considered in Part 3 of this book. This point has been recognized by Arrow and Hahn, as evidenced by their statement: "If a serious monetary theory comes to be written, the fact that contracts are indeed made in terms of money will be of considerable importance."[6] It is also the rationale for Paul Davidson's *Money and the Real World*.[7]

The disequilibrium analysis of Patinkin, Clower, and Leijonhufvud falls into the category of "contemporaneous causality." Each developed his analysis in the framework of Walrasian general equilibrium, though the concept of equilibrium can make room for disequilibrium. For instance, in his *Value and Capital*, Hicks did not suppose that equilibrium prices are established immediately; rather he suggested that a good deal of "false" trading might occur before they are established. While the prices adjust, expectations are adapting themselves to the information that becomes evident in the course of trading. In the cases of the disequilibrium analyses of Patinkin and Leijonhufvud, the final outcomes of their respective theories are consistent with those of the "standard" model of the "neoclassical synthesis." Only during the transitional period does disequilibrium come in to its own. Clower's analysis may be "more Keynesian" than Keynes, for his "dual decision hypothesis" supplied the missing chapter in the *General Theory*. However, the causality in his model is not different from that of Keynes.

Monetarism is very much at home with "contemporaneous causality." The Monetarists' perpendicular aggregate supply curve (corresponding to the natural rate of unemployment) and the associated neutrality of money thesis fit the equilibrium method much better than

Keynes's theory. Their adaptive expectations hypothesis is also consistent with the framework. In essence, it may be viewed as a temporary equilibrium model in which the exogenous element is allowed to vary, while other things, as far as possible, are unchanged. Monetarism breaks away from the confines of "contemporaneous causality" when Milton Friedman delves into the question of the optimal quantity of money.[8] In this connection, monetarism joins the company of the "golden rule of accumulation" and sails into the realm of "static causality" in which both cause and effect are permanencies in the Hicksian sense.

Under the strong rational expectations hypothesis, economic agents are assumed to have perfect information about the behavior of the economy at the present and in the future. If one could penetrate its impressive stochastic mask, one could say that the strong rational expectations hypothesis (like the "classical" model) is very much at home with "contemporaneous causality."

With regard to the Austrian school, their economics does not fit into the pigeon-hole of "contemporaneous causality." Practically all modern Austrian economists reject the equilibrium analysis of the "neoclassical synthesis." They stress that the central concept of Austrian economics is a market process taking place over historical time. The unpredictable nature of knowledge and unfulfilled expectations in a world of uncertainty are also emphasized. Thus, one may say that their verbal economics (for they abhor mathematical formulations and econometrics) seems to be at home with "sequential causality."

Part III

Contemporary
Reinterpretations of
Post-Keynesianism

CHAPTER 8

The Post-Keynesian Alternative
Paradigm

The Post-Keynesians may be viewed as more revolutionary than the
revisionists of the "neoclassical synthesis."* Instead of simply altering
the Walrasian general equilibrium framework, they would like to over-
turn the entire microfoundations of the "neoclassical synthesis." Post-
Keynesians argue that Walras and the neoclassical synthesis omit the
very factor that Keynes contributed—historical time.† The views of the
Post-Keynesians on this point are aptly summarized by Joan Robinson:

> A system of simultaneous equations need not specify any date nor does its
> solution involve history. But if any proposition drawn from it is applied to

*The advocates of Post-Keynesian economics have been called by various names,
such as "neo-Keynesians," "neo-Ricardians" and the "Anglo-Italian School." The
writers of this school prefer to be called "Post-Keynesians." Some of the leading
figures are: Joan Robinson, N. Kaldor, L. Pasinetti, D. M. Nuti, P. Sraffa, and
G. C. Harcourt in England; J. A. Kregel in the Netherlands; P. Garegnani,
L. Spaventa, and A. Roncaglia in Italy; A. Bhaduri and K. R. Bharadwaj in India;
T. K. Rymes and A. Asimakopulos in Canada; and S. Weintraub, Paul Davidson,
E. J. Nell, A. S. Eichner, J. Cornwell, P. Kenyon, B. Moore and many others in
the United States. Axel Leijonhufvud is not included in this group. As pointed out
by Joan Robinson, "Leijonhufvud has made an heroic effort to show how a theory
of unemployment could be derived from a Walrasian model—Walras without the
auctioneer. But this in fact was not the basis of the argument." See her Richard T.
Ely Lecture, "The Second Crisis of Economic Theory." *The American Economic
Review*, May 1972, reprinted in Joan Robinson, *Contributions to Modern Economics* (New York: Academic Press, 1978), p. 4.

†Joan Robinson in 1962 wrote: "Keynes brought back time into economic theory.
He woke the Sleeping Princess from the long oblivion to which 'equilibrium' and
'perfect foresight' had condemned her and led her out into the world here and
now." See her *Economic Philosophy* (Chicago: Aldine Publishing Company, 1963),
copyright 1962 by Joan Robinson, p. 76.

an economy inhabited by human beings, it immediately becomes self-contradictory. Human life does not exist outside history and no one has correct foresight of his own future behavior, let alone of the behavior of all other individuals which will impinge upon his.*

Thus, the Post-Keynesians couch their analysis in historical time and emphasize the all-pervading influence of uncertainty on economic behavior and economic institutions. This orientation leads to two basic tenets of Post-Keynesian economics, namely (1) the critical role of investment at both macroeconomic and microeconomic levels, and (2) sequential causality.

In historical time, the influence of past history and current expectations about the uncertain future are linked together through the act of investment. Keynes confined his investment theory to the short run (the Keynesian investment multiplier or the "demand-generating effect" of investment). By combining Keynes's insight with Ricardo's vision, the Post-Keynesians treat investment as the leading determinant of both income distribution and economic growth.† Furthermore, the Post-Keynesians, like the Institutionalists, carefully monitor institutional changes in the capitalist economy.‡ Wallace Peterson observes:

I like to view Keynesianism and institutional economics as two trains which started out on parallel tracks toward a common destination. That destination is an understanding of the workings of our complex, but essentially capitalist system. One train—the Keynesian train—spurted

*Robinson, *Contribution to Modern Economics*, p. 127. Alfred S. Eichner and J. A. Kregel in their paper, "An Essay on Post-Keynesian Theory: A New Paradigm in Economics," *Journal of Economic Literature*, *13* (4), December 1975, point out: "Post-Keynesian theory, in contrast to other types of economic analysis, is concerned primarily with the depiction of an economic system expanding over time in the context of history." (p. 1294).

†Alfred S. Eichner points out: "This follows from an underlying belief that in a dynamic, expanding economy (paraphrasing neoclassical terminology), the income effects produced by investment and other sources of growth far outweigh the substitution effects resulting from price movement." See his *Guide to Post-Keynesian Economics* (Armonk, New York: M. E. Sharpe, Inc., 1979), p. 12.

‡John Cornwall observes: "Post-Keynesian macrodynamics can be seen as an attempt to incorporate both the institutional framework of an advanced market economy and the manner in which this institutional framework changes over time into the explanation of growth and cyclical process. Unlike neoclassical macrodynamics, it strives to encompass the real world of uncertainty, oligopolies, new products and technologies, a world in which the 'human element' is reflected in the quality of the entrepreneurial class." See John Cornwall, "Macrodynamics," in Eichner, ed., *Guide to Post-Keynesian Economics*, pp. 29–30.

ahead, but was almost imperceptibly shunted onto another track, one which took it further and further away from its original destination. This was the neoclassical synthesis. What is now needed is to get the trains back on parallel tracks.*

The Post-Keynesian emphasis on the critical role of investment together with the impact of institutional change on economic activities is clearly reflected in their specific doctrines. A schematic representation of the Post-Keynesian alternative paradigm is depicted in Figure 8.1. In the following sections of this chapter we shall address these specific doctrines.

The Post-Keynesian theory of distribution

Recall that the so-called "neoclassical parables" described in Chapter 5 laid the foundations of the orthodox marginal productivity theory of distribution. "For marginal productivity to be a determinate quantity," observes K. R. Ranadive, "the factors need to be capable of variation by small increments and also substitutable at the margin, so that the same output could be obtained by a number of alternative combinations of factors. For the validity of both the assumptions, viz., divisibility of factors and variability of coefficients, the factors need to be defined in their ultimate rather than their intermediate form."[1] In other words, the classical concept of capital as a collection of commodities must be rejected; the Sraffian analysis in *Production of Commodities by Means of Commodities* has to be ignored.

The neoclassical parable of capital-deepening (the assertion that there is an association between lower rates of profit and higher capital per man) requires the applicability of the marginal productivity theory to be confined to the long period. As pointed out by Ranadive, "Not only is it necessary to confine the applicability of the Cobb-Douglas production function to the long period, but a unique aggregate production function also cannot be postulated except under conditions of long

*Wallace C. Peterson, "Institutionalism, Keynes and the Real World" in *Challenge*, 20 (2), May/June 1977, p. 23. Peterson writes further: "Although the institutionalism cannot boast of a precise structure of theory, there is one viewpoint common to institutionalists of nearly every persuasion. This is the rejection of the idea that the economic system can be adequately organized through markets and the free play of individual self-interest. . . . Economic activity is part of an ongoing process, not part of a mechanistic system tending toward a state of balance or equilibrium. . . . We cannot ignore history and time. When we bring history and time into our analysis it means that the economic system never returns to the same condition, as much as we might wish otherwise" (pp. 23–25).

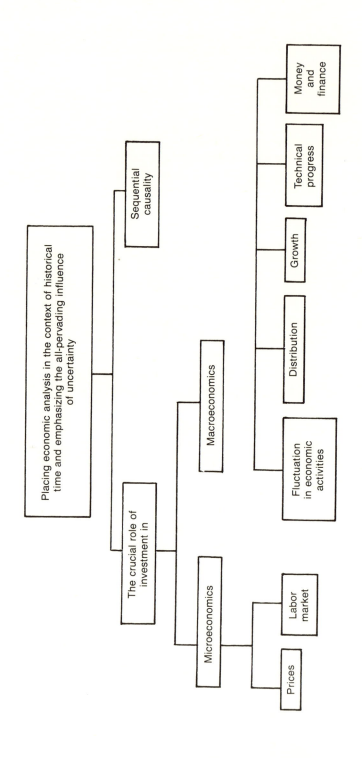

Figure 8.1

The Post-Keynesian alternative paradigm

period equilibrium of the system as a whole, which, ipso facto, entails equilibrium for every decision-making unit."[2] This means that the rationalization of the unique aggregate production function which is the foundation of the beautiful edifice of neoclassical theory (borrowing a phrase from Ferguson) requires the long-run general equilibrium of the system.

The Post-Keynesians have argued that the neoclassical parables have many limitations. The opening rounds of the debate were concerned with the question of reswitching of techniques.[3] However, as emphasized by Eichner and Kregel, the Post-Keynesian arguments are not tied to the question of capital reswitching.* In addition to the theoretical problems noted by Ranadive, there is a deeper logical weakness in the marginal productivity theory of distribution, namely, in the treatment of capital as a mere instrument of production (in the aggregate production function). Borrowing from Marx's treatment of capital, A. Bhaduri writes:

> The central consequence of treating "capital" as a mere physical instrument of production results in the prevalent neo-classical methodology of treating "production" and "distribution" as two separable branches of inquiry. The conventional "production function" is supposed to depict the pure production aspect of an economy, and the profit-maximizing behavior leading to marginal calculations gives a corresponding "marginal productivity theory" of distribution. The single most important consequence of accepting the Marxian definition of "capital," on the other hand, is to recognize the logical untenability of the separation between "production" and "distribution" in a general conceptual scheme.†

*Eichner and Kregel write: "Trying to grasp the potential [of the alternative paradigm] from the arguments about capital reversal and double-switching, however, is likely to be just as treacherous as trying to understand the marginalist revolution . . . from the debate over the 'wages fund' doctrine" ("An Essay on Post-Keynesian Theory," in Eichner, ed., *Guide to Post-Keynesian Economics*, p. 1294).

†A. Bhaduri, "On the Significance of Recent Controversies on Capital Theory: A Marxian View," *Economic Journal*, 79, 1969, pp. 532–539; reprinted in G. C. Harcourt and N. F. Laing, eds., *Capital and Growth* (Middlesex, England: Penguin Books Ltd., 1971), p. 254. Marx claimed that capital as an aid to labor in the production process should be viewed in the context of a social organization. Each type of economic organization develops its own "relations of production" or "rules of the game," often sanctioned by law or religion. Economic theory which ignores such "rules of the game" is ahistorical in spirit. Distribution is also related to the "relations of production," for it is a social ownership relation giving rise to capitalists' income. In the Marxian view, means of production are not "capital" unless owned by the capitalists. This is the reason why Marx criticized Ricardo for ignoring the concept of "mode of production."

Bhaduri then proceeds to demonstrate the artificiality of the marginal productivity theory of distribution as follows:[4]

(1) $y = rk + w$. This is a definitional equation depicting the distribution of the net national income, y, between profits, rk, and wage income, w. The equation is stated in per capita terms.

(2) $dy = rdk + kdr + dw$. This equation is obtained by totally differentiating equation (1) and shows that the marginal product of capital, dy/dk, does not in general equal the rate of profit, r.

Bhaduri points out that "it is clear that the 'marginal productivity' relation will hold provided, by fluke or by assumption,"

(3) $kdr + dw = 0$, which in turn implies $dw/dr = k$. This expression is equivalent to Samuelson's condition that the elasticity of the "factor-price frontier" equal the distributive shares, when the factors are paid according to their marginal products in an economy with a homogeneous production function of degree one in labor and capital.[5]

Bhaduri further points out that the Samuelson condition is based on very restrictive assumptions and employs P. Garegnani's diagram (1970) to illustrate this point.[6]

In Figure 8.2, the wage-profit frontier for a technique is represented by the curve AB. Samuelson needs a linear relation between profit and wage in order to rationalize the marginal productivity theory of distribution. This point can be developed as follows:

(4) The value of capital per man is: $k = (y - w)/r$. This equation is derived from Equation (1). In Figure 8.2, the value of capital is given by $\tan \phi$, which is the slope joining the points A and P.

(5) From Equation (1), by setting $r = 0$, the maximum wage is depicted by $0A$ in the diagram. Similarly, setting the wage to 0, one obtains the maximum profit $0B$.

(6) The slope of the AB wage-profit frontier at point P is given by $\tan \psi$, which does not coincide with $\tan \phi$.

(7) Therefore, only a linear relation between wage and profit will make

$$-dw/dr = k = \frac{y - w}{r}$$

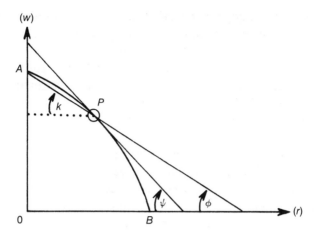

Figure 8.2

The Garegnani diagram showing the restrictive assumptions of the Samuelson condition

Source: P. Garegnani, ''Heterogeneous Capital, the Production Function and the Theory of Distribution,'' *Review of Economic Studies, 37*(3), 1970, pp. 407–436.

or

$$\tan \psi = \tan \phi.$$

Bhaduri further points out: ''The assumption which Professor Samuelson makes to produce a straight-line frontier is the uniform 'capital-labour ratio' in all lines of production. In Marx's terminology this is equivalent to the assumption of uniform 'organic composition of capital' in all lines of production—exactly the assumption which Marx himself made in the first two volumes of his *Capital* to avoid the famous 'transformation problem' that appears only in the third volume. Professor Samuelson rediscovered the importance of this assumption about a hundred years later!''[7]

   The Post-Keynesian rejection of the marginal productivity theory of distribution is, in effect, an indirect challenge to the entire microfoundations of the ''neoclassical synthesis.'' In order to offer an alternative explanation of income distribution, the Post-Keynesians seek its determinants outside the sphere of market exchange. They have found them in investment and oligopolistic market structure. As observed by J. A. Kregel, the following relations make up the central core of the Post-Keynesian approach to the distribution of income:

(1) the control of investment, and thus growth, by profit recipients (either entrepreneurs or large corporations) and the control of prices by producers (oligopolistic corporations);

(2) the dependence of the rate of change of output per worker on the rate of gross investment and technical progress;

(3) an interdependence between the growth of output on the one hand and the distribution of income between wages and profits on the other hand (with that interdependence affecting the willingness and ability of entrepreneurial organizations to carry out investment).[8]

Nicholas Kaldor's "widow's cruse" theory of distribution can be considered as the basic model of the Post-Keynesian approach to distribution. Using S_w and S_c to represent aggregate savings out of wages and profits respectively, Kaldor formulates the following identities:

(1K)
$$Y = W + P,$$

where W stands for wage-earners' income and P represents capitalist's income.

(2K)
$$S = S_w + S_c,$$

the definitional equation for aggregate savings.

(3K)
$$S_w = s_w W.$$

(4K)
$$S_c = s_c P$$

(5K)
$$I = \bar{I},$$

stating investment to be a exogenous variable.

As pointed out by Kaldor, "the interpretative value of the model depends on the 'Keynesian' hypothesis that investment, or rather, the ratio of investment to output, can be treated as an independent variable, invariant with respect to changes in the two savings propensities.[9]

(6K)
$$\bar{I} = S,$$

the condition for dynamic equilibrium.

It should be noted that this equilibrium condition is that of the "steady-state" or "golden age" growth path. The Post-Keynesians recognize the "steady state" to be an artificial setting and try to avoid it to the extent possible. The objective in employing this device here is to provide a theoretical framework for highlighting the determinants of the rate of profit other than those given by the marginal productivity theory. Only in the "steady-state" setting are the rate of profit on capital (which is ex ante and forward-looking, expressing expectations of returns to be obtained from the finance invested) and the ex post rate of profit (which is a calculation of the returns actually realized) the same. Only in such an artificial setting can the determinants of the equilibrium rate of profit be more precisely identified. By substitution, Kaldor obtains:

(7K)
$$\bar{I} = s_c P + s_w W = s_c P + s_w(Y - P) = (s_c - s_w) P + s_w Y.$$

Dividing Equation (7K) by Y, we derive the equation for the profit share in income:

(8K)
$$\frac{P}{Y} = -\frac{s_w}{s_c - s_w} + \frac{1}{s_c - s_w}\frac{\bar{I}}{Y}.$$

The equation for the rate of profit is obtained by dividing Equation (7K) by K:

(9K)
$$r = \frac{P}{K} = \frac{s_w}{s_c - s_w}\frac{Y}{K} + \frac{1}{s_c - s_w}\frac{I}{K}.$$

Equation (8K) states that, given the wage-earners' and capitalists' propensities to save, the share of profit in income depends on the ratio of investment to output. This is the so-called "widow's cruse" theory of distribution* for the equation indicates that the more capitalists

---

*The expression "widow's cruse" is derived from Keynes's *Treatise of Money*, Vol. 1 (London: Macmillan, 1930), p. 139, wherein Keynes considered profits as a "widow's cruse." Keynes wrote: "If entrepreneurs choose to spend a portion of

invest, the higher will be profit's share of income. This proposition is
described graphically in Figure 8.3.

Kaldor points out that in the limiting case where $s_w = 0$ and $s_c = 1$,
Equation (8K) can be rewritten as:

$$(10K) \qquad \frac{P}{Y} = \frac{1}{s_c} \frac{I}{Y} .$$

The "widow's cruse" idea is brought out in sharp relief by this equation. Furthermore, this is what Pasinetti considers the "new answer to
the old Ricardian problem." "For Ricardo the wage rate is fixed
exogenously and all that remains (after paying rent) goes to profits. For
Kaldor the rate of profit is determined exogenously by the natural rate
of growth of output and the capitalists' propensity to save; and all that
remains goes to wages. For the former it is profits that take up the
feature of residual category; for the latter it is wages."[10]

Kaldor's "new answer" is most explicit in the limiting case where
$s_w = 0$:

$$(11K) \qquad r = \frac{P}{K} = \frac{1}{s_c} \frac{I}{K} , \text{ or } \frac{P}{K} = \frac{1}{s_c} \frac{K}{K} .$$

In "golden age" growth (Harrod's "natural rate of growth"), $\dot{K}/K = \dot{L}/L = n$. Substituting this equation into Equation (11K), one obtains:

---

their profits on consumption . . . the effect is to increase the profits on the sale of
liquid consumption goods. . . . Thus, however much of their profits entrepreneurs
spend on consumption, the increment of wealth belonging to entrepreneurs remains
the same as before. Thus profits, as a source of capital increment for entrepreneurs,
are a widow's cruse which remains undepleted however much of them may be devoted to riotous living. When on the other hand, entrepreneurs are making losses,
and seek to recoup these losses by curtailing their normal expenditure on consumption, i.e. by saving more, the cruse becomes a Danaid jar *which will never be filled
up*; for the effect of this reduced expenditure is to inflict on the producers of con-
sumption-goods a loss of an equal amount." Kaldor observes in the footnote of p.
227, "Alternative Theories of Distribution," *Review of Economic Studies, 23,* (2),
1955–56, "This passage, I think, contains the true seed of the ideas developed in
the *General Theory*—as well as showing the length of the road that had to be tra-
versed before arriving at the conceptual framework presented in the later work."

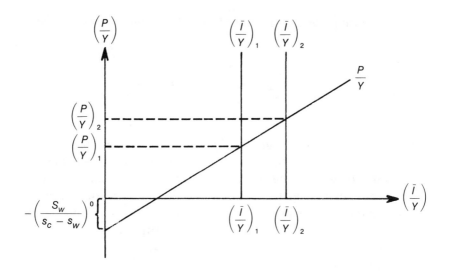

Figure 8.3

The "widow's cruse" distribution

Source: Charles E. Ferguson, *The Neoclassical Theory of Production and Distribution* (London: Cambridge University Press, 1969) p. 315. Reprinted by permission.

$$
\text{(12K)} \qquad r = \frac{P}{K} = \frac{n}{s_c},
$$

which pinpoints the determinants of the rate of profit beyond those given by the marginal productivity theory.

This basic model can also be employed to demonstrate the linkage between distribution and growth through the common critical determinant of investment. Recall that Harrod's growth model depicts the inherent instability of the capitalist system. This instability is the result of a divergence between the warranted growth rate of output and the natural growth rate. This has been termed the "knife-edge" problem. The "widow's cruse" theory of distribution is one resolution of the Harrodian problem.

Expressing the savings function $[S = s_w Y + (s_c - s_w)P]$ in a different form we have:

$$
\text{(13K)} \qquad s = \frac{S}{Y} = s_w + (s_c - s_w)\frac{P}{Y}.
$$

Incorporating the growth rate of output into this equation yields:

$$(14K) \qquad \frac{s}{\beta} = \frac{s_w + (s_c - s_w) \dfrac{P}{Y}}{\beta} = n$$

where s/β is Harrod's "warranted growth rate" and n represents the "natural rate." Kaldor emphasizes that "the 'warranted' and the 'natural' rates of growth are not independent of one another; if profit margins are flexible, the former will adjust itself to the latter through a consequential change in P/Y."[11] What causes P/Y to change? The answer is given by Equation (8K), or its simplified version, Equation (10K). In the case where $s/\beta < n$, an increase in investment exceeding ex ante saving implies excess aggregate demand. Consequently, prices will rise and profit margins (P/Y) will also increase. If $s_c > s_w$, this redistribution of income in favor of profits will increase aggregate real saving and the "warranted" and "natural" rates will be brought into equality again. The redistribution effect is applicable to the converse case as well. However, it is evident that $s_c > s_w$ is the stability condition.

In his theory of distribution Kaldor recognizes real world institutional developments more than most of the writers of the "neoclassical synthesis." For example, he imposes the following constraints on his model:

$$(15K) \qquad\qquad w > w_{min}$$

reflecting the influence of labor unions or government policy, and

$$(16K) \qquad\qquad P/Y > m,$$

where m represents minimum profits.

Kaldor thereby stresses that there are limits to this equilibrium mechanism. The first limit is that the real wage cannot fall below a certain minimum and the second is that "the indicated share of profits cannot be below the level which yields the minimum rate of profit necessary to induce capitalists to invest their capital."[12] These constraints are illustrated by Figure 8.4.*

*This is Kaldor's diagram adopted by G. C. Harcourt with slight modifications.

Post-Keynesian growth theory

Post-Keynesian growth theory is still in the formative stage. However, there are certain discernible features of its central core that can be outlined. The framework of this central core was laid out by Joan Robinson. We will attempt to restate some of the important contributions of this pioneering Post-Keynesian theorist.

Joan Robinson emphatically rejects what she calls the "pseudo-causal models" of economic growth constructed by theorists of the "neoclassical synthesis." She writes:

> In a model depicting equilibrium positions there is no causation. It consists of a closed circle of simultaneous equations. The value of each element is entailed by the values of the rest. At any moment in logical time, the past is determined just as much as the future. In a historical model, causal relations have to be specified. Today is a break in time between an unknown future and an irrevocable past. What happens next will result from the interactions of human beings within the economy. Movement can only be forward. [13]

Joan Robinson urges that "to build a causal model, we must start not from equilibrium relations but from rules and motives governing human behavior. We therefore have to specify to what kind of economy the model applies, for various kinds of economies have different sets of rules." [14]

The causal model that Joan Robinson outlines represents her initial attempt to analyze the growth process of the modern capitalistic world. She groups the determinants of the growth process under seven headings: (1) technical conditions, (2) investment policy, (3) thriftiness conditions, (4) competitive conditions, (5) the wage bargain, (6) financial conditions, and (7) the initial stock of capital goods and the state of expectations formed by past experience. The purpose of highlighting these determinants is twofold: (a) to distinguish the factors responsible for long-run growth of output from those responsible for short-run fluctuations around a trend line and (b) to show the possibility of various alternative growth paths to that of the "golden age" path, such as the "limping golden age"—representing growth at less than full employment, "leaden age"—describing growth with rising rates of unemployment, "bastard golden age," and so on. [15]

The causal links of Joan Robinson's model may be described as follows: "The dynamic force of a capitalist economy is capital accumu-

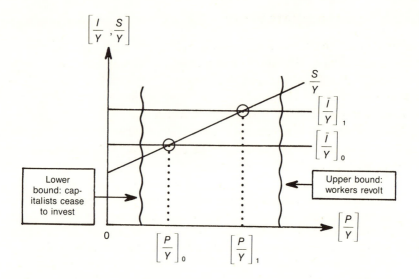

Figure 8.4

The Kaldorian constraints

Source: G. C. Harcourt, *Some Cambridge Controversies in the Theory of Capital* (London: Cambridge University Press, 1972) p. 209. Reprinted by permission.

lation and growth. The accumulation going on in a particular situation determines the level of profits obtainable in it, and thus determines the rate of profit expected on investment. The rate of profit in turn influences the rate of accumulation.''[16] This is the double-sided relationship between the rate of profit (P/K) and the rate of accumulation (I/K) which Robinson depicts in Figure 8.5.

The diagram shows the ''short-period situations which chances and changes of history throw up''[17] and is the central mechanism of Joan Robinson's causal model. Why did she use a short-period model to analyze long-run growth?—because Joan Robinson's view is similar to that of Michal Kalecki, who stated: ''The long-run trend is but a slowly changing component of a chain of short-period situations; it has no independent entity.''[18] The short-period she employs is the Marshallian theory of the firm in the short run. The double-sided relationship between the rate of profit and the rate of accumulation is derived from the short-period production and pricing decisions of the firm. The Robinsonian short-period model is depicted in Figure 8.6.

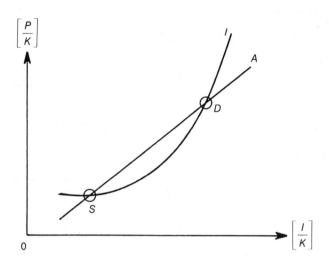

Figure 8.5

The double-sided relationship between r and $\dot{K}/K$

Source: Joan Robinson, *Essays in the Theory of Economic Growth* (New York: St. Martin's Press, 1962) p. 48. Reprinted by permission of Macmillan, London and Basingstoke.

In Figure 8.6 the vertical axis measures aggregate supply (Z) and aggregate demand (D). The horizontal axis measures quantities of workers employed (N). The aggregate supply curve (Z_e) indicates alternative aggregate supply prices (expected sales-proceeds) which would leave producers satisfied for the alternative levels of employment that they could maintain. The market wage rate is assumed to be historically determined $(\bar{w})$, and $0\bar{w}N$ is the wage bill line. The vertical distance $0A$ indicates the normal profits expected on the committed finance in the current period. The expected supply price of output is equal to the sum of the total wage bill and normal profits $(p = \bar{w}N + P$, where p represents supply price and P denotes normal profits).

Suppose that expected aggregate demand is given by Ed_e. The point of intersection of aggregate supply and demand is Y. Then N workers will be hired to produce the total output YN. The expectations of the producers are fulfilled; the realized supply price consists of YG normal profits and GN in total wages. Under the conditions of "tranquillity" where expectations are not disappointed, the double-sided relationship between the rate of profit and the rate of accumulation can be derived.

158

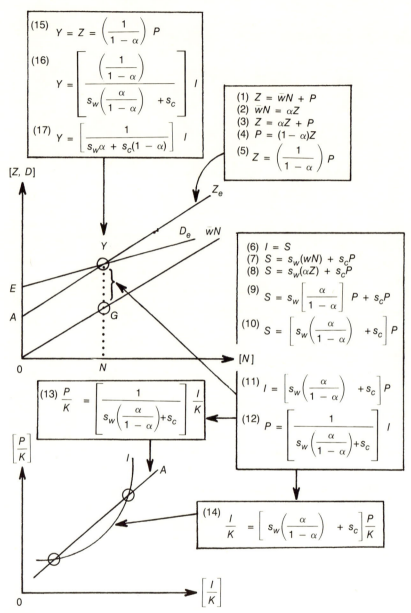

Figure 8.6

Joan Robinson's short-period model

Source: Adapted from Paul Davidson, *Money and the Real World*, 2nd ed. (New York: John Wiley & Sons, 1979), pp. 120–129.

Following Paul Davidson's treatment,[19] the aggregate supply price can be defined symbolically as:

(1R) $$Z = \bar{w}N + P.$$

Let $\bar{w}N$ be some constant proportion (α) of Z; i.e.,

(2R) $$\bar{w}N = \alpha Z.$$

Substituting (2R) into (1R), one obtains:

(3R) $$Z = \alpha Z + P.$$

Rearranging terms, we have:

(4R) $$P = (1 - \alpha)Z,$$

or

(5R) $$Z = \left(\frac{1}{1 - \alpha} \right) P.$$

Under conditions of "tranquillity," ex ante saving equals ex ante investment, or

(6R) $$I = S.$$

Total savings (S) is defined as:

(7R) $$S = s_w (\bar{w}N) + s_c P.$$

Substituting (2R) into (7R), we have:

(8R) $$S = s_w (\alpha Z) + s_c P.$$

Substituting (5R) into (8R), the following is derived:

(9R) $$S = s_w \frac{\alpha}{1 - \alpha} P + s_c P.$$

Rearranging terms, we obtain the following three equations:

(10R)
$$S = \left[s_w \left(\frac{\alpha}{1 - \alpha} \right) + s_c \right] P.$$

(11R)
$$I = \left[s_w \left(\frac{\alpha}{1 - \alpha} \right) + s_c \right] P.$$

(12R)
$$P = \left[\frac{1}{s_w \left(\dfrac{\alpha}{1 - \alpha} \right) + s_c} \right] I.$$

Dividing (11R) by K, we obtain an equation stating that the rate of profit depends on the rate of capital accumulation:

(13R)
$$\frac{P}{K} = \left[\frac{1}{s_w \left(\dfrac{\alpha}{1 - \alpha} \right) + s_c} \right] \frac{I}{K}.$$

Obtained by dividing (11R) through by K, Equation (14R) states that the rate of accumulation is influenced by the rate of profit:

(14R)
$$\frac{I}{K} = \left[s_w \left(\frac{\alpha}{1 - \alpha} \right) + s_c \right] \frac{P}{K}.$$

The equilibrium level of output is given by

(15R)
$$Y = \left[\frac{1}{s_w \alpha + s_c(1 - \alpha)} \right] I.$$

which can be transformed into the Keynesian investment multiplier:

(16R)
$$\Delta Y = \left[\frac{1}{s_w \alpha + s_c(1 - \alpha)} \right] \Delta I.$$

Having derived the symbolic representation of the double-sided relationship between the rate of profit and the rate of capital accumulation, consider Figure 8.5. Curve A is the locus of all possible expected rates of profit that justify the investment plans drawn up by firms, oligopolistic or otherwise. Curve I is the locus of all possible investment plans of firms that are fulfilled by the realized rate of profit. Consequently, the "golden age" growth rate is indicated by point D in Figure 8.5. However, Joan Robinson warns: "The fact that the desired and actual rates of accumulation coincide in a particular short-period situation does not by itself guarantee that they will continue to do so.[20] "Uncertainty, through the volatility of expectations to which it gives rise, is continually leading the firms into self-contradictory policies. Now it needs no chance shocks to set an upswing going. The model is inherently unstable and fluctuates even in otherwise tranquil conditions."[21]

Joan Robinson's ultimate concern is with the analysis of the economy in disequilibrium, which is a salient attribute of historical time. Paul Davidson observes:

> Mrs. Robinson has cautioned that these neo-Keynesian models (such as those of Kaldor and Pasinetti) are only applicable to economies growing at constant rates through time and that in the current state of the economic arts these formal models could not readily explain how economies traverse from one growth rate to another, or how adjustments to disequilibrium are made when tranquility conditions are disturbed. Accordingly, the Cambridge [England] philosophy is to use these models to make comparisons between economies each growing at a uniform but different rate in conditions of tranquility as preliminary to attempting disequilibrium path analysis.*

---

*Paul Davidson, *Money and the Real World*, 2nd ed. (New York: John Wiley & Sons (1978), p. 132. Davidson's observation may also provide an explanation as to why Joan Robinson did not employ any mathematical formulation in her two books *The Accumulation of Capital* (1956) and *Essays in the Theory of Economic Growth* (1962). In fact, Robinson did not employ any mathematical formulation in any of her writings on capital and growth.

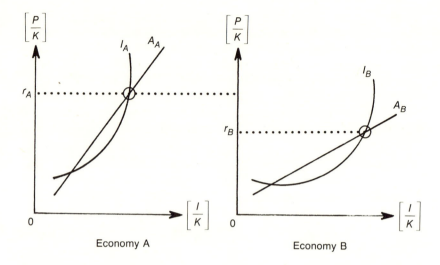

Figure 8.7

Two economies: an example

Preliminary to her ultimate disequilibrium analysis, Joan Robinson employs the "golden age" model to make comparisons between economies, each growing at a uniform but different rate. One of her objectives in this is to provide a theoretical framework for investigating the determinants of the rate of profit beyond those given by marginal productivity theory. In this sense, her methodology is similar to those of Kaldor and Pasinetti. The comparative dynamics can be simply stated as follows: If firms in two "golden age" systems have the same "animal spirit" as reflected in identical I-curves in Figure 8.7, and if the average propensity to save is higher in Economy B than it is in A, then the rate of profit and the rate of accumulation will be lower in Economy B than in Economy A. The higher average propensity to save in Economy B is depicted by an A-curve that lies below the A-curve of Economy A. Consequently, r_B is lower than r_A. If one adopts the Ricardo–von Neumann–Kalecki assumption that $s_w = 0$, the determinants of the rates of profit of the two economies would be the "natural growth rate," (n), and the average propensity to save out of gross profit, (s_c). It should be noted that these determinants are the same as those in Kaldor's special case. Joan Robinson's views on economic growth can be summarized by the schematic representation (Figure 8.8) of the key causal relationships in her theory.

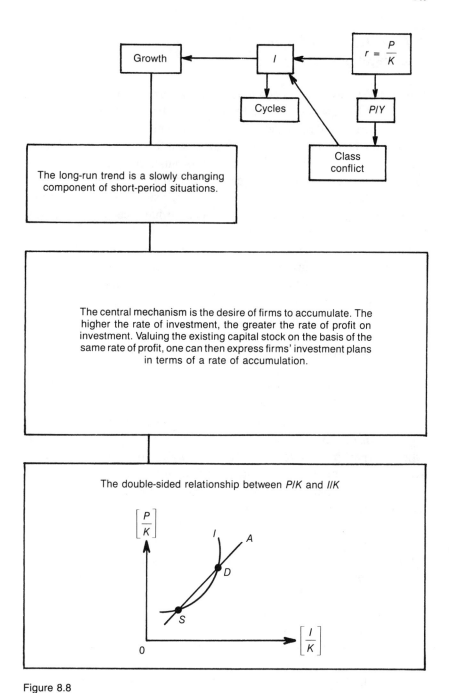

Figure 8.8

A schematic representation of Joan Robinson's causal model

The Post-Keynesian approach
to technical progress

The Post-Keynesian approach to technical progress varies significantly from those approaches adopted by writers of the "neoclassical synthesis." A representative model of the latter is Robert Solow's model with embodied technical progress. In an important theoretical paper, Solow shows that the neoclassical aggregate production function with its aggregate homogeneous capital can be modified to accommodate machines of different vintages.[22] The necessary and sufficient conditions for the aggregation of heterogeneous capital have been subsequently given by F. M. Fisher as follows:[23]

(a) linearly homogeneous production for every industry;

(b) capital-augmenting technical progress everywhere; and

(c) optimal allocation of the labor force so that the marginal product of labor is the same for all vintages of capital equipment in existence.

The vintage model that satisfies these conditions has been called the "putty-putty" case. The name reflects the fact that the model requires substitutability between machines and labor at all times before and after installation, according to the same Cobb-Douglas production function. Furthermore, labor is allocated to different vintages of machines under conditions of perfect competition. Less labor is allocated to older machines than to new machines. Thus the question of scrapping old machines does not arise. "In this case," quipped R. G. D. Allen, "machines (like old soldiers) never die but simply fade away."[24] It should be noted that, even though Solow treats investment as the transmission mechanism of technical progress, the source of technical progress remains exogenous to his model.

Representative of the Post-Keynesian approach to technical progress is the technical progress function of N. Kaldor and J. A. Mirrlees (1962).[25] In their paper "A New Model of Economic Growth," Kaldor and Mirrlees present a "putty-clay" vintage model incorporating the concept of endogenous technical progress. Some important differences between the Kaldor-Mirrlees model and that of Solow can be summarized:

(a) Whereas the question of obsolescence does not arise in the Solow model, this question is taken into consideration in the Kaldor-Mirrlees model. In the Kaldor-Mirrlees model, factor substitution is impossible ex poste (after installation). Labor will not be released from older machines to man the machines of the latest vintage. The solution is, therefore, to scrap some old machines. Thus, the economic life of a machine of given vintage becomes an additional endogenous variable to be determined. The criterion for scrapping the machine as obsolescent is its quasi-rent. Along the "golden age" growth path, the real-wage rate rises and the quasi-rents of old machines continue to decline and eventually become zero. Hence, the additional equilibrium condition emerges, i.e., the obsolescence condition of zero quasi-rent.

(b) Kaldor and Mirrlees give more emphasis to uncertainty and expectations than does Solow's 1960 model. This point is highlighted by their investment function. Under conditions of continuous technical progress, expectations concerning the future are uncertain and hazardous. "Hence, investment projects which qualify for adoption must pass a further test—apart from the test of earning a satisfactory rate of profit—and that is that the cost of the fixed assets must be 'recovered' within a certain period—i.e., that the gross profit earned in the first h years of the operation must be sufficient to repay the cost of investment."[26] In other words, the authors invoke a fixed pay-off period criterion as a simple "rule of thumb" for investment decisions.

(c) The concept of the aggregate production function and the marginal productivity theorems derived therefrom are absent in the Kaldor-Mirrlees model. The authors write: "A 'production function' in the sense of a single-valued relationship between some measure of capital, K_t, the labour force N_t and of output Y_t (all at time t) clearly does not exist. Everything depends on past history, on how the collection of equipment goods which comprises K_t has been built up. Thus Y_t will be greater for a given K_t (as measured by historical cost) if a greater part of the existing capital stock is of more recent creation; this would be the case, for example, if the rate of growth of population has been accelerating.[27]

The main thrust of the Kaldor-Mirrlees model is to show that the "golden age" solution is possible only if appropriate assumptions are made about its functional relationships. The following is a simplified version of their model.

(1K-M) $$S_t = s_c P_t.$$

Equation (1K-M) is the classical saving function assumed by the architects of the model. This savings assumption leads to the "widow's cruse" theory of distribution. Hence, we have the following equation:

(2K-M)
$$P_t/Y_t = \frac{1}{s} \frac{I_t}{Y_t} .$$

As in any vintage model, two time variables are needed: one for time in the usual sense denoted by t and the other, τ, for the dating of vintage machines in use at time t.

(3K-M)
$$L_t = L_0 e^{nt}$$

and

(3'K-M)
$$L_t = \int_{t-\tau}^{t} L_\tau d_\tau.$$

Equation (3K-M) incorporates the Harrodian assumption about the growth of the labor force while (3'K-M) defines the total labor force.

(4K-M)
$$\frac{1}{q_t} \frac{dq_t}{dt} = F \left(\frac{1}{i_t} \frac{di_t}{dt} \right) .$$

Equation (4K-M) is the technical progress function. The term $(1/q_t)(dq_t/d_t)$ stands for the annual rate of growth in gross investment per worker operating on new machines; and $(1/i_t)(di_t/dt)$ denotes the rate of growth in gross investment per worker.

The microfoundations of the Kaldor-Mirrlees model consist of two equations: one behavioral equation depicting the firm's decision to invest and a second expressing the condition for obsolescence.

(5K-M)
$$i_t = hq_t - \int_t^{t+h} w_x dx.$$

Equation (5K-M) is the investment function. The fixed payoff period set in advance is indicated by the symbol h. The symbol x is a running time variable for integration from t to $t + h$; q_t stands for output per worker produced by the new machine; and w represents the real-wage rate. Defining p_t to be profit per worker, the initial level of profit per worker from the new machine can be expressed as: $p_t = q_t - w$. This is the identity equation behind Equation (5K-M). Note that Equation (5K-M) is stated in per capita terms. The total function is:

(6K-M)
$$I_t = hQ_t - L_t \int_t^{t+h} w_x dx.$$

(7K-M)
$$Q_{t-T} - wL_{t-T} = 0,$$

or

(7'K-M)
$$q_{t-T} = w.$$

Equation (7K-M) is the obsolescence condition, while Equation (7'K-M) is the same condition stated in per capita terms. The symbol T stands for the economic life of a machine of given vintage. Figure 8.9 indicates that the "golden age" solution of the model depends upon the assumption of a well-behaved technical progress function.

The technical progress function is nonlinear, showing the tendency toward diminishing returns. This is not the same as diminishing marginal productivity of capital. The nonlinearity merely indicates that there is a limit to the learning process. Implicit in the technical progress function is the idea that technical progress is partly the result of a learning process on the part of the entrepreneurs. The more investment undertaken by entrepreneurs, the greater the opportunities for them to explore the existing technical knowledge. Furthermore, increased investment also provides the impetus for faster technical advance. The intercept on the vertical axis signifies that some innovation is possible, through a "learning-by-doing" process, even when there is zero gross investment.

The "golden age" growth path is indicated by the point m at which the technical progress function intersects the 45° line.

(8K-M)
$$m = \frac{1}{q_t} \frac{dq_t}{dt} = \frac{1}{i_t} \frac{di_t}{dt}.$$

The "golden age" growth rate of aggregate output per worker can be written as:

(9K-M)
$$\frac{1}{y_t} \frac{dy_t}{dt} = \frac{1}{Y_t} \frac{dY_t}{dt} - n = m.$$

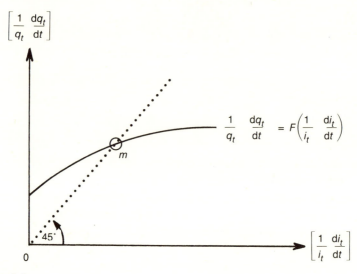

Figure 8.9

The Kaldor-Mirrlees model of technical progress

Source: Adapted from Nicholas Kaldor and James A. Mirrlees, "A New Model of Economic Growth," *Review of Economic Studies*, 29, June 1962.

It follows that along the "golden age" growth path aggregate output will grow at the rate of $m + n$.

$$(10\text{K-M}) \qquad \frac{1}{Y_t} \frac{dY_t}{dt} = m + n.$$

By the same reasoning, the "golden age" growth rates for gross investment per man and aggregate gross investment are respectively:

$$(11\text{K-M}) \qquad \frac{1}{i_t} \frac{di_t}{dt} = \frac{1}{I_t} \frac{dI_t}{dt} - n = m,$$

and

(12K-M)
$$\frac{1}{I_t} \frac{dI_t}{dt} = m + n.$$

The real-wage rate along the "golden age" growth path will also grow at the same rate m. This result is derived as follows:

(13K-M)
$$w = q_{t-T} = q_t e^{-mT}.$$

This is the obsolescence condition.

(14K-M)
$$\ln w = \ln q_t + \ln e^{-mT}.$$

Equation (14K-M) is obtained by taking the natural log of Equation (13K-M). Differentiating (14K-M) with respect to time we have:

(15K-M)
$$\frac{d}{dt} \ln w = \ln q_t + \left(-\frac{d}{dt} mT \right).$$

Since m and T are constants, the time derivative of mT is zero. Therefore,

(16K-M)
$$\frac{1}{w} \frac{dw}{dt} = \frac{1}{q_t} \frac{dq_t}{dt} = m.$$

We know that in the "golden age" q_t grows at the constant rate m. Thus,

(17K-M)
$$\frac{\dot{w}}{w} = m.$$

Why does Kaldor conduct his analyses in terms of the "golden age" growth path? A partial answer is provided by Eichner and Kregel:

Approaching the problem of disequilibrium in this manner gives rise to the distinction found in the post-Keynesian literature between long-period analysis, focusing on the determinants of the warranted growth rate; and the short-period analysis, focusing on cyclical deviations in the actual rate relative to the warranted rate. The methodological point is that the deviations cannot be understood except with respect to some reference growth path.[28]

Post-Keynesians and monetary theory

The Post-Keynesians have exposed some hidden weaknesses in orthodox monetary theory. Although a formal Post-Keynesian monetary theory is still in the embryonic stage, their devastating criticisms pave the way for a realistic reformulation of monetary theory in the not-too-distant future. This optimistic observation is substantiated by conclusions reached by some of our most distinguished theorists. For instance, Arrow and Hahn have concluded that in a "world with a past as well as a future in which contracts are made in terms of money, no equilibrium may exist."[29] Hicks confessed: " . . . I must say that diagram [IS-LM] is now much less popular with me than I think it still with many other people. It reduces the *General Theory* to equilibrium economics; it is not really 'in' time."[30] Clower stressed: "Our first order of business is to state explicitly just what aspects of experience we should want to have 'explained' by any theory that claims to provide even a minimally adequate description of a monetary economy."[31] One of the mandatory requirements for an adequate monetary theory according to Clower is that "the theory should imply that trade is an ongoing process in time rather than a once-for-all affair that ends in the permanent elimination of incentives for further trade."*

A survey of the writings of these leading economists leaves us little doubt that a central thrust of Post-Keynesian protest is the concept of historical time. The Post-Keynesian case is most forcefully stated by Paul Davidson in his *Money and the Real World* (1978). Davidson's

---

*Robert W. Clower, "The Anatomy of Monetary Theory," *American Economic Review*, Papers and Proceedings of the 89th Annual Meeting, September 16–18, 1976 (February 1977), p. 206. The other mandatory requirements are: "(2) The theory should imply that, on average over any finite time interval, each individual holds positive stocks of all goods that are regularly traded. (3) The theory should imply that the bulk of all trades occur not through essentially random airing of individuals who happen to share a double coincidence of wants, but rather through systematic pairing of specialist with nonspecialist traders in a small number of organized, continuously operating markets. (4) The theory should imply that at least one and at most a few distinctive 'money' commodities are transferred (or promised for future delivery) by one party to another in virtually all exchange transactions" (pp. 206–207).

main arguments are outlined in the schematic representation of Figure 8.10. He stresses:

> It is in a world of uncertainty and disappointment that money comes into its own as a necessary medium for deferring decisions.[32]

> Money plays an essential and peculiar role only when contractual obligations span a significant interval of calendar time. If the economic system being studied permits only *spot* transactions, i.e., contracts that require payments at the immediate instant, then even if its members utilize a convenient medium of account and/or exchange, such a *numéraire* is *not* money in the full sense of the term. Spot transaction economies—which are equivalent to Hicks' flexprice economies—have, as Keynes insisted, "scarcely emerged from the stage of barter."[33]

Davidson further points out that only in real world market-oriented monetary economies where production takes time does "the existence of market institutions that permit (and encourage) contracting for future payment create the need for money, and liquidity."[34] This essential feature of real world monetary economies has been overlooked by orthodox general equilibrium theory. "Since orthodox neoclassical theory neglects the fact of contracting over calendar time in organized markets for future delivery and payment, the ubiquitous liquidity provision of entrepreneurs in capitalist economies is left unattended by mainstream economists in their nonmonetized theory of the firm. Consequently, they are irresistible targets of the businessman's gibe: 'They never met a payroll!'"[35]

The store-of-value function of money, according to Davidson (who follows Keynes faithfully), depends upon the flow supply prices of producers, which, in turn, are a function of their expectations about future production costs. In the central core industrial sector of an advanced capitalist economy, future costs of production are tied to money wage rates and the average productivity of labor. "Only a contractually fixed wage and product price system permits capitalist economies to engage in the time-consuming production process; for such a system provides the sticky (meaning normal) price level of producible goods that are the basis of decisions involving future economic consequences. This was the focal point of Keynes' view on the workings of a monetary capitalist economy."[36]

In the same vein, Sidney Weintraub emphasizes that the money wage rate is not just one of the prices in the economy. Rather, it is a parameter

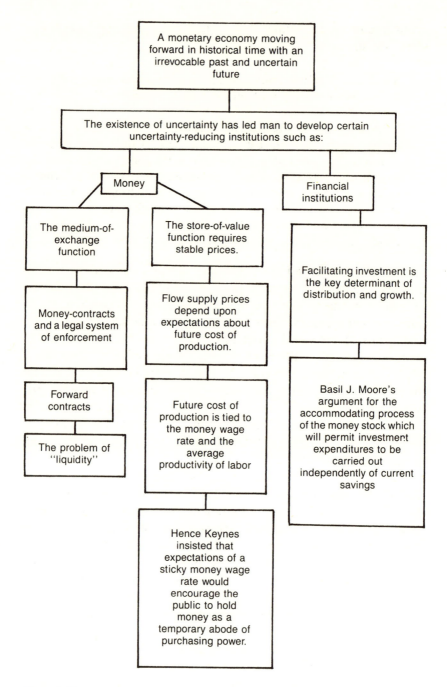

Figure 8.10

A simplified schematic representation of Paul Davidson's arguments affecting aggregate demand and aggregate supply.[37] This assertion is demonstrated by the accompanying simple model.

Aggregate supply	Aggregate demand
(a) $Z = kWN = Py.$	(e) $D = \alpha WN$ $+ I + G + X - M.$
(b) $P = kW\left(\dfrac{N}{Y}\right).$	
(c) $\dfrac{N}{Y} = \dfrac{1}{Y/N} = \dfrac{1}{A}.$	
(d) $P = k\ \dfrac{W}{A}.$	

Aggregate supply (Z) is depicted by Equation (a) as some fixed multiple (k) of total labor cost (WN). The symbol k can be interpreted as the "markup" of unit labor costs or the targeted profit margin. Rearranging terms in (a) yields Equation (b) defining the price level (P). The expression (N/Y) denotes the reciprocal of average labor productivity (Y/N). Let A represent Y/N. Substituting (c) into (b) yields (d), which is an alternative way of stating the price level equation.

On the demand side, aggregate demand (D) is defined as: $C + I + G + X - M$ as usual. The component C is assumed to be some constant proportion of labor income (αWN). "Clearly," Weintraub points out, "a shift in the wage parameter will dislodge Z and nudge demand (with investment-good prices being 'cost-determined,' and civil servant wages in G, the money wage also enters G)."[38] Since prices of exportable goods are also "cost-determined" and relative prices influence the volume of imports, a change in the money wage rate also affects ($X - M$).

Thus, a sticky money wage rate is *not* a cause of involuntary unemployment in contrast to views generally held by writers of the "neoclassical synthesis." Davidson's work casts "rigid wages" as a necessary stability condition for a monetary economy. Not only does the flow supply price of commodities require a sticky money wage rate, but the store-of-value function of money also depends on it.

Davidson observes that "problems of liquidity and finance are the hallmarks of everyday business decision making in a monetary economy.''[39] He writes:

> Liquidity involves being able to have the means of settlements to meet all one's contractual obligations when they come due. Since money is the only thing that will discharge contract commitments (by definition), for any store of value besides money to be liquid, it must be easily resalable for money in a spot market. . . . *Liquid assets* are durables traded in well-organized and orderly markets. Hence, what are liquid assets of any economy depends on the social practices and institutions that exist in that economy.[40]

Post-Keynesian monetary theorists like Paul Davidson, Hyman P. Minsky, and Basil J. Moore argue that in a modern monetary economy investment decisions are intricately related to the portfolio preferences of financial managers.[41] Davidson writes:

> For accumulation to occur, two conditions must be fulfilled: (1) entrepreneurs must have the "animal spirits" which encourage the belief in additional profit opportunities and (2) entrepreneurs must be able to command sufficient resources to put their projects into execution. Animal spirits may depend at least in part on non-monetary phenomena but the obtaining of command of resources requires the cooperation of the banking system and financial markets. If the banking system and related financial institutions acquiesce, then there will be net investment as the output of the capital goods industry increases.[42]

In the same spirit, Basil J. Moore insists on the endogenous nature of the money stock. He points out that, while the high-powered monetary base is exogenous in the control sense, it is endogenous in the real world and hence in the statistical sense. The accommodation process of the money stock is demonstrated by Moore as follows:[43]

Over the long run, assuming considerations of variable velocity can be ignored, the growth rate of demand for money can be expressed tautologically as:

(1M)
$$\frac{\dot{M}}{M} = \frac{\dot{P}}{P} + \frac{\dot{Y}}{Y},$$

where M is the demand for the nominal money stock; P is the price level; and Y is real output. This equation can be rewritten as:

(2M)
$$\frac{\dot{P}}{P} = \frac{\dot{M}}{M} - \frac{\dot{Y}}{Y},$$

which represents the famous rule of Milton Friedman that, to ensure price stability ($\dot{P}/P = 0$), the rate of growth of the nominal money stock should be increased at a rate parallel to the rate of growth of real output ($\dot{M}/M = \dot{Y}/Y$).

In view of the cost-determined prices of the central core industries, the proximate determinant of inflation may be viewed as the rate at which nominal money wages rise in excess of the growth rate of average labor productivity. This relationship is depicted by the following equation:

(3M)
$$\frac{\dot{P}}{P} = \frac{\dot{W}}{W} - \frac{\dot{A}}{A},$$

where $\dot{A}/A$ is the rate of growth of average labor productivity.

Substituting Equation (3M) into (1M) or (2M) and rearranging terms, we have:

(4M)
$$\frac{\dot{Y}}{Y} = \frac{\dot{M}}{M} - \frac{\dot{P}}{P} = \frac{\dot{M}}{M} - \left[\frac{\dot{W}}{W} - \frac{\dot{A}}{A} \right].$$

Equation (4M) states that, if the monetary authorities do not permit the nominal money stock to accommodate the rate of increase of money-wages (which is determined exognenously), aggregate demand will not be sufficient to maintain the secular growth of real output. Consequently there will be (a) downward pressure on the growth of real income, (b) a rise in interest rates, and (c) an accompanying rise in the rate of unemployment.

The endogenous nature of the money stock can be seen from a different angle. According to Hyman P. Minsky, "Innovations in financial practices are a feature of our economy, especially when things go well. New institutions, such as Real Estate Investment Trusts (REITs), and new instruments, such as negotiable Certificates of Deposit, are developed; old instruments, such as commercial paper, increase in volume and find new uses. But each new instrument and expanded use of old instruments increases the amount of financing that is available and that can be used for financing activity and taking positions in inherited assets. Increased availability of finance bids up the prices of assets relative to the prices of current output and this leads to increases in investment. The quantity of relevant money in an economy in which money conforms to Keynes' definition, is endogenously determined.''[44]

Minsky further distinguishes between hedge and speculative finance. "Speculative finance takes place when the cash flows from operations are not expected to be large enough to meet payment commitments, even though the present value of expected cash receipts is greater than the present value of payment commitments. Speculating units expect to fulfill obligations by raising funds by new debt.''[45]

Minsky observes that the investment boom in the mid-1960s was made possible by speculative finance.[46] However, speculating units are vulnerable to increases in the interest rates for a rise in interest rates can cause their cash payment commitments to rise relative to their cash receipts. Furthermore, a rise in long-term interest rates will lead to a fall in the market value of long-term asset holdings. These combined outcomes often cause the speculating units to make a sudden revaluation of their debt structure. Thus, "a robust financial system was transformed into a fragile system during the long expansion of the 1960s. As a result of the fragility, shocks that might well have been absorbed without serious repercussions in a more robust financial structure triggered insipient financial crises in the United States in 1966 and in 1969–70.''[47]

The focal point of Post-Keynesian analysis is on the credit side of bank intermediation. Their views are diametrically opposite to those of the Monetarists. The current debate is reminiscent of the "Bullionist controversy" in the nineteenth century.* The Post-Keynesians are the heirs of the anti-Bullionists and the subsequent "Banking School."

*For a lucid analysis of the debate between the Banking School and the Currency School, see Mark Blaug, *Economic Theory in Retrospect* (Homewood, Ill.: Irwin, 1968), pp. 201–204. The leaders of the Currency School were Samuel Jones Loyd, Lord Overstone (1796–1883), Colonel Robert Torrens (1780–1864), and Norman. The spokesmen for the Banking School were Thomas Tooke (1774–1858) and John Fullarton (1780–1849). Blaug wrote, "Ricardo had laid down the currency principle: a mixed gold-paper currency should be made to vary in the same way as a purely metallic currency so that it responds automatically to any inflow or outflow of gold. . . . The Banking School denied that it was possible to overissue a convertible paper currency inasmuch as 'needs of trade' automatically controlled the volume of notes issued" (p. 201).

The policy implications of the Post-Keynesian monetary theory may be viewed as variations of the original prescriptions of Keynes, which are succinctly summarized by Davidson as follows:

> In both the *Treatise* and *General Theory*, Keynes emphasized the money wage/money supply nexus. He noted that if we have control of both the earnings system [incomes policy] and the monetary system [monetary policy], and if we can control the pace of investment, we can "stabilize the purchasing power of money, its labour power, or anything else— without running the risk of setting up social and economic frictions or of causing waste."[48]

The microfoundations of Post-Keynesian economics

The distinguishing feature of Post-Keyenesian microeconomics is that it is growth-oriented both in its short- and long-period analyses. Post-Keynesian long-period analysis shows a return to the classical approach. Recall that the role of classical "natural price" (normal price) was to assure the viability (reproducibility) and surplus (growth) of the economic system. In our time, the works of Sraffa, Leontief, and von Neumann clearly reflect this classical spirit.[49] Alfred S. Eichner points out that a short-period Post-Keynesian theory of prices is now emerging. "With its emphasis on the role of prices in assuring reproducibility and expansion of the system—rather than in allocating resources—this new theory diverges sharply from the models of pricing behavior found in economics textbooks. Since the price level depends, via the need for funds to finance investment, on the rate of economic expansion, the post-Keynesian theory of price formation is a dynamic one."[50]

While an explanation of the trend in relative prices is essential, it is the emerging short-period Post-Keynesian theory that is most relevant to the real world of oligopolies, multinational corporations, and diversified conglomerates. The pioneers of this short-period analysis are Kalecki, Steindl, Eichner, and Levine.[51] J. A. Kregel observes:

> Kalecki's contributions, while essentially similar, are generally more concise and compact than Keynes'. Kalecki has the same views as Keynes concerning (1) the wage bargain, (2) the futility of effecting employment through reduction of the money wage, (3) the emphasis on time and (4) the concern with effective demand, etc.[52]

Kalecki made a clear distinction between "cost-determined" and "demand-determined" prices in the short run. He wrote:

> Generally speaking, changes in the prices of finished goods are "cost-determined" while changes in the prices of raw materials inclusive of primary foodstuffs are "demand-determined." The prices of finished goods are affected, of course, by any "demand-determined" changes in the prices of raw materials but it is through the channel of costs that this influence is transmitted.[53]

Kalecki's "cost-determined" price is given by the following formula:

$$(1Ka) \qquad\qquad p = mu + n\bar{p}$$

where p is the "cost determined" price, u is the prime cost per unit, and $\bar{p}$ is the weighted average price of all firms (for the firm must make sure that the price does not become too high in relation to prices of other firms). The coefficients m and n characterizing the price-fixing policy of the firm reflect what may be called the degree of monopoly of the firm's position.[54]

Building on the work of Kalecki, Eichner, and Steindl, Levine and others have made further contributions to the formulation of Post-Keynesian short-period analysis. The institutional setting of their analyses is the dynamics of American industry structure. A simple schematic representation of this new microfoundation is shown in Figure 8.11.

According to Robert T. Averitt, the contemporary American economy is a composite of two distinct business systems: (a) the "center" firms and (b) the "periphery" firms. "The center firm is large in economic size as measured by number of employees, total assets and yearly sales. It tends toward vertical integration (through ownership or informal control), geographical dispersion (national and international), product diversification and managerial decentralization."[55] The pricing decisions of the "center" firms are growth-oriented. As aptly put by Nina Shapiro:

> Continuous and accelerating growth is the overriding goal of the capitalist enterprise. This goal pushes the firm toward a long-run perspective in its pricing decisions. All actions must be judged in terms of their effect on the ongoing expansion of the firm. Their future, rather than immediate economic consequences, is the decisive consideration.[56]

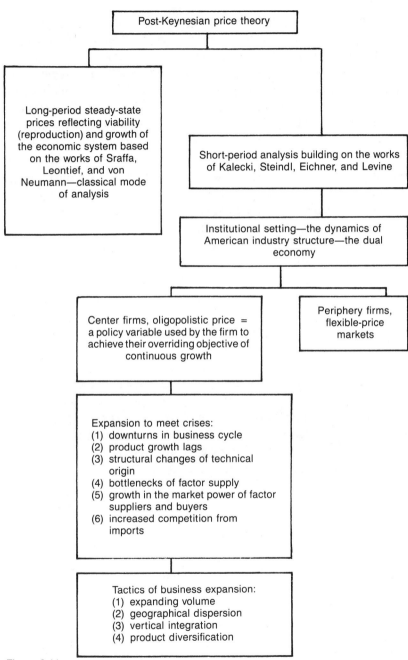

Figure 8.11

The microfoundations of Post-Keynesian economics

Expansion is a strategy to reduce uncertainty confronting the oligopolistic "center" firm. Averitt observes that the "center" firm has to face six crises: (i) downturns in the business cycle; (ii) product growth lags; (iii) structural changes of technological origin; (iv) bottlenecks of factor supply; (v) growth in the market power of factor suppliers and buyers; and (vi) increased competition from imports. "Fortunately these six crises types can be met with a single strategy: expansion. The four tactics of business expansion—expanding volume, geographical dispersion, vertical integration and product diversification—when used in correct proportions and with careful timing, guarantee initial protection."[57]

Post-Keynesians like Nina Shapiro and Nai-Pew Ong revitalize the Marshallian analogy comparing business survival to the maturation of young trees in a forest.[58] With a view of maintaining viability and expansion in the long run, the dominant firms frequently employ the strategy of target pricing. As observed by Ong, there are two types of price strategy: (a) defensive target pricing strategy, which is aimed at depriving the marginal producers of accumulation funds necessary to keep up with market growth, and (b) offensive target pricing strategy, which is aimed at eliminating them altogether in a destructive price war.[59]

The markup pricing formula, $p = k(w/A)$, mentioned earlier is just the tip of the iceberg. Peter Kenyon observed that "the mark-up is not only readily explained, but also the result of a complex set of economic forces operating to produce the growth and distribution observable at the macroeconomic level."[60] In other words, the markup is an important link in the chain of causal relationships of Post-Keynesian microeconomic theory (see diagram).

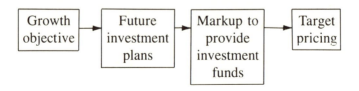

Thus, decisions about markups and prices are linked directly with the firms' expectations about the future. The theory views investment as an overriding goal of the firm and is stated in the context of historical time. It is indeed an alternative of orthodox microeconomics. As aptly summarized by Shapiro:

The notion of strategic price contains the seeds of a viable theory of capitalist exchange. The consummation of this theory requires, on the "micro" side, the construction of a concrete treatment of the relation of pricing to technical change. On the "macro" side it requires a theory of growth which takes in the centrality of product development to the character and pace of capital accumulation. When technical progress is systematically integrated into the conception of capitalist expansion, economics will gain its first real account of market operations in a capitalist economy.[61]

Turning to the question of factor price determinants, we find that the Post-Keynesians reject the marginal productivity theory of wages and profits. Recall that both Joan Robinson and Nicholas Kaldor seek the determinants of the rate of profit outside the sphere of exchange. In the same vein, Post-Keynesians deny that the money wage rate is determined by the supply and demand forces in the labor market. Eileen Appelbaum emphasizes:

The labor market is not a "market" as that term is usually understood, for the labor market does not possess a market-clearing price mechanism. Variations in either money wages or in the real wage rate are unable to assure a zero surplus of labor, and thus eliminate unemployment. In the context of (1) an industrial structure that is largely oligopolistic, (2) fixed technical coefficients in production and (3) markup pricing, the demand for labor depends on the level of aggregate economic activity. It has little, if anything, to do with the marginal product of labor. The supply of labor, meanwhile, depends largely on demographic and other sociocultural factors, though it is somewhat responsive to changes in employment opppor-tunities.[62]

In other words, the Post-Keynesian theory of wage determination combines Keynesian demand analysis and the institutional approach to labor supply. Michael J. Piore points out that "wage rates perform certain basic social and institutional functions. They define relationships between labor and management, between one group of workers and another, among various institutional entities (the locals in a national union, the various branch plants of a national company, the major employers in a local labor market, the major international unions which compose the American labor movement) and last, the place of individuals relative to one another in the work community, in the neighborhood and in the family. The role of wages in this respect results in a series of fixed relationships among the wage rates of certain groups of jobs and workers; these relationships are known as wage contours."[63]

Sidney Weintraub argues that Keynes conceived the money wage to be an exogenous variable only vaguely resolvable by the tools of economic analysis.[64] In view of the fact that the economist lacks exact details on motivation, strategic maneuvering, and ideological rationalization whenever wage bargains are struck, history alone can enable us to "predict" money wage outcomes. Thus, Weintraub calls attention to the lamentable situation that "one of our theories is missing," namely, a theory of money wages. He writes:

> There is thus an imposter in the textbook literature, surviving as a disguised marginal productivity theory, dressed in (W/P) and fed by a question-begging $P = \bar{P}$; or entering in a quantity theory of money context, with $Q = \bar{Q}$, which is a curious logic for $\Delta N \gtrless 0$. Too, despite sentimental longings for "competitive" labor markets to resolve w, the dreamers who wish away unions forgo the necessary probe of the interactions of ΔW and ΔP in the one-sided power state of unbalanced exploitative bliss.[65]

Post-Keynesian analysis of money wages and unemployment draws heavily on "segmented labor market theories."[66] It covers the spectrum of ideologies but the common thread tying them together is the historical process which led to dualism in the American economy. The segmentation of the labor market into primary and secondary sectors may be attributed to the coexistence of "center" firms and "periphery" firms. Glen G. Cain observes that the various segmented labor market hypotheses generally invoke the following theoretical ideas—"the demand-determined allocation of jobs, the key role of on-the-job training, employer discrimination and the downgrading of observable human capital characteristics as determinants of wage levels."[67] In addition, dualists like Peter B. Doeringer, Michael Piore, and others emphasize "the roles of workers' attitudes, motivations and work habits and the way these interact with community 'variables,' such as the welfare system and illegal activities."[68] The dual market idea in the hands of the radical wing is "sometimes expressed in terms of an analogy with an underdeveloped economy or even a colony that is exploited by an imperialistic primary sector."[69]

Sequential causality in Post-Keynesian economics

Sequential causality, in which cause precedes effect, is tied to historical time. In a monetary economy traveling through historical time, "the inherited stocks of durables, contractual obligations and the existing stock of money provide a continuity between irrevocable past economic behaviors and the current environment, while the existence of durable goods, contracts and money provides the essential link between an uncertain perfidious future and present activity."[70] Sequential causality is clearly conveyed by the accompanying diagram of the causal links.

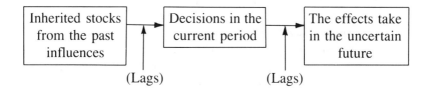

Hicks observes that "even the simplest case of sequential causation in economics has two steps in it: a prior step, from the objective cause to the decisions that are based on it, or influenced by it, and a posterior step, from the decisions to their (objective) effects."[71] Frequently, each of these steps involves time lags. "The characteristic form of a modern economy is one in which many of those who make decisions (households, firms, nations) have some reserves. They are accordingly not bound to respond to (market) signals; even if the signal persists, they have time to react. So the signal is less imperative, and therefore less dependable."[72] Thus, Arrow and Hahn draw the conclusion that in "a world with a past as well as a future in which contracts are made in terms of money, no equilibrium may exist."[73] This is also the reason that Hicks states that "liquidity is freedom."[74] In other words, the existence of reserves gives decisionmakers time to interpret market signals and to meet their contractual commitments before they make decisions to change courses of action. In the words of Paul Davidson, "thus liquidity is essential in a world of nonpredictable change and sequential causality."[75]

In his book *Causality in Economics*, Hicks points out:

I have tried to show that there are different kinds of causality in economics; and that to each kind there is, or can be, a kind of theory that corresponds.

To static causality corresponds static theory: the part of economic theory that is most completely developed (neoclassical economics), but which leaves even those most devoted to it unsatisfied, since its field of application is so narrow. To contemporaneous causality corresponds the (formal) theory of Keynes, and in "micro" contexts that of Marshall. . . .It is nevertheless not surprising that economists, even the most "Keynesian" ones, have become dissatisfied with it. . . . I have been trying to show that the further development of theory, which I agree is required, should begin with an attempt to identify the questions it will have to be concerned with. These, I have tried to show, are in essence questions of sequential causality.[76]

The questions raised by Post-Keynesian writers are essentially those of sequential causality. The centerpiece of their analysis is the workings of a monetary economy progressing through historical time. Not only in their approach to the monetary factor, but in interrelated specific questions, they have continually focused on historical time and uncertainty. For instance, Post-Keynesian price theory highlights the causal links among prices, profits, investment, and growth. Post-Keynesian macrodynamics emphasizes the direction of causation from rate of profit to distribution which, in turn, effects growth. In the Kaldor-Mirrlees analysis of technical progress, a sense of history is reflected in the inherited fixed-coefficient vintage machines, and uncertainty about future outcomes is lurking behind the fixed-payoff-period investment decision rule. Undoubtedly, Post-Keynesian economics is answering Hick's challenge and represents the beginning of a theory consistent with sequential causality.

Part IV

The Widening Common
Ground in Economic Analysis

Jean-Pascal Benassy's Analysis of Expectations and Temporary Fixprice Equilibria

Since the 1960s economists of different persuasions have been attempting to reconstruct the microfoundations of macroeconomics. This literature is voluminous and expanding rapidly. It is beyond the scope of this book to make a complete survey of this ongoing area of research.[1] Our objective is to concentrate on a few representative models of non-tâtonnement theories with the goal of conveying the main thrusts of this exciting development. The representative models considered here are schematically described by Figure 9.1. The temporary fixed price and quantity rationing model of Jean-Pascal Benassy will be considered in this chapter.[2] Franklin Fisher's stability analysis will be presented in Chapter 10. Other representative non-tâtonnement models will be discussed in Chapter 11.

Predecessors of the Benassy model

The roots of Benassy's analysis can be traced chronologically from Patinkin (1965), to Clower (1965, 1967), to Leijonhufvud (1966, 1969), to Barro and Grossman (1971, 1976).[3] Some aspects of these disequilibrium approaches were described briefly in Part 2. Robert Clower's early work, "The Keynesian Counterrevolution: A Theoretical Appraisal" (1965) provides Benassy with the important distinction between "notional demand" and "effective demand." In his "Reconsideration of the Microfoundations of Monetary Theory" (1967), Clower provides Benassy with the distinction between a barter and a monetary economy. Clower writes:

188

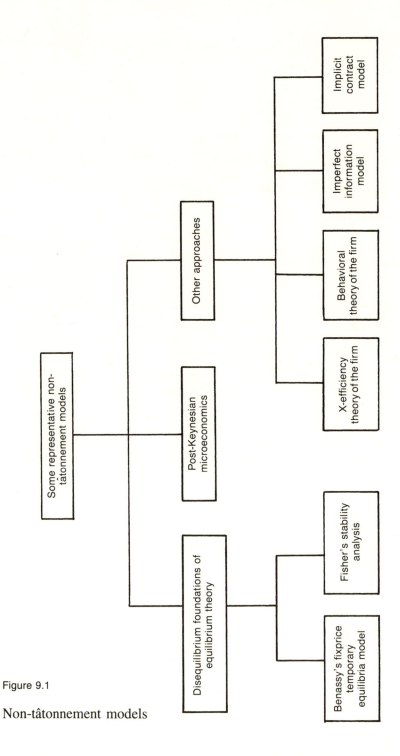

Figure 9.1

Non-tâtonnement models

. . . the peculiar feature of a money economy is that some commodities (in the present context, all but one) are denied a role as potential or actual means of payment. To state the same idea as an aphorism: Money buys goods and goods buy money; but goods do not buy goods. This restriction is—or ought to be—the central theme of the theory of a money economy. The task of reformulating microeconomic analysis to accommodate those aspects of experience that are commonly supposed to distinguish a money from a barter economy consists, indeed, of little more than an elaboration of the implications of this one restriction.[4]

Clower's postulate is embraced by Axel Leijonhufvud, who writes:

Even if the ratio of money wages to money prices comes out as the GE (general equilibrium) real wage, we may be caught in the vicious circle where the unemployed cannot make their consumption demand effective until they have sold their services for money, and producers with excess capacity cannot bid for labor until they have sold their goods—which the unemployed do not have the cash to purchase, and so on. This failure of the markets to transmit messages about desired transactions from one side to the other is what we mean by the phrase "effective demand failure."[5]

Leijonhufvud's argument was subsequently adopted by Benassy as the basic cause for inefficiency of temporary general equilibrium with fixed price and quantity rationing.

Benassy attributes the following properties of the market rationing schemes to the suggestions made by Clower (1960, 1965), Barro–Grossman (1971), and particularly Grossman (1971).

(i) One cannot force any agent to exchange more than he wants ("voluntary exchange").

(ii) Market efficiency.

(iii) Individuals on the "short" side (i.e., suppliers if there is excess demand, demanders if there is excess supply) can realize their demands ("frictionless market").

(iv) All rationing functions are continuous in their arguments.[6]

The "short-side rule" is illustrated by Figure 9.2. The diagram is the familiar Marshallian cross. If the price is P_1, the market is in disequilibrium. Quantities supplied (Q_1^s) are greater than quantities demanded (Q_1^d). Since trading is voluntary, suppliers cannot force the demanders to absorb the unsold goods indicated by the distance AB. The "short-side rule" is now invoked. The quantity actually traded would be Q_1^d. Similarly, if price is P_2, which is lower than the equilibri-

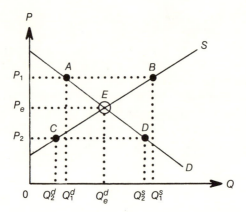

Figure 9.2

The "short-side rule"

Source: Mark Casson, Unemployment: A Disequilibrium Approach (New York: John Wiley & Sons, 1981) p. 41. Reprinted by permission of Mark Casson and Basil Blackwell Limited.

um price (P_e), the market will again be in disequilibrium. In this case, the quantity actually traded will be Q_2^d. This rationing scheme is lucidly stated by Mark Casson (1981) as follows:

> In general, because transactions are voluntary, the quantity traded cannot exceed either the amount demanded or the amount supplied. And because traders will not forego opportunities for mutually beneficial transactions, the quantity traded will never be less than the minimum of the demand and supply. It must therefore be equal to the minimum of demand and supply. This proposition is summarized by saying that "quantity is set at the short end of the market." A corollary of this is that transactors on both sides of the market cannot be quantity-constrained at the same time.[7]

The predecessors of Benassy also include Keynes. Benassy best states Keynes's influence on the Benassy process:

> We may remark that the structure of temporary non-Walrasian equilibrium corresponds exactly to the usual notion of Keynesian equilibrium. Indeed in such an equilibrium the consumption, employment, and production plans of households, firms, and government have adjusted to each other on the current markets via income movements. However, their future plans are independent of each other and are usually inconsistent.[8]

In attempting to integrate historical time and expectations in his model, Benassy further stresses the similarities between his analyses and those of Keynes:

> The period considered is not isolated in time; it has a past and a future, and we shall now see how these influence current trading. The legacy of the past comprises stocks of accumulated physical and financial assets. The future is represented by expectations about trading opportunities, themselves functions of past observations. These expectations are very important elements in Keynesian macroeconomic theory, where they are embedded, at least implicitly, in the schedule of the marginal efficiency of capital and the demand function for money.[9]

The broad resemblance between Keynes's theory of the marginal efficiency of capital and Benassy's analysis of expectations and temporary fixprice equilibria is made explicit in the next sections.

Benassy's analysis of expectations and temporary fixprice equilibria

The institutional framework

The setting of Benassy's analysis of expectations and temporary fixprice equilibria is a pure exchange (no production) monetary economy with n traders, indexed by $i = 1, 2, \ldots, n$; and r current markets for nonmonetary goods, indexed by $h = 1, 2, \ldots, r$. On each of the r markets the money price p is given. Each trader has a two-period horizon and plans for the current and future periods. Variables for the future (second) period are indexed by the symbol e indicating "expected." In the current (first) period trader i has an initial endowment of nonmonetary goods and a given stock of money holding $\bar{m}_i \geq 0$. The nonmonetary goods are assumed to be nonstorable. The only link between the present and the future is the quantity of money (analogous to Keynes's capital stock) which serves both as a medium of exchange and as a store of value.

Trader i is a utility maximizer. His utility function depends on his end-of-the-period holdings of money denoted by the symbol m_i and final holdings of goods for consumption denoted by the symbol x_i. The vector x_i is usually referred to as the consumption vector, since the goods are nonstorable. The utility function is represented by $U_i = U_i(x_i, m_i)$, which is continuous and concave in its arguments.

Trader i's vector of net transactions of goods against money is represented by the symbol z_{ih} which is defined as $z_{ih} = d_{ih} - s_{ih}$ where d_{ih} indicates the trader's demand for goods in market h and s_{ih} stands for his or her supply of goods in the same market. Then z_{ih} is positive in the case of a purchase and negative in the case of a sale; x_i and m_i are related to z_i through the following relations:

$$x_i = w_i + z_i,$$

and

$$m_i = \bar{m}_i - pz_i,$$

where w_i represents trader i's initial endowment of goods.

Trader i's net effective demand is represented by the symbol $\tilde{z}_{ih}$. In this non-Walrasian approach net effective demand and net transactions are not the same. Benassy points out: "Transactions, that is, purchases and sales on a market, are exchanges actually carried out on the market. They are thus subject to all traditional material and accounting identities. In particular, in each market transactions must balance as an identity."[10] The identity is written as

$$\sum_{i=1}^{n} Z_{ih}^* \equiv 0$$

for all h. As Benassy states: "Effective demands, on the contrary, are signals transmitted by each agent to the market before exchange takes place."[11] Thus they are "tentative trades" and need not balance on a market. Symbolically:

$$\sum_{i=1}^{n} \tilde{Z} \neq 0$$

Benassy further points out: "Each market has a particular organization through which possibly inconsistent demands and supplies are converted into consistent transactions. This organization can be represented by a rationing scheme."[12] The rationing scheme in the Benassy model is a set of n number of functions stating that actual transactions are functions of the n traders' effective demands:

$$Z_{ih}^* = F_{ih}(\tilde{Z}_{ih}, \tilde{Z}_{2h}, \tilde{Z}_{3h}, \ldots, \tilde{Z}_{nh}), \quad i = 1, 2, 3, \ldots, n.$$

This rationing function which causes the effective demands to be consistent with supplies has the fundamental property that

$$\sum_{i=1}^{n} F_{ih} (\tilde{Z}_{ih}, \tilde{Z}_{2h}, \tilde{Z}_{3h}, \ldots, \tilde{Z}_{nh}) = 0 \text{ for all } \tilde{Z}_{1h}, \ldots, \tilde{Z}_{nh}.$$

The rationing scheme can be written in more compact form:

$$Z^*_{ih} = F_{ih}(\tilde{z}_{ih}, \tilde{Z}_{ih})$$

with $\tilde{Z}$ representing the set of all effective demands on market h, except trader i's, which is $\tilde{z}_{ih}$.

Benassy identifies two types of rationing schemes: manipulable and nonmanipulable. According to Benassy, "A scheme is nonmanipulable if each trader faces in its trades upper and lower bounds that he cannot manipulate. A scheme is manipulable if a trader can, even if he is rationed, increase his transactions (actual trades) by increasing his demand."[13] In order to keep the analysis manageable, Benassy chooses to deal mainly with nonmanipulable schemes. These can be written as:

$$Z^*_{ih} = \min (\tilde{z}_{ih}, \bar{z}_{ih}) \text{ if } \tilde{z}_{ih} \geq 0$$
$$\max (\tilde{z}_{ih}, \underline{z}_{ih}) \text{ if } \tilde{z}_{ih} \leq 0$$

or, more compactly,

$$Z^*_{ih} = \min [\bar{z}_{ih}, \max (\underline{z}_{ih}, \tilde{z}_{ih})].$$

where $\bar{z}_{ih}$ and $\underline{z}_{ih}$ represent the upper and lower bounds of his trades, that is, the quantity constraints as subjectively perceived by the trader.

Both the upper and lower bounds of his trades are functions of the demands of other traders:

$$\bar{z}_{ih} = \bar{G}_{ih} (\tilde{Z}_i) \geq 0,$$
$$\underline{z}_{ih} = \underline{G}_{ih} (\tilde{Z}_i) \leq 0.$$

In more compact form as vector functions (because we are dealing with multi-markets in general equilibrium analysis), one can write:

$$z_i^* = F_i (\tilde{z}_i, \tilde{Z}_i),$$
$$\bar{z}_i = \bar{G}_i (\tilde{Z}_i),$$
$$\underline{z}_i = \underline{G}_i (\tilde{Z}_i).$$

In summary, Benassy states: "The fixprice equilibrium concept will involve for each trader three types of quantities:"[14]
   (i) effective demand vectors $(\tilde{z}_i)$,
   (ii) perceived constraints $(\bar{z}_i, \underline{z}_i)$, and
   (iii) transactions (z_i^*).
"Their equilibrium values may be thought of as the outcomes of some process of 'quantity tâtonnement,' *working simultaneously on all markets.*"[15] In other words, the process of "quantity tâtonnement" can be described as a continuous searching and revision of the trader's perceived constraints. Since the realized transactions (z_i^*), and the perceived constraints $(\bar{z}_i, \underline{z}_i)$ are all continuous functions of effective demands $(\tilde{z}_i, \tilde{Z}_i)$, the inconsistencies between demands and supplies can be eliminated after the trader obtains more and more realistic information about the quantity constraints. In this "tâtonnement" process, all three properties of the rationing scheme (voluntary exchange, market efficiency, and the "short-side-rule") play essential roles.

In the two-period case, trader i initially has vectors of endowment goods w_i and w_i^e. The second vector represents his expected endowment in the second period. His consumption vectors are denoted by x_i for the first period and w_i^e for the second. They are related to his transactions by the following relationships:

$$x_i = w_i + z_i \geq 0,$$

and

$$x_i^e = w_i^e + z_i^e \geq 0.$$

At the beginning of the first period, the trader has an initial quantity of money $\bar{m}_i$. If he does not spend all his money holdings during the first period, he transfers the unused quantity to the second period. Final money holdings at the end of the first period is denoted by $m_i = \bar{m}_i - pz_i \geq 0$. Planned transactions in the second period must satisfy the condition: $p^e z_i^e \leq m_i$.

Benassy's intertemporal choice-theoretic model

In historical time, stocks are the physical link between successive periods. Valuation of stocks in the current period depends upon expectations about future tradings and rates of return. In the case of the Keynesian marginal efficiency of capital, the expected net rate of return from investment influences current investment decisions. In the Benassy model, the only stock that links the first and second periods is the quantity of money. In the first period the trader has to make an optimal choice as to his consumption and the quantity of money (m_i) to be transferred to the second period. The trader's decision will be influenced by his expected future trading opportunities made possible by the transferred money holdings. Stated in utility terms, the utility of money entering into the utility function of each trader will have to be derived indirectly from the utility of transactions in the second period. Thus Benassy asserts:

> . . . we shall construct a utility function via a multiperiod optimization program taking expectations about future prices and quantities into account. Our construction will thus provide a formalization of the role of money as a store of value in situations where markets do not clear. The current equilibrium will have the character of temporary equilibrium, since it depends on future expectations.[16]

The procedure of constructing such a multiperiod optimization program for the first period is as follows:

(1) For a price taker, expected trading opportunities in the second period depend on (a) the vectors of expected prices p^e and (b) the expected quantity constraints ($\bar{z}_i^e$, $\underline{z}_i^e$). Letting σ_i^e denote the expected trading opportunities in the second period, we can write the relation as:

$$\sigma_i^e = (p^e, \bar{z}_i^e, \underline{z}_i^e).$$

(2) Since these expectations are based on the information available from the past, σ_i^e may be described as a function of the information available in the first period:

$$\sigma_i^e = \psi_i(\sigma_i)$$

where $\sigma_i = (p, \bar{z}_i \underline{z}_i)$.

(3) Given σ_i^e, the optimization problem for the second period is:

Maximize $U_i^e = U_i^e(x_i, x_i^e)$

subject to:
(i) budget constraint: $x_i^e = w_i^e + z_i^e \geq 0$, $p^e z_i^e \leq m_i$, and
(ii) quantity constraint: $\underline{z}_i^e \leq z_i^e \leq \bar{z}_i^e$.

The solution of the optimal (expected) consumption vector for the second period is:

$$x_i^e = x_i^e (x_i, m_i, \sigma_i^e) \text{ where } \sigma_i^e = (p^e, \bar{z}_i^e, \underline{z}_i^e).$$

(4) Substituting the function $x_i^e = x_i^e (x_i, m_i, \sigma_i^e)$ into the utility function $U_i^e = U_i^e (x_i, x_i^e)$, we obtain: $U_i^e = U_i^e (x_i, m_i, \sigma_i^e)$. Since $\sigma_i^e = \psi_i (\sigma_i)$, we can write:

$$U_i^e = U_i^e [x_i, m_i, \psi_i (\sigma_i)].$$

(5) The multiperiod utility function in the first period can now be written:

$$U_i = U_i (x_i \, m_i, \sigma_i].$$

It should be noted that the expected utility function, $U_i^e = U_i^e [x_i, m_i, \psi_i (\sigma_i)]$, has been subsumed under the multiperiod utility function via the assumption that $\sigma_i^e = \psi_i (\sigma_i)$. Therefore, we can say: $U_i (x_i, m_i, \sigma_i) = U_i^e [x_i, m_i, \psi_i (\sigma_i)]$. This is Benassy's "indirect utility function." It "has money as an argument, together with first-period consumption x_i. It also depends on expected prices and quantity constraints."[17] We should add that money in the utility function also has "indirect utility."

Having derived the indirect utility function, we find that the problem is to derive the optimal vector of effective demands in the current (first) period. Once this optimal vector is attained, the optimal final money holdings (to be transferred to the second period) follows.

Recall that transactions and perceived constraints are all functions of effective demand. In the Benassy model, trader i's effective demand on market h is formulated by ignoring the constraints on the market in question (namely, market h) and taking into consideration the perceived constraints in other markets. This definition of effective demand may appear puzzling. However, it does seize on some important aspects of economic theory. It is in some respects similar to the theory of imperfect information and search unemployment of Armen A. Alchian (also Leijonhufvud).[18] All three writers (Benassy, Alchian, and

Leijonhufvud) conduct their analyses in the choice-theoretic framework. Just like the unemployed worker in the Alchian and Leijonhufvud models, Benassy's trader is a utility maximizer. The "quantity
tâtonnement" of Benassy is analogous to Alchian and Leijonhufvud's
"searching" and adjustments of the worker's "reservation wage."
The effective demand initially expressed by Benassy's trader is higher
than his or her optimal transactions simply because he or she does not
have perfect information about the "true" quantity constraints on
market h. Gradually as better and more accurate information becomes
available, Benassy's trader (just like the Alchian-Leijonhufvud unemployed worker) has to make downward adjustments in his or her expressed effective demands until consistency between demands and supplies is reached. This is a recursive "quantity tâtonnement" process.
Eventually it will reach a temporary equilibrium. More specifically, the
recursive searching process may be described as follows.

Assume that all traders have expressed demands on all markets
$z_i, i = 1, 2, \ldots, n$. From these expressed demands the traders obtain
information on the perceived constraints given by the functions:
$\bar{z}_i = \bar{G}_i (\tilde{Z}_i); \underline{z}_i = \underline{G}_i (\tilde{Z}_i)$. The traders now have some perceived
quantity signals: $\bar{z}_i \geq z_i \geq \underline{z}_i$. On the basis of these quantity signals,
they express a new set of effective demands from which they derive a
more accurate perception of the quantity constraints. This process of
revision continues until they obtain the "true" quantity signals. Finally, an optimal set of effective demands is obtained which can be stated
as a function:

$$\tilde{z}_i = \phi_i (p, \bar{z}_i, \underline{z}_i).$$

This effective demand function is the solution in $z_i$zi of the following
program:
Maximize $U_i = U_i (x_i, m_i, \sigma_i)$
subject to:

$$x_i = \underline{w}_i + z_i \geq 0,$$

$$m_i = \bar{m}_i - pz_i \geq 0, \text{ and}$$

$$\bar{z}_i \geq z_i \geq \underline{z}_i.$$

A temporary general equilibrium can eventually be obtained as a
fixed point of the recursive quantity tâtonnement process. What is a

"fixed point"? It is a solution to the problem of existence of equilibrium. The best nontechnical explanation of the "fixed point theorem" is that given by William J. Baumol.[19] Baumol writes:

> First, let us see what is meant by a "fixed point." Suppose we have some functional relationship $Y = f(X)$ which associates different values of Y and X. Then a fixed point is a specific value of X, say $X = X^*$ (some number), for which $Y^* = f(X^*) = X^*$, i.e., for which the value of Y is equal to the value of X. The reason such a value of X is called a fixed point can be made clear with the accompanying illustrative table which gives Y as a function of X.

X	1	2	5	6
Y	9	7	5	11

Source: William J. Baumol, *Economic Theory and Operation Analysis*, 4th ed. ©1977, p. 551. Reprinted by permission of Prentice-Hall, Inc., Englewood Cliffs, N.J.

By employing the fixed point theorem Benassy succeeds in expressing temporary fixprice equilibrium for a given set of prices (p) and rationing schemes (F_i) as a set of effective demand vectors $\tilde{z}_i$, transactions z_i^*, and quantity constraints $\bar{z}_i$ and $\underline{z}_i$ such that

$$\tilde{z}_i = \phi_i\,(p,\,\bar{z},\,\underline{z}_i) \quad \text{for all } i$$

$$z_i^* = F_i\,(\tilde{z}_i,\,\tilde{Z}_i) \quad \text{for all } i$$

$$\bar{z}_i = \bar{G}_i\,(\tilde{Z}_i) \quad \text{for all } i$$

$$\underline{z}_i = \underline{G}_i\,(\tilde{Z}_i) \quad \text{for all } i.$$

CHAPTER 10

Franklin M. Fisher's Stability Analysis

Early predecessors

Stability analysis began with Leon Walras, who presented the first formulation of the stability of competitive equilibrium for a two-commodity economy. The equilibrium condition of the Walrasian analysis is that excess demand in the aggregate should be zero; the stability condition is that a price reduction (increase) should increase excess demands (supplies). The Walrasian stability analysis was extended by Sir John Hicks in 1939. In *Value and Capital*, Hicks reformulated stability analysis for a multiple-commodity exchange economy.[1] His method was essentially that of comparative statics.

Paul A. Samuelson suggested a new approach to the problem and laid the foundation of modern stability analysis in *Foundations of Economic Analysis* (1948). Samuelson introduced his "correspondence principle" and led stability analysis into the realm of dynamics. In explaining the common assumption "that if at any price demand exceeds supply, price will rise; if supply exceeds demand, price will fall," Samuelson wrote the following differential equation:[2]

$$\dot{p} = \frac{dP}{dt} = H(q_d - q_s) = H[D(p, \alpha) - S(p)],$$

where $H(0) = 0$ and $H' > 0$ and suggested the stability properties of the differential equation could be found by taking the linear terms of the Taylor expansion of the right-hand side of the equation about the equilibrium point. Samuelson writes: "In the neighborhood of the equilibrium point this can be expanded in the form

$$\dot{p} = \lambda(D_{p^0} - S_{p^0}) \, (\bar{p} - p^0) + \ldots ,$$

where $\lambda = (H')^0 > 0$, and where terms involving higher powers of $(p - p^0)$ are omitted. The solution of this simple differential equation for initial price $\bar{p}$ at time zero can be written at sight:

$$p(t) = p^0 + (\bar{p} - p^0) \, e^{\lambda \, (B_{p^0} - S_{p^0})t}.$$

If the equilibrium is to be stable,

$$\lim_{t \Rightarrow \infty} p(t) = p^0.$$

This is possible if, and only if,

$$D_{p^0} \, t > \infty \; - S_{p^0} \leq 0.$$

If we rule out neutral equilibrium in the large and in the small, the equality sign may be omitted so that $D_{p^0} - S_{p^0} < 0$. If the supply curve is positively inclined, this will be realized. If it is negatively inclined, it must be less steep than the demand curve. If our stability conditions are realized, the problem originally proposed is answered. Price must rise when demand increases."[3]

It should be noted that Samuelson's linear approximation procedure establishes only "local stability" and not "global stability." According to Michael D. Intriligator, "local stability" occurs "if the equilibrium is eventually attained starting from a set of prices sufficiently close to the equilibrium point."[4] This is the case with the linear approximation procedure. On the other hand, "the equilibrium is globally stable if the equilibrium is eventually attained regardless of the starting point."[5] A weaker notion of "global stability" is so-called "quasi-stability." Franklin M. Fisher defines "quasi-stability" as follows:

> For convenience of language, let us suppose that the variables involved are prices only. . . . Starting with an initial condition, consider an infinite sequence of prices. Such a sequence may not have limit (unless prices converge), but it may nevertheless have one or more limit points (roughly,

points to smaller and smaller neighborhoods of which the sequence keeps returning). If every limit point of every such sequence is a rest point of the adjustment process, then that process is said to be quasi-stable.[6]

Investigations of "local stability" did not get very far. Interest waned after the publication of Arrow and Hurwicz's paper, "On the Stabilty of the Competitive Equilibrium, I" (1958) and its sequel, "On the Stability of the Competitive Equilibrium, II" (1959) by Arrow, Block, and Hurwicz.[7] They demonstrated that "global stability" results could be obtained if all commodities were "gross substitutes" for each other.* The distinguishing feature of their proof is that they employ the entire properties of the competitive system, such as Walras's law, and the zero homogeneity of the individual demand functions. Their work put an end to the first phase of the history of stability analysis.

The mathematical technique employed by Arrow, Block, and Hurwicz to prove "global stability" is Lyapounov's second (or direct) method, which is explained by E. Roy Weintraub as follows:

> Consider, for example, the differential equation $\dot{x} = f(x)$, $x(0) = x_o$. . . . An equilibrium is a function of time (i.e., a state), such that $\dot{x}_e(t) = 0$; alternatively, it is a root or zero of the function $f(x)$. To find out whether a given equilibrium $x_e(t)$ is stable, one needs to examine whether other "nearby" motions of the system "get close" to $x_e(t)$. . . . [In other words, it is] a study of whether, over time, the distance between an arbitrary motion and equilibrium grows smaller; if so, then the system's rules mean that non-equilibrium states approach equilibrium, and thus the equilibrium is stable.[8]

Arrow, Block, and Hurwicz made no explicit formulation of the Lyapounov (or Liapunov) function. It was Lionel McKenzie (1960) who constructed the following Lyapounov function for the proof of the stability of a competitive equilibrium:[9]

$$V(t) = \sum_{i=1}^{n} p_i \mid f_i(p) \mid , i = [p_1, p_2, \ldots , p_n]$$

where $V(t)$ is the sum of the absolute values of the excess demands,

*Franklin M. Fisher explains "gross substitutability" as follows: "a rise in the price of any one good increases the demand for every other (goods), including income effect." See *Disequilibrium Foundations of Equilibrium Economics* (New York: Cambridge University Press, 1983), p. 23, footnote 7.

$f_i(p)$, multiplied by their prices, p_i. And V would be equal to zero when an equilibrium price vector prevails.

E. Roy Weintraub formulated the following Lyapounov function for the same purpose:[10]

$$(1) \qquad V(p) = \tfrac{1}{2} \sum_{i=1}^{n} (p_i - p_i^*)^2$$

where p^* is the equilibrium price of commodity i, $i = (1, 2, \ldots, n)$; and p_i is the price of the i-th commodity. The following inequalities hold for all p in the open region around p^*:

$$(2) \qquad V(p) \geq 0, \text{ and } V(p) = 0 \text{ only at } p^*,$$

and

$$(3) \qquad \dot{V}(p) \leq 0, \text{ and } \dot{V}(p) = 0 \text{ only at } p^*,$$

where p denoted a column n-vector of prices.

$$(4) \qquad \dot{V}(p) = \sum_{i=1}^{n} (p_i - p_i^*) \, \dot{p}_i = \sum_{i=1}^{n} (p_i - p_i^*) f_i(p),$$

or

$$(5) \qquad \dot{V}(p) = \sum_{i=1}^{n} p_i f_i(p) - \sum_{i=1}^{n} p_i^* f_i(p)$$

where $f_i(p)$ is excess demand functions for commodity i;

$$\sum_{i=1}^{n} p_i f_i(p)$$

denotes the sum of excess demands multiplied by the price of the i-th commodity. If Walras's law holds, then

$$\sum_{i=1}^{n} p_i f_i(p) = 0.$$

Thus, we are left with

$$(6) \qquad \dot{V}(p) = -\sum_{i=1}^{n} p_i^* f_i(p),$$

or

$$\dot{V}(p) < 0.$$

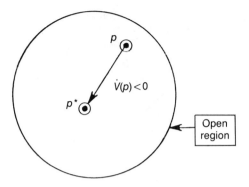

Figure 10.1

A representation of the Lyapounov method

Following Intriligator, $V(p)$ can be interpreted as a measure of the distance between the disequilibrium price and the equilibrium price within the open region around the equilibrium price.[11] Equation (6) means that the distance falls over time, so equilibrium is eventually attained. At p^*, $\dot{V}(p) = 0$. The inward direction of $\dot{V}(p) < 0$ is depicted in Figure 10.1.

Fisher's immediate predecessors

The 1960s saw a renaissance of stability analysis. The prime movers in this new wave were F. H. Hahn, H. Uzawa, and T. Negishi.[12] The distinguishing new features of this literature are that:

(1) they give more consideration to trade out-of-equilibrium and to disequilibrium behavior;

(2) price adjustments and non-tâtonnement stability are attained via the Lyapounov functions. However, according to Franklin M. Fisher, "Such Lyapounov functions have tended to go from geometrically interpretable measures of the distance from equilibrium to economically more interesting functions such as the sum of the utilities which households would expect to get if their mutually inconsistent plans could be realised";[13]

(3) the institutional framework is a pure exchange economy. Fisher observes:

It is important to remember that, while this stage of development permits trading out of equilibrium, most of the work to be discussed does not permit consumption or production to take place until equilibrium has been

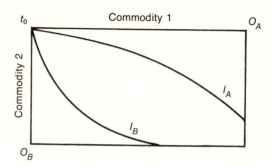

Figure 10.2

The Edgeworth-Bowley box

reached. One must think of participants as swapping titles to commodity stocks while prices (and, of course, possessions) adjust. Only after the music stops do people go home and enjoy what they have. Such a model is obviously most suited to pure exchange with no firms.[14]

Two representative non-tatonnement processes (Fisher prefers to call them "trading process") are the "Edgeworth Process" used by Uzawa (1962) and the "Hahn Process" named by Hahn and Negishi (1962).[15] Before we consider the modern Edgeworthian disequilibrium adjustment process, a review of the Edgeworth exchange process is in order. Following Vivian Charles Walsh,[16] the Edgeworth bilateral exchange process can be explained by the Edgeworth-Bowley box diagram as shown in Figure 10.2.

Walsh writes:

> The simplest possible model for the theory of an exchange system is one involving only two parties and two comodities—a system of bilateral exchange. Each of our two parties is thought of as possessing a commodity bundle, his object being to exchange this for a more preferred bundle. The total stock of commodities held by the two traders collectively is assumed to be fixed throughout the analysis.[17]

In Figure 10.2 quantities of commodity 1 are measured horizontally while quantities of commodity 2 are measured vertically. The symbol O_A represents the origin for trader A; O_B denotes the origin for trader B. Assume that each individual initially holds only one commodity. Hence, the initial position of the system is indicated by the northwest corner point t_0. The indifference curves, I_A and I_B, have special significance: both end at t_0 and are attained without trade. Trader A will not be interested in any curve of his below I_A, nor will trader B be interested in any curve below curve I_B. According to Walsh, "they will trade only by moving to points in the better set with their indifference curves through t_0."[18] The better sets associated with the initial endowment for the two traders are shown in Figure 10.3. The better sets for trader A are depicted by the shaded area of Figure 10.3(a); the better sets for trader B are indicated by the shaded area of 10.3(b). The two better sets overlap $(B_A \cap B_B)$ and form closed convex sets.

The bilateral exchange process involves the two traders bargaining directly with each other over price. If both parties agree on a price, a transaction (a two-party coalition) is set up. The portion of the contract curve which does not lie below I_A or above I_B is called the "core." In the words of E. Roy Weintraub, "the core consists of those allocations that no coalition (the coalitions are A, B, and (A,B)) finds more desirable and can, in fact, affect. . . . It is a subset of the set of Pareto-efficient allocations."[19] A coalition that can affect the allocation (transaction) is called a "blocking coalition." The range of the "core" becomes smaller as the number of traders is increased in this pure exchange economy.[20]

The coalition formation in the bilateral exchange model is the source of modern Edgeworthian disequilibrium analysis. Weintraub observes:

> Without a central market, and market maker, one is left with agents attempting to make themselves better off through trade. The process involves inter-agent communication, tentative offers, contracting, recontracting, and transacting. There is no information center, no one but other similar agents to whom a given agent can turn. . . . The Edgeworth model, with its lack of a central coordinator, thus may be well suited to the posing of macroeconomic questions. . . . The Edgeworth model thus seems to hold some promise of being able to capture the essence of Leijonhufvud's "corridor" behavior.*

*E. Roy Weintraub, *Microfoundations: The Compatibility of Microeconomics and Macroeconomics* (New York: Cambridge University Press, 1979), pp. 133–134. Concerning the "corridor" behavior, Leijonhufvud writes: "The (economic) system is likely to behave differently for large than for moderate displacements from the 'full coordination' time-path. Within some range from the path (referred to as 'the corridor' for brevity), the system's homeostatic mechanism works well, and deviation-counteracting tendencies increase in strength. Outside that range these tendencies become weaker as the system becomes increasingly subject to 'effective demand failures.' If the system is displaced sufficiently 'far out,' the forces tending to

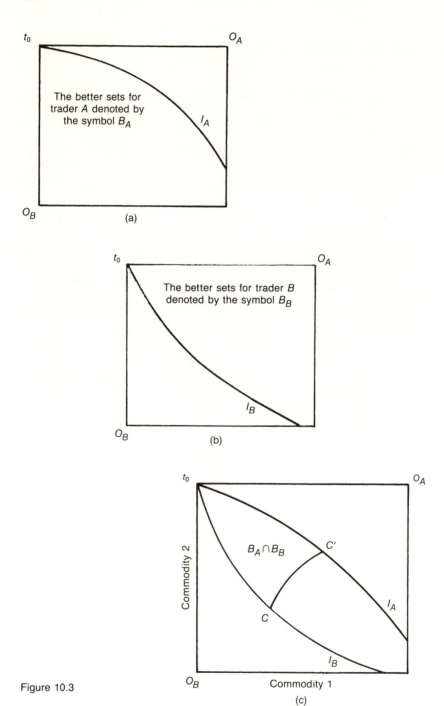

Figure 10.3

The Edgeworth bilateral exchange process

The disequilibrium "trading process" in the Edgeworthian framework was first examined by Uzawa (1962). As pointed out by Weintraub, "There are two adjustment mechanisms. One changes prices in the direction of excess demands, where those demands are now functions of individual stocks. In the other, stocks change via trade when trade would increase the utility of the participants.[21] These mechanisms were investigated by Leo Hurwicz, Roy Radner, and Stanley Reiter in 1975.[22] In the same year Daniel A. Graham and E. R. Weintraub studied the properties of the final allocation of the disequilibrium adjustment process in a monetary theoretic theme.[23]

Turning now to the "Hahn Process," we see that the central assumption is best summarized by F. M. Fisher as follows:

> At any one time, after trade has taken place, there may of course be either unsatisfied demand or unsatisfied supply for some commodity, say, apples. However, we suppose that markets are sufficiently well organized that there are not both . . . Markets are sufficiently well organized that willing buyers and willing sellers can and do come together and consummate a trade very quickly relative to the rate at which the disequilibrium adjustment equations operate; such deals are to be thought of as consummated instanteously or *outside of* [*historical or real*] *time*.[24]

---

bring it back may, on balance, be so weak and sluggish that—for all practical purposes—the Keynesian 'unemployment equilibrium' model is as sensible a representation of its state as economic statics will allow . . . although within the corridor market forces will be acting in the direction of clearing markets. Institutional obstacles of the type familiar from the conventional Keynesian literature may, of course, intervene to make them ineffective at some point. Thus a combination of monopolistic wage-setting in unionized occupations and legal minimum-wage restrictions could obviously cut the automatic adjustment process short before 'equilibrium employment' is reached" (Axel Leijonhufvud, *Information and Coordination: Essays in Macroeconomic Theory* [New York: Oxford University Press, 1981], pp. 109–110).

E. Roy Weintraub further observes: "Macroeconomics has not been on the research agenda for most 'core' theorists. Their work has generalized and extended the exchange model to economies permitting production, public goods, externalities, monopoly, and oligopoly. The work has concentrated on basic microeconomics, and has tended to show satisfying unities in the structure of economic theory. Arrow's Impossibility Theorem, external diseconomies and public goods problems can all be linked to the failure of some structurally similar games to possess a core (William H. Riker and Peter C. Ordeshook [*An Introduction to Positive Political Theory* (Englewood Cliffs, N.J.: Prentice-Hall)], 1973, and Robert Wilson ["The Game Theoretic Structure of Arrow's General Possibility Theorem," *Journal of Economic Theory*, 5 (1), August 1972, pp. 14–20], 1972). Since core allocations are produced by the Invisible Hand, their nonexistence and 'market failures' are inextricably linked" (*Microfoundations*, p. 134).

Quasi-stability is again proved by means of a Lyapounov function which is no longer viewed as the geometrically interpretable measure of the distance from equilibrium. It is now the sum of "target utilities" bounded from below. "Target utility" in the "Hahn Process" means the utility which the trader expects to get if he can complete all his transactions. Since prices adjust in the same direction as aggregate excess demand, the frustrated trader in disequilibrium will find that the things he wishes to buy and cannot buy are getting more expensive. The reverse situation will apply to the frustrated seller. The frustrated trader will find his "target utility" decreasing. This is the basis for the Lyapounov function. As Fisher states, "In the 'Hahn Process,' the adjustment is such that people have to lower their expectations until equilibrium is reached and everyone can in fact attain the utility he anticipates."[25]

In their *General Competitive Analysis* (1971), K. J. Arrow and F. H. Hahn constructed a revised version of the "Hahn Process" by introducing a money commodity. They demonstrated that "global stability" for the "Hahn Process" would be attained if no one ever runs out of money. Franklin Fisher names this condition of stability the "Positive Cash Assumption."[26] Fisher points out that a further stability condition is necessary to prove "global stability," that being the "Present Action Postulate." "Households in this model must act now to make some nonzero part of every nonzero target demand an active excess demand."[27] "Target" excess demands mean those excess demands attainable in a world without money constraints (the result of the introduction of money into the process); "active" excess demands are those excess demands that are expressed by actual offers to buy (the same as Clower's effective demand).

The major problem faced in the revised version, in the opinion of Franklin M. Fisher, is that all trading opportunities will cease once equilibrium is attained. The implication is that in equilibrium there is no reason for traders to hold money. Fisher writes:

> Now, money as such makes its appearance in the present model as a medium of exchange: All transactions take place for money. This gives agents a reason for holding money while they are still making transactions. However, since equilibrium in this model involves an exhaustion of trading opportunities, once equilibrium is reached, all money that will ever change hands has already done so. Hence, without further assumptions, no agent will have a reason to hold money in equilibrium. To make

matters worse, agents always believe that the system is already in equilibrium so that all they need to do is to complete their current transactions. . . . Hence there is no reason for agents ever to plan to hold money.
. . . All this is very awkward. It makes the Positive Cash Assumption that
agents never run out of money quite artificial. Further, it makes money
quite unsuitable as a numeraire good since nobody wants to hold it in
equilibrium. Hence Arrow and Hahn follow the usual unsatisfactory
practice of assuming that money enters the utility function—in effect, that
it is an ordinary good which just happens to be used as the medium of
exchange.*

Fisher's generalized "Arrow-Hahn Process"

Franklin M. Fisher observes that the "Arrow-Hahn Process" rests on
two insights: (a) that markets are orderly so that there are no frustrated
demands or supplies after trade; and (b) that all agents "naively"
believe that the economy is in equilibrium. He says, "In effect, the
orderly market assumption plus the naive expectations of agents leads
to a situation in which the opportunities which agents perceive disappear as they are acted on—even though the 'arbitrage' involved is not
deliberate."[28]

Fisher points out:

> We must allow production and consumption to take place out of equilibri-
> um. More important, we must allow agents to realize that they are not in
> equilibrium and to act on arbitrage opportunities as they occur. This
> fundamentally requires that agents be permitted to do two things. First,
> they must recognize that prices may change. Second, they must recognize
> that they may not be able to complete their desired transactions. In
> forming their consumption and production plans, agents must take these
> things into account.[29]

In Fisher's view it is possible to incorporate disequilibrium production
and consumption into the "Arrow-Hahn Process" without disrupting
the stability analysis. His explanation is as follows: Production and
consumption decisions involve taking actions which are likely to be

*Fisher, *Disequilibrium Foundations*, pp. 35–36. Fisher stresses: "Despite these
problems, the Arrow-Hahn introduction of money as a sole medium of exchange is
a considerable step forward . . . [among other things] it has a modicum of realism,
if *not monetary theory*; and it is probably indispensable for the introduction of firms
into trading processes" (p. 26). The emphasis is ours.

irreversible. These actions are taken under given expectations about prices and trading opportunities. Since no one has perfect foresight, expectations may not be realized. Consequently, such regrettable actions inevitably lead to lower profits or utilities. This state of affairs can only reinforce Hahn's assumption of declining target profits and utilities in disequilbrium. Hence, a similar Lyapounov function can be formulated to prove the "quasi-stability" of the system.

The Fisherian refined stability analysis is certainly more sensible than that of Arrow and Hahn. The price adjustment is no longer entrusted to a deus ex machina, the "auctioneer"; rather it is based on the optimal decisions of agents. In Fisherian stability analysis, agents do not have "naive expectations." They are constantly aware of disequilibrium (Fisher's "disequilibrium consciousness") and are allowed to make price offers and to arbitrage whenever they perceive favorable new opportunities. Fisher maintains that such arbitraging activities do not prevent the system from converging to equilibrium. The only restriction necessary is that such activities should be consistent with the condition of "no favorable suprise." Fisher writes:

> Following Schumpeter, we cannot suppose it to be true that an economy in which new opportunities constantly arise will converge to equilibrium. Such "new opportunities" are to be broadly interpreted; apart from the traditional forms of Schumpeterian innovation—technology, new raw materials, new markets, new forms of organizations, and so on—they include the weakening of previously binding constraints. A leading example here is that of the effect of windfall gains on constraints on borrowing. Further, it is agents' perceptions of new opportunities that matter rather than their reality. Finally, since agents plan over time, what must be ruled out is sudden optimistic revisions in agents' expectations. There must be no favorable surprise.[30]

Although the Fisherian Lyapounov function is similar to that of the "Arrow-Hahn Process," there are two important differences. The first has to do with the role of firms. In the "Arrow-Hahn Process," the target profits of firms fall when the firms are out of equilibrium. The fall in target profits, in turn, trickles down to the households through decreases in dividend payments and other related households' incomes. Consequently, the target utilities of households fall also. The sum of these utilities serves as a Lyapounov function which is continuous, bounded below, and decreasing through time except at rest points. (A rest point of an adjustment process is a point at which the process does not move.) As pointed out by Fisher, "In the present case, however, this is not necessarily so. Firms and their shareholders can have different expectations [no more naive expectations] about future profits. Hence it is possible that a firm might not be in monetary personal equilibrium while its shareholders feel no effect on their target utilities."[31]

Fisher further states:

> The result of this is that the sum of target utilities alone will not do as a Lyapounov function. Such a sum can fail to decrease even if firms are not in monetary personal equilibria provided that households are all in such equilibria [which is the case in the Arrow-Hahn process]. Instead, we must include firms as equal personae, reflecting the fact that they have been given independent abilities to form expectations. This means taking as our Lyapounov function not the sum of target utilities but the sum of target utilities plus the sum of target profits.[32]

The second difference also concerns differences in the treatment of expectations. It is possible in the Fisherian adjustment process that "all agents can temporarily complete their transactions and find their near-term expectations as to prices and other relevant magnitudes fulfilled while some (or all) of their longer-term expectations will not come true. In such a circumstance, the system—and the proposed Lyapounov function—will stop moving, but only temporarily. Eventually, agents will either change their expectations or find that they cannot go on completing their transactions."[33]

In the opinion of Fisher, there is one overriding fact that is far more important than the technical details of convergence. That overriding fact is the "hysteresis effects" or "path dependence effect." The role of historical time is firmly grasped by Fisher in his consideration of the "hysteresis effect":

> The study of stability theory also casts a somewhat negative light on the usefulness of computational algorithms for the calculation of points of general equilibria even on their own grounds. Such algorithms as that of Scarf (1973) provide a method of finding general equilibrium points given (among other things) the endowments of the agents. In a real economy, however, trading, as well as production and consumption, goes on out of equilibrium. It follows that, in the course of convergence to equilibrium (assuming that occurs), endowments change. In turn this changes the set of equilibria. Put more succinctly, the set of equilibria is path dependent— it depends not merely on the initial state but on the dynamic adjustment process.[34]

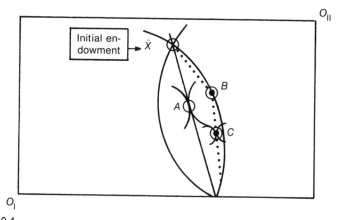

Figure 10.4

The "hysteresis effect"

Source: Franklin M. Fisher, *Disequilibrium Foundations of Equilibrium Economics* (London: Cambridge University Press, 1983), p. 14. Reprinted by permission.

The "hysteresis effect" is illustrated by the Fisherian two-person exchange economy shown in Figure 10.4. The initial endowment point is represented by X. Corresponding to the initial endowment is a unique equilibrium point, A. If starting at X, prices happen to be the right equilibrium prices shown by the solid line, then the two agents, I and II, will trade until they reach the equilibrium point, A. What if the initial prices are not the equilibrium prices but are instead the prices given by the dotted line? If prices again shift shown by the dotted line below point B, trade would take place until point C is reached. Points B and C are competitive equilibrium prices, but they are not the same as the equilibrium point A, which, in the static sense, corresponds to the initial endowment X. It should be noted that the equilibrium point C corresponds statistically to the new endowment point B, which was the result of trade in the first step. In other words the endowment point has changed over time. Fisher writes:

> In more general models, there will be more than two steps (indeed, there can be continuous change) and the situation will be more complex; however, the point should now be clear. An algorithm that predicts that the economy with endowment X will get to A will simply be wrong.[35]

In the context of historical time, the optimal decisions (plans) of agents involve three things: (a) the optimal timing of consumption (households), (b) the optimal timing of production (firms), and (c) the optimal timing of transactions (firms and households). The optimal production plans of arbitraging firms are the solution of the following program:

Maximization of the present discounted value of profits

Subject to:

(i) technical constraints
(ii) "short constraints," and
(iii) "money constraints."

The "short constraints" and "money constraints" are both necessary restrictions for the stability of the system.*

The optimal arbitrage behavior of households in disequilibrium, in spite of certain differences, parallels that of the firm. They face similar constraints and they both speculate. One of the common threads tying the two theories together is the "money constraint." Because of the "money constraint," as pointed out by Fisher, "the true price of money is neither unity nor totally reflected in the instantaneous interest rate. Rather it is the shadow price of money (the Lagrange multiplier of money constraint) which reflects the value of future opportunities to use it."[36] The shadow price of money is important in the speculative activities of the firm as well as in those of the household.

In his generalization of the "Arrow-Hahn Process," Fisher also investigates other aspects of the optimal arbitrage behavior of agents in disequilibrium. One of these is the connection between "transaction constraints" and "conjectured monopoly power." The analysis is reminiscent of Arrow's earlier considerations of price adjustment (1959).[37] Kenneth J. Arrow stresses: "In disequilibrium, the market consists of a number of monopolists facing a number of monopsonists. The most general picture is that of a shifting set of bilateral monopolies."[38] However, Fisher goes a step further than Arrow and considers the impact of monopoly power on the stability result. His tentative conclusion is that "the stability result turns out to hold when monopoly

---

*The "short constraints" require the arbitraging firm to deliver on its promise. It should not let its short position (selling things that it does not already have) last beyond the dates of the commodities involved. The "money constraint" means essentially that the firm's planned money stock must always be nonnegative. The firm should not issue new equity.

power is present—whether the power is real or merely perceived.''*

Downplaying the importance of his own work, Fisher gives the following evaluation of his scholarly efforts:

> Unfortunately it is not nearly enough. Both in terms of stability analysis itself and in terms of other aspects of the analysis of disequilibrium there is a great deal more that needs to be done before we have a sound basis for equilibrium analysis. I consider these matters in the hope that the present model can provide the framework for further research. . . . What is certain is that work in this area must continue. The issues involved in disequilibrium analysis are too important to economics to be avoided. They must be faced head on rather than assumed away in the course of a desire to do what economists do best—analyze equilibrium without regard for the foundations on which such analysis must rest.[39]

---

*Fisher, *Disequilibrium Foundations*, p. 213. Fisher writes: ''When we consider how the agent sets his selling price, however, this optimizing condition turns out to have a very familiar interpretation. The shadow price of the transaction constraint is the amount which the seller would just be willing to give up in order to be able to sell an additional unit. . . . Hence, price will be set so that the shadow price of the constraint just equals . . . the difference between price and marginal revenue. When this is done, the optimizing condition that virtual price (price less constraint shadow price) equal marginal cost is seen to be the familiar monopoly condition that marginal revenue equal marginal cost'' (p. 154).

CHAPTER 11

Post-Keynesian Microfoundations and Some Other Non-Walrasian Approaches

In the Post-Keynesian camp, there is increased awareness of the limitations of the Sraffian and other neo-Ricardian arguments about the set of "normal" prices which must prevail in the long run if the system is to be capable of maintaining steady-state growth. As pointed out by Alfred S. Eichner (1981):

> Equilibrium models of this sort are not enough. Such models offer little or no insight into what happens over the cycle. They also are inadequate for explaining the observable changes in trend over time. It is for this reason that, following Kalecki, one must also have models that are "out of equilibrium"—whether they are of the purely short-period sort, such as those used to account for the cyclical movements of . . . the economy, or [whether] they are of an intermediate nature and, abstracting from any cyclical movements, focus on the change in trend over time.[1]

Eichner's observations seem to have nudged Post-Keynesian microeconomics toward the line of reasoning expounded by Robert J. Gordon:

> Prices are neither perfectly fixed nor perfectly flexible, and variations over time and across countries with regard to the degree of flexibility require explanation as well.*

*Robert J. Gordon, "Output Fluctuations and Gradual Price Adjustment," *Journal of Economic Literature*, *13* (2), June 1970, p. 495. Gordon points out: The phenomena the theory must explain is a long and daunting one: "(1) Some markets have prices that are set at the same level over weeks, months, or years. (2) Some prices, even though they are marked on price tags, are changed every day (e.g., the price of lettuce in a supermarket), and yet other pre-set prices remain sufficiently fixed to be

The increasing sophistication of Post-Keynesian price theory has led Nina Shapiro, Josef Steindl, Nai-Pew Ong, and others to study changes in markup pricing over time.[2] As observed by Eichner, "To develop pricing models of this intermediate sort, Shapiro and Ong have relaxed two of the critical assumptions usually made in long-period analysis: (1) equalized rates of return on capital investment, and (2) absence of technical progress."[3]

In her paper "Pricing and Growth of the Firm" (1981), Nina Shapiro writes:

> Continuous and accelerating growth is the overriding goal of the capitalist enterprise. The goal pushes the firm toward a long-run perspective in its pricing decisions. All actions must be judged in terms of their effect on the ongoing expansion of the firm. Their future, rather than immediate economic consequences, is the decisive consideration.[4]
>
> This discussion is not intended to suggest that prices always remain fixed in the event of short-run demand fluctuations. The point is not the "rigidity" of prices but the prevalence of long-run pricing policies. Such policies and the market quantity adjustments they imply become fully intelligible when grasped in the light of the growth orientation of the capitalist firm.[5]

Shapiro emphasizes that diversification and product competition are important vehicles in revitalization of the growth process. Diversification provides investment outlets, and the introduction of cost-reducing technical innovation can reinforce the diversification process. Shapiro asserts: "Technical change does not merely add another dimension to competitive relationships. Product competition does not stand next to

---

printed in catalogues and on product containers. (3) The division of nominal GNP changes between prices and quantitites varies across countries, with evidence of a greater price response in Europe both during the Great Depression and more recently (Robert J. Gordon and James A. Wilcox, 'The Monetarist Interpretation of the Great Depression: An Evaluation and Critique' in *The Great Depression Revisited*, edited by Karl Brunner (Hingham, MA: Martinus Nijhoff, 1981, pp. 49–107). (4) The division of nominal GNP changes between prices and quantities has varied over time in the United States, with a rapid price response during and after World War I, and after the OPEC oil shock in 1974, but virtually no price response to high unemployment in 1938-40 and 1970-71. (5) Prices, although set in advance and marked on price tags, nevertheless have the potential to move fast enough to allow hyperinflation to occur (Thomas J. Sargent, 1981)." Thus "*any adequate framework must go beyond the fixed-price paradigm which has no ingredient that would explain variations over time* in the degree of price responsiveness. Similarly, the facts of price-setting and quantity-taking cannot be explained by the new classical paradigm, which simply assumes them away" (pp. 494–495).

price competition. Rather, it radically reorganizes the pricing system
. . . .Price formation is dichotomized into the pricing of new and old
products, with the specific growth strategy of the individual firm unifying the process. The notion of 'strategic price' replaces that of competitive price."[6] "The firm is always intent on sustaining the strategic
price," Shapiro maintains, "and does whatever is in its power to
convince its customers that the strategic price is the 'real worth' of the
good."[7] Shapiro is confident that "the notion of strategic price contains the seeds of a viable theory of capitalist exchange."[8]

As mentioned earlier in this book, the Post-Keynesians are in many
ways the pioneers of our time, campaigning for the reconstruction of
microfoundations of Keynesian macroeconomics. We say "of our
time," for there had been voices in the recent past protesting the
orthodox treatment of uncertainty and historical time.*

Orthodox economists have stressed the importance of expectations
formation in macroeconomics. As pointed out by David K. H. Begg
(1982): "In the past, the adoption of various ad hoc assumptions about
the process of expectations formation has allowed the development of
simple macroeconomic models whose dynamic properties might be
analyzed. Yet ad hoc assumptions are troubling for they are arbitrary.
The recent work on the hypothesis of Rational Expectations has commanded considerable attention because it seems to rely on a good
optimizing principle: individuals should not make systematic mistakes
in forecasting the future."[9]

Post-Keynesians question the foundation of the Rational Expectations hypothesis. Paul Davidson regards it as "a fallacious foundation
for studying the crucial decision-making process." Davidson argues
that the Rational Expectations hypothesis is based on the theory of
stationary stochastic process:

> Stochastic processes can be defined as families of random variables de-
> pending upon a parameter. The random variables can assume certain

---

*See Douglas Vickers, "Uncertainty, Choice, and the Marginal Efficiencies," *Jour-
nal of Post Keynesian Economics*, 2 (2), Winter 1979–80. Vickers calls attention to
the views of Frank Knight (1948) on the differences between "uncertainty" and
"risk," the criticisms of Tjalling C. Koopmans (1957) on the failure of traditional
economic analysis in shedding light on the core problem of economic organization
of society, namely, that of how to deal with uncertainty, and the 1960 broader methodological conclusion of T. W. Hutchinson that the method of deduction from
some "fundamental assumptions" of economic conduct is more or less useless
(pp.241–242).

given values with *definite* probabilities. If the random variables are well defined for all points of time, and if all their distribution functions (cumulative probability distributions) are independent of time, then the stochastic process is called *stationary* in *the strict sense* . . . The concept of stationarity means the probability structure of a stationary process is independent of absolute (historical) time. . . . This implies that when an experiment is performed should not *per se* affect the outcomes.[10]

Unfortunately, the economic process moves through historical time and therefore it is not stationary. The very conditions necessary to make the probability assumptions meaningful generally do not exist in the economic decision situation at all. This view of uncertainty, which is sometimes referred to as the Keynes–Shackle–Hicks view, is generally upheld by economists of the Post-Keynesian persuasion, such as Paul Davidson, Douglas Vickers, G. L. S. Shackle, James R. Wible, and others.[11] Davidson cites Keynes's 1937 defense of *The General Theory*:

By "uncertain" knowledge, let me explain, I do not mean merely to distinguish what is known for certain from what is only probable. The game of roulette is not subject in this sense, to uncertainty. . . . The sense in which I am using the term is that in which the prospect of a European war is uncertain, or the price of copper and the rate of interest twenty years hence, or the obsolescence of a new invention. . . . About these matters there is no scientific basis on which to form any calculable probability whatever. We simply do not know! (*The Collected Writings of J. M. Keynes*, Vol 14 [London: Macmillan, 1973], pp. 114–115)[12]

Again in his review of Hicks's *Causality in Economics* (1980) Davidson mentions Keynes's discussion of time series regression analysis in which he said such "analysis is but a pseudoscience, since the material is 'not homogeneous through time' [Keynes, *Collected Writings*, Vol 14], 1973, p. 296."[13]

Accepting Keynes's views on uncertainty, G. L. S. Shackle wrote:

Frequency-ratios give us foreknowledge of the outcome of an experiment which is going to consist of the aggregation of many separate but similar acts. . . . The application of frequency ratios only makes sense if the individual can feel sure that there will be many repetitions, that there will be a divisible experiment in which the immediate act, with which he is now concerned, will be swallowed up.[14]

Shackle observes that there are situations which cannot be predicted by the Bayes-LaPlace theorem. He asserts that sometimes a decision-maker has to make crucial choices which are in effect unique and never to be repeated.* Shackle points out further that "time" is not just one dimension of space "where distinct points do not, a priori, differ from each other in their general essential nature and properties. . . . Yet plainly time is not of this character when viewed from the human standpoint. . . .In the experience of human individuals each of these moments is in a certain sense solitary. There is for us a moment-in-being, which is the locus of every actual sense-experience, every thought, feeling, decision and action."[15]

It is interesting to note that the Shacklean approach is highly subjective and individualistic and therefore rather similar to that of Ludwig von Mises. As observed by Ludwig M. Lachmann:

> In their emphasis on the spontaneous, and thus unpredictable nature of human action, in their rejection of mechanistic notions of time and prob-

---

*In his "Probability and Uncertainty," Shackle illustrated the "crucial choice" by a borrowed parable. Shackle wrote: "In his novel *The Widows of the Magistrate*, Keith West tells how certain Chinese officials plotted rebellion against their Emperor. The brief passage that I am going to reproduce describes the thoughts of a certain sentry, who had to decide whether to obey his immediate superior, the treacherous Captain of the Guard, or to stand alone against the rebels in loyal defence of the Emperor's representative, the lady Hibiscus:

> "I am a man who seizes opportunity," he told the admiring women and the sleeping children. "If I obey the Captain of the Guard, two things may happen. Either the rebellion succeeds, and I remain a soldier in the guard, or the rebellion fails, when I lose my head. Whereas if I obey the Lady Hibiscus, two things may happen. Either the rebellion succeeds, and I lose my head, or the rebellion fails, when I shall receive rewards quite beyond my imagination to conceive. Now of these four possibilities, the last only attracts me. So I shall strive to hold this tower unentered, as long as possible, until the arrival of help from elsewhere. That is the course of wisdom, as well as the course of courage, and I am deficient in neither wisdom nor courage."

This eminently wise and sensible decision, reached with such incisive logic, might not have been so readily attained had the sentry been acquainted with the theory of probability. For then he might have argued thus: 'I find in the record of history a thousand cases similar to my own, wherein the person concerned decided upon treachery, and in only four hundred of these cases the rebellion failed and he was beheaded. On balance, therefore, the advantage seems to lie with treachery, provided one does it often enough.' The parable of the sentry is clearly a case of unique crucial choice" (*Metroeconomica*, 1949, 1, reprinted in *Uncertainty in Economics and Other Reflections* [Cambridge: Cambridge University Press, 1968], p. 3).

ability, our two authors are completely at one. They also agree that a science of human action requires a methodology sui generis.[16]

However, there are also differences between the two thinkers, the most important difference being that Shackle has extended the scope of subjectivism from taste to expectations. "Mises hardly ever mentions expectations, though entrepreneurs and speculators often enough turn up in his pages. Thus from 1939 onwards Shackle had to take on expectations more or less single-handedly without much benefit of support from the Austrian side."[17]

Shackle's approach to expectations and decision-making is original. He writes:

> By decision I do not mean the act of choosing between alternatives whose character is felt by the chooser to be certainly and perfectly known to him in all respects which matter to him. To make a decision is to commit oneself to the first step in an action-scheme about whose relevant consequences the decision-maker has in mind a plurality of rival (mutually exclusive) hypotheses none of which he regards as impossible.[18]

Shackle asserts that subjective probability considerations are not applicable to an individual's important and unique decisions made under conditions of uncertainty. He constructs a decision framework that replaces subjective probability with the notion of "the potential surprise." His potential surprise function is designed to measure the consequences of a decision under uncertainty. In the Shacklean framework, an important and unique decision may have many alternative outcomes. Some of the potential outcomes are deemed to be improbable by the decision maker. Should such improbable consequences occur, he would certainly be surprised. The occurrence of an outcome the decision maker deems as highly possible would not have any potential surprises. The Shacklean decision-making process is most aptly summarized by Douglas Vickers:

> He [the decision maker] stands at his "solitary moment" in which the imagination of possible outcomes holds rein. But his perceptions of the possibilities that bound his penumbral uncertainty are determined by the economic inheritance which brings him to the present and by his memory of, and appreciation for, real world histories, data, and the limits of possibility in the natural events that might unfold. The decision maker, in

his moment of responsibility, stands undetermined and free . . . and his choice, now legitimized by its referents in his personally delineated set of possible results, establishes his act. The results he envisages, however, are described not by the spurious distributional variables of the probability calculus, but by what must be termed nondistributional variables. What therefore must be grasped is that, in the context of the decision framework thus established, *possibility* can never be mapped into probability, and the "potential surprise function" cannot be translated into probability distributions.[19]

Shackle's "potential surprise function" is depicted in Figure 11.1. In Figure 11.1(a) the payoffs which might occur are measured along the horizontal axis. The symbol X represents such possible payoffs. The potential surprises associated with these payoffs, depicted by the symbol Y, are measured along the vertical axis. Shackle explains:

> What I have been saying is that the decision-maker can be supposed to have in mind for each action-scheme a function $Y = Y(X)$ of a shape like a vertical section through a flat-bottomed basin. The flat-bottom represents the inner range or *perfectly possible* values of X, the rising sides of the basin represent those intermediate ranges of cloudy possibility which merge into the outer ranges of impossibilities, where Y attains an "absolute maximum" value $Y = \bar{Y}$.[20]

The degree of potential surprise for perfectly possible outcomes or payoffs is zero and the decision maker will not be concerned with such payoffs. The perfectly possible range is indicated by the range bounded by the points K and L on the horizontal axis in Figure 11.1(a). The point N is one of a number of points within the inner range.

The decision maker focuses his attention on those possible outcomes (Shackle's "focus outcomes") outside of the inner or perfectly possible range. Let the symbol ϕ represent the "attention arresting power" of each pair of X and Y. The relationships are summarized by $\phi = \phi(X, Y)$ where it is asumed that ϕ is an increasing function of X and a decreasing function of Y. It is also assumed that ϕ will be zero for all totally improbable outcomes $\bar{Y}$. Since ϕ is a function of two variables (similar to the utility function, $U = U(X,Y)$), Shackle regards it as a surface (similar to the iso-utility map). The contours of the surface are depicted by the curves in Figure 11.1(b). There are two sets of ϕ functions: one of them indicating all the possible desirable payoffs (or gains), the other depicting all the possible undesirable payoffs (or losses).

222

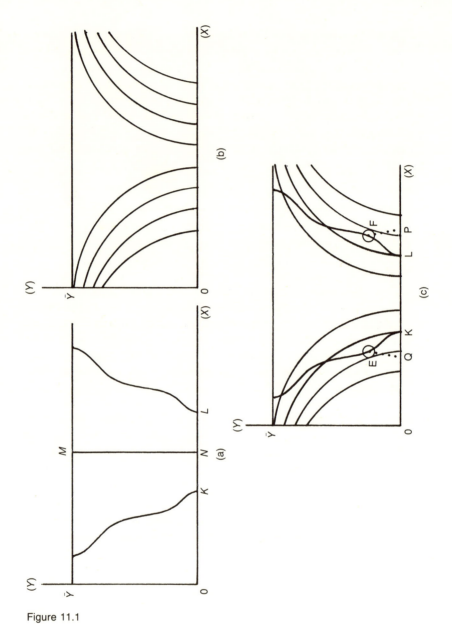

Figure 11.1

Shackle's "potential surprise"

Source: G. L. S. Shackle, *Time in Economics* (Amsterdam: North-Holland, 1958), p. 52. Reprinted by permission of the author and North-Holland Publishing Company.

In Figure 11.1(c) the potential surprise function and the surface are put together. The two tangency points are indicated by E and F (Shackle's "primary focus outcomes"). By dropping a perpendicular vector from E and Q, and from F to P, one can state the outcomes in terms of X (payoffs) alone. Points Q and P are Shackles's "standard focus outcomes," or the optimal choice of the decision maker.

Shackle's analysis is the point of departure for the Post-Keynesian theory of expectations under uncertainty. However, his individualistic and subjective approach to decision making under uncertainty and his view of economic process in a kaleidic society do not give sufficient attention to other important Post-Keynesian building blocks such as technological progress, viability and growth, investment, and Paul Davidson's "seven wonders" (uncertainty-reducing institutions) in a real monetary economy.[21] The interrelationships between distribution, growth, and investment are also absent in the Shacklean analysis. Fernando Carvalho is correct when he observes:

> The Shacklean expectational time approach must face a difficult problem: the concept of mechanism, fundamental to the idea of evolution and evolutionary time, necessarily reduces the solitariness of individuals. There is a conflict between the order of mechanism and the imagination of the solitary person which must be resolved.*

The task is indeed a very difficult one especially in relation to questions of historical time. The problem of how to deal with historical time has been occupying the attention of philosophers ever since the time of Zeno. Arthur Eddington observes:

> Our knowledge of space-relations is indirect, like nearly all our knowledge of the external world—a matter of inference and interpretation of the impressions which reach us through our sense-organs. We have similar indirect knowledge of the time-relations existing between the events in the world outside us; but in addition we have direct experience of the time-

---

*Fernando Carvalho, "On the Concept of Time in Shacklean and Sraffian Economics," *Journal of Post Keynesian Economics*, 6 (2), Winter 1983–84, pp. 265–280. "Shackle created a four-way classification of Time," Carvalho writes. "Firstly, we have *mechanical* time: this is the time of the external observer, who knows everything, the future as well as in the past. With this concept all moments become 'co-valid' . . . in the sense that past, present, and future are just moments of a known sequence." The other three concepts are: *evolutionary* time, which refers to a segment of history, *timeless* models, and *expectional* time, which attracted Shackle's primary attention (pp. 267–268).

relations that we ourselves are traversing—a knowledge of time not coming through external sense-organs, but taking a short cut into our consciousness. When I close my eyes and retreat into my inner mind, I feel
myself enduring, I do not feel myself extensive. It is this feeling of time as
affecting ourselves and not merely as existing in the relations of external
events which is so peculiarly characteristic of it; space on the other hand is
always appreciated as something external.

That is why time seems to us so much more mysterious than space. We
know nothing about the intrinsic nature of space, and so it is quite easy to
conceive it satisfactorily. We have intimate acquaintance with the nature
of time and so it baffles our comprehension. It is the same paradox which
makes us believe we understand the nature of an ordinary table whereas
the nature of human personality is altogther mysterious.[22]

Nicholas Georgescu-Roegen expresses the same view in his scholarly
book *The Entropy Law and the Economic Process* (1971).*

If the Post-Keynesian approach is to become a viable, encompassing
alternative to the neoclassical paradigm, it must develop a more precise
methodology of dealing with historical time than that initiated in Joan
Robinson's causal model (considered in Chapter 8).†

The micro-micro theory of Harvey Leibenstein

Three implict assumptions of the neoclassical theory of the firm are: (a)
complete control of all variables on which the extrema (maxima and

---

*Nicholas Georgescu-Roegen, *The Entropy Law and the Economic Process* (Cambridge, Mass.: Harvard University Press, 1971). Georgescu-Roegen writes: "The
peculiarly unique feature of Time is its fleeting nature combined with its ever-
presentness. Time flows; yet it is always present. That is why the problem of Time
has tormented the minds of all great philosophers far more than its correlative,
Space" (p. 130).

†The Post-Keynesian writers have been asking hard questions in this area. A tentative methodology is beginning to emerge. For instance, Randall Bausor suggests:
"A more promising model [of historical-time behavior] consists of a functional net-
work linking four sets, representing perceptions, expectations, strategies, and outcomes, in a logical loop. Expectations govern choice but are themselves shaped by
perceptions of the past rather than knowledge of the future. Those perceptions, in
turn, depend on the outcomes of earlier decisions. In short, strategies depend on
current expectations, which in turn depend on current perceptions, themselves tied
to past outcomes, while current outcomes depend on past strategies. Clearly, considerable detail is imperative for this structure to mimic phenomena in historical time"
("Time and the Structure of Economic Analysis," *Journal of Post Keynesian Economics*, 5 (2), Winter 1982–83, p. 167).

mimima) depend, (b) sole concern for physical production and physical output, and (c) price efficiency. Harvey Leibenstein rejects all three assumptions in his analysis. With regard to assumption (a), Leibenstein argues that traditional theory ignores "the question of how individuals in multiperson firms influence firm decisions" p. (447).[23] Leibenstein writes further: "A frequently-used metaphor is that the firm behaves as if it possesses a 'black box' which drives the firm as if it were an individual irrespective of size. One way of looking at micro-micro theory is to suggest that the micro-micro problem is the study of what goes on inside the black box." In other words, "micro-micro theory is concerned with intra firm behavior and relations or with the interaction of persons within the firm and their influence on firm behavior."[24]

Leibenstein observes that a firm does not have complete control of all relevant variables for profit maximization. He points out:

> Implicit to neoclassical theory is the notion that contracts are complete. Under the X-efficiency viewpoint firm-membership contracts or employer-employee contracts are incomplete. Rather, they are likely to be asymmetrical. The payment part of the contract is frequently well specified, but the work part is not. Thus effort is a discretionary variable. Individuals have to interpret their jobs. . . . This involves the choice of an "effort position"—that is, a subset of effort points that allows the individual to take into account a variety of demands on his effort capacity.[25]

With regard to assumption (b) mentioned above, the micro-micro theory of Leibenstein is not solely concerned with physical production. It is concerned with the problems of how to increase worker motivation, internal organizational improvements, and refinements in a wide range of business decisions, including promotions, recruiting salaries and bonuses, and so forth. It is concerned with the removal of inefficiencies inside the firm. The main differences between the neoclassical theory and X-efficiency theory are stated by Leibenstein in the accompanying table.[26]

Leibenstein suggests that X-efficiency theory is based on the following four postulates:

(1) The individual, not the firm, is the basic decision unit. This includes individuals participating in committees which make decisions.

(2) Individuals have some discretion with respect to the nature and amount of effort put forth within certain bounds because employment contracts are generally incomplete. For instance, the payment part is

Components	X-Efficiency theory	Neoclassical theory
1. Psychology	1. Selective rationality	1. Maximization or minimization
2. Contracts	2. Incomplete	2. Complete
3. Effort	3. Discretionary variable	3. Assumed given
4. Units	4. Individuals	4. Households and firms
5. Inert areas	5. Important variable	5. None
6. Agent-principal	6. Differential	6. Identity of interests

Source: Harvey Leibenstein, "The General X-Efficiency Paradigm and the Role of the Entrepreneur," in Mario J. Rizzo, ed., *Time, Uncertainty, and Disequilibrium* (Lexington, MA: D. C. Heath, 1979), p. 130. Reprinted by permission.

known in a contract situation, but the effort part is either fuzzy or not stated. Contract incompleteness would therefore imply the existence of effort discretion.

(3) Within certain bounds, inertia will exist. Therefore a position taken within these bounds, associated with a certain utility, will not result in a movement to another position, even if this other position is associated with a higher utility.

(4) Individuals do not behave as maximizers. Instead individual behavior depends on a balance of internal and external pressures. Pressure internal to the individual also depends on a balance of opposing motivational forces—on such factors as conscience, self-interest, and the desire for approval, on the one hand, and on "animal spirits," including the urge to avoid responsibility, on the other.

Leibenstein further insists:

> If the individual is the decision-maker with respect to effort (he has some effort discretion), then he is in a position to make an effort decision that is not necessarily in the best interest of the firm. Furthermore, this is true of all firm members. Hence, there is no fixed relation between inputs and outputs. . . . The first conclusion is that for given inputs there is a variety of outputs possible.[27]

It is interesting to note that the behaviorist postulates of Leibenstein have provided him with an important criticism of the neoclassical production function which is quite different from that of Joan Robinson.[28] By emphasizing the role of the entrepreneur, X-efficiency addresses an activity not within the purview of neoclassical theory. Leibenstein breaks the categories of entrepreneurial activities into three classes:

These are: (1) gap filling and "obstacle overcoming," (2) input completing, and (3) uncertainty bearing on the organization and its environment.
Clearly if there are holes in the input market, the entrepreneur has to
somehow make up such holes. Where the imperfections are in terms of
obstacles to inputs, these have to be overcome. . . . A necessary and
simultaneous responsibility for the entrepreneur is to be an input com-
pleter. This is critical. That is to say, the entrepreneur must fill enough of
the gaps so that all necessary inputs can be marshalled in order to produce
the commodity in question.[29]

   The attempt of Leibenstein to rescue the entrepreneurial role from
oblivion receives warm comments from the neo-Austrian camp. According to Israel M. Kirzner:

Austrians as far back as Carl Menger have refused to view market participants as errorless maximizers, instantaneously selecting the optimum
option from the array that confronts them. Where there is room for error,
there is surely room for the exercise of the entrepreneurial function. So
that here, too, Leibenstein's paradigm might appear to be one the Austrian should find both comfortable and congenial.[30]

However, there are certain differences of emphasis between the Austrians and Leibenstein. For Leibenstein, the rediscovery of the entrepreneur is a corollary of his X-efficiency hypothesis, whereas for the
Austrians, "entrepreneurship is at the very heart of the economic
process."[31] In spite of the differences, here is another evidence of the
widening common ground for dialogue in the economic profession.

The behavioral theory of the firm

The behavioral approach, like the X-efficiency theory, is concerned
with the internal operations of the firm. However, there are some major
differences between the two approaches. Harvey Leibenstein considers
the behavioral approach as "semi-micro-micro theory" for "what we
have is a set of ingredients; we are asked to work out specific recipes of
our own from these ingredients. Sample recipes already exist. These
are simulation models presented in Cyert and March's *Behavioral
Theory of the Firm* and elsewhere. . . . Each simulation model represents a single case. Since the bounds of the simulation model are not
constrained by a more general theory, it would seem reasonable to
assume that we cannot determine in advance whether the simulation
model is consistent with the neoclassical model."[32]

The behavioral theory of Richard M. Cyert and James G. March is the outgrowth of research conducted by Herbert Simon and his colleagues at Carnegie-Mellon University. A major concern of this research is organizational theory, the basic characteristics of the Carnegie school ideas being: (1) satisficing, (2) bounded rationality, (3) multiplicity of goals, (4) sequential attention to goals, (5) feedback, (6) standard operating procedures, (7) resistance to change except under "duress," (8) coalitions to resolve conflicts, (9) organizational slack to stabilize coalitions, and (10) maintenance of viability.[33] According to Leibenstein:

> In Day's list, eight of the ten characteristics are not necessarily related to an essential micro-micro approach. Most of them are related to the departure from the perfect rationality assumption. The two that are related to the insides of the firm are (8) "coalitions to resolve conflict," and (9) "organizational slack to stabilize coalitions." But we are not presented with a theory of intra-firm coalitions.[34]

Cyert and March focus on the processes of organizational decision making. They point out:

> Like the theory of the firm, organization theory means different things to different people. Only those meanings of the term that emphasize the empirical study of behavior in organizations are relevant to our purpose.[35]

Accordingly, the three branches of organizational theory they address are:

(a) sociological—mainly on the phenomena of bureaucracy;

(b) social psychological—which "has been built primarily on an experimental base with an emphasis on an 'efficiency' criterion."[36]

(c) administrative—"focuses on the problems of the executive in dealing with an organization and is centered on classic administrative axioms."[37]

The basis of their theory "is that it has (1) the firm as its basic unit, (2) the prediction of firm behavior with respect to such decisions as price, output, and resource allocation as its objective, and (3) an explicit emphasis on the actual process of organizational decision making as its basic research commitment."[38]

The four building blocks of the Cyert and March theory are:

(a) a theory of organizational goals which would consider how goals arise in an organization, how they change over time, and how the organization attends to them;

(b) a theory of organizational expectations which explain the information searching procedure and information processing through the organization;

(c) a theory of organizational choice to treat the organizational selection of alternatives and the decisions made among them;

(d) a theory of organizational control.

More or less in the spirit of the "Edgeworth Process," Cyert and March view the business firm as a coalition of individuals. Cyert and March write:

> Let us view the organization as a coalition. It is a coalition of individuals, some of them organized into subcoalitions. In a business organization the coalition members include managers, workers, stockholders, suppliers, customers, lawyers, tax collectors, regulatory agencies, etc.
>
> This conception of an organization fits a number of recent formulations: the inducement-contributions schema, game theory, and the theory of team.[39]

Organization goals are established through a bargaining process among coalition members. Cyert and March further point out that organization goals change over time and that they are multiple rather than single. These goals of the firm (production, inventory, sales, market share, and profit) are satisficing rather than maximizing constraints. These goals also shift with changes in aspiration levels.

Cyert and March assert that a theory of the firm cannot neglect the role played by business expectations. In their view, the firm is an adaptive organization constantly striving to resolve conflicts between the coalitions and to avoid uncertainty by reliance upon feedback and rules. Following Herbert Simon, we see that the firm is a satisficer rather than a maximizer. The firm's decisions depend upon its expectations and upon the information possessed by it. Cyert and March write:

> Expectations are by no means independent of such things as hopes, wishes, and the internal bargaining needs of subunits in the organization. Information about the consequences of specific courses of action in a business organization is frequently hard to obtain and of uncertain reliability. As a result, both conscious and unconscious bias in expectations is introduced. . . . Organizations seem to protect themselves from the worst effects of bias by focusing on easily verified data in lieu of uncertain

estimates and by using easily checked feedback information instead of more remote anticipations.[40]

The incomplete-information paradigm

The models of disequilibrium macroeconomics considered in Chapter 6 are part of what Herschel I. Grossman called the "non-market-clearing paradigm.[41] The principal alternative to this paradigm is the incomplete-information paradigm. Grossman observes: "In the existing literature, the development of the incomplete-information paradigm within the framework of competitive markets has used three different, but mutually consistent stories."[42] The three stories are:

(1) Milton Friedman's "natural rate hypothesis" and his analysis of "adaptive expectations."

(2) Armen A. Alchian's concept of "search unemployment,"[43] Edmund S. Phelp's "island parable,"[44] and the separate but mutually consistent research of Dale T. Mortensen[45] and Charles C. Holt.[46]

(3) Robert E. Lucas, Jr., and Leonard A. Rapping's analysis of workers' misinformation concerning the difference between the real wage rate and nominal wage rate and its effect on employment and inflation.[47]

Phelps points out:

> A common thread runs through all these models. The actors of each model have to cope ignorant of future or even much of the present. Isolated and apprehensive, these Pinteresque figures construct expectations of the state of the economy—over space and over time—and maximize relative to that imagined world. The supply prices of outputs and of labor services and, similarly, the demand prices for labor, are linear homogeneous in known and expected prices (including expected mean demand prices in the stochastic case)—present and future. Quantity decisions are homogeneous of degree zero in these variables.

> On adaptive or other error-correcting expectations hypotheses, a change of aggregate demand alters the relations between sampled prices and expected prices. The implied alternation of expected relative price—of expected wage rates elsewhere relative to sampled rates, of expected real rates of interest, etc.—causes a change in quantity decisions, hence changes in employment and output.[48]

A fourth line of development in the incomplete-information paradigm is represented by Frank H. Hahn's analysis of conjectural equi-libria.[49] In his paper "On Non-Walrasian Equilibria," Hahn writes:

> The central difficulty in studying non-Walrasian economics, which to some extent is shared with Walrasian sequence economics, is the distinction between the trading possibilities as perceived by an agent and the "true" trading possibilities. [Note that in this respect Hahn stands on the same ground as Benassy.][50]

The trading possibilities as perceived by some agents include a conjectural demand curve for the goods sold by them. But the conjectured demand curve is not necessarily the same as the "true" demand curve due to "incomplete" information. The conjectural non-Walrasian equilibrium is a situation in which the conjectural demand curve coincides with the "true" demand curve. Unfortunately, conceptual and technical difficulties forced Hahn to give up the criterion of "global rationality" and settle for the more realistic assumption that economic agents behave sensibly. Hahn writes:

> By sensible I mean two things: (a) a small agent must not be expected to have "general equilibrium theories" embodied in his conjectures. Thus he believes that a change in his budget situation consequent upon his wishing "to break a ration" in any one market can be conjectured with reference to events in only that market. (b) an agent does not have "perverse" conjecture.[51]

The essential difference between Hahn's analysis and the Benassy model considered earlier lies in the simultaneous determination of price and quantity as an integral part of the agent's attempt to overcome perceived quantity constraints. In Hahn's model, the agent takes over the price-setting role. As pointed out by Hahn, "I do not wish to make imperfect competition intrinsic to the model. The conjectures I consider always permit Walrasian equilibrium. What I show is that there are also non-Walrasian equilibria."[52]

The concept of "reasonable conjecturers" advanced by Hahn appears very promising. However, Hahn regrets that he has "nothing of a formal nature to report on reasonable conjecturers."[53] In the opinion of Allan Drazen, "the inability to implement it (reasonable conjecture) may indicate that it's a dead end. My belief is that non-Walrasian models of unemployment will stand and fall on the issue of rationality of behavior."[54]

Following Grossman, we see that the attractiveness of the "incomplete-information paradigm" lies in its choice-theoretic explanation for the relation between aggregate demand and aggregate employment. The main difficulty of the theory is its basic assumption of significant information costs, which is derived only from casual evidence.[55]

The theory of implicit contracts

The macroeconomic problem of "stagflation" has confronted economists with many thorny problems of interpretation and has prompted renewed efforts to seek out the microeconomic foundations of macroeconomics. The incomplete-information paradigm is one interpretation of this vexing problem. Implicit contract theory provides another useful explanation. In the view of Grossman, if the theory of implicit contracts is incorporated into the incomplete-information paradigm, the integrated theoretical framework would be a very forceful one. Grossman writes:

> Research in macroeconomics has witnessed persistent disagreement about the usefulness of specific non-Walrasian paradigms for modeling the determination of aggregate employment. This disagreement reflects basic differences in perceptions of the essential characteristics of the actual economy that are responsible for non-Walrasian behavior of aggregate employment. . . . A resolution of this paradigm conflict is presently at hand . . . this impending settlement involves recognition that incomplete information is the critical factor in the generation of non-Walrasian fluctuations in employment, together with explicit allowance for the implications of implicit contractual arrangements for efficient shifting and pooling of risk in labor and product markets.[56]

Implicit contract theory was born during the inflationary era of the 1970s. As observed by Arthur M. Okun, in numerous instances during the period "we have observed nonunion employers with no contractual obligations granting general pay increases when they had abundant applicants, no vacancies, and negligible quit rates."[57] The explanation is that the employers "find it worthwhile to make an investment in personnel relationships; they seek a reputation as a good employer to maintain an experienced and reliable work force for the long run."[58] Okun named this sensible behavior on the part of the nonunion employers in the labor market "the invisible handshake."

The explanation for workers' acceptance of implicit contractual arrangements is given by exponents of this approach as follows according to Benjamin Klein:

> Most labor market relationships are de facto long term, and workers are risk averse. A labor contract is considered similar to a mortgage with the wage merely an installment payment on a long-term "implicit" commitment to transfer a certain amount of wealth in exchange for a certain amount of labor services (see Robert Hall, 1980).[59]

From the employer's standpoint, as observed by Benjamin Klein, explicit contracts are more costly than implicit contracts. The costs involved in explicit contracts are transaction costs and enforcement costs. Concerning transaction costs, Klein points out: "These costs refer not merely to ink costs involved, but, in an uncertain world with a large number of contingencies, to the significant real resource costs of discovering all the possible things that can happen in the future, and figuring out the optimal response by the transacting parties for all these hypothetical, largely irrelevant, states."[60] As to the enforcement costs, Klein refers to the costly measurement of qualitative worker performance, such as the level of energy an employee is to devote to a complex task, as well as various legal costs. Furthermore, Klein asserts:

> Another cost of explicit contracts compared to implicit contracts is the increased rigidity of such arrangements. This implies that an explicit contract term, such as price is more likely to differ from the "perfectly competitive" level. This results in costly resource misallocations which may be avoided by more flexible implicit contract terms.[61]

According to Okun, "the same insights [of implicit contractual arrangements] also help to solve puzzles about [the firm's] behavior in many product markets.[62] In periods of boom, the firm will forego large markups with a view of building a clientele and establishing a reputation that helps to retain customers when markets ease. "In many industries, firms feel obligated to justify price increases to their customers in terms of cost increases; they want to convince their customers that they are not exploiting a tight market to capture a large share of the benefits from continuing relationships. The cost-oriented pricing in product markets geared to customer relationships offers a dramatic contrast with the behavior of prices for products traded on auction markets."[63] Okun's view is shared by Bengt Holmstrom, who writes: "Once all firms recognize the value of long-term contracts, wage auctions get replaced by contractual auctions in which the market will be equilibrated through the expected utility contracts offer.''[64]

It is clear that implicit contract theory implies important amendments to traditional concepts of market efficiency. The following two points are food for thought:

(1) ''Implicit contracts can be effective only in a social atmosphere that incorporates a sense of mutual respect and a consensus on principles of fair play and good faith. Equity is thus not an extraneous irritant imposed upon the market by political institutions, but rather a vital lubricant of market process.''[65] Equity and efficiency may no longer be the ''big tradeoff'' if we take an optimistic view.

(2) ''Fundamentally, our economy is more efficient because it is guided by the invisible handshake as well as the invisible hand. And it will work even better when policy-makers and theorists recognize the implications for the cure of chronic inflation—in short, when they choose to act as wise owls rather than fierce hawks or passive doves.''[66]

CHAPTER 12

The Widening Common Ground of Dialogue

Since the Cambridge controversies in the theory of capital, writers of the conflicting paradigms have been able to see their way clear to appreciate some of the strong points made by their antagonists. The increasing technical sophistication of economic analysis has make the common ground for discourse possible. Supplementing the major points made throughout this book, we present below additional evidence of a widening ground for dialogue.

(A) Historical time

The Post-Keynesians deserve major credit for bringing historical time back to economics. At present, a significant number of economists have clearly recognized the difference between "logical time" and "historical time." For instance, Franklin M. Fisher in his stability analysis stresses that there is one overriding fact that is far more important than the technical details of convergence to equilibrium. That overriding fact is the possibility of the "hysteresis effect," or the "path dependent effect." Again in his criticism of the "Present Action Postulate," Fisher writes: "The Arrow-Debreu world is one in which all markets and trades occur at the beginning of time and never again. Elegant as such a model is, however, it is not truly satisfatory when applied to *real economies developing over time*."[1] In addition, Fisher introduces "disequilibrium consciousness" into his adjustment process, which is a definite advance beyond the assumption that economic agents naively believe that the world is always in equilibrium.

Jean-Pascal Benassy is also fully aware of the problem of historical time. He takes pains to emphasize that methodologically his analysis of expectations and temporary fixed-price equilibria is similar to Keynes's analysis of marginal efficiency of capital and Keynes's treatment of under-employment equilibria.

In spite of their attacks on ''neo-Ricardianism,'' the common thread that ties the various Austrian doctrines together is the notion of historical time. It is also the central thrust of the neo-Austrian critique of the ''neoclassical synthesis.'' Their praxeology is stated in the context of historical time. This point is made clear by Murray N. Rothbard's statement: ''All action in the *real world* . . . must take place through *time*; all action takes place in some *present* and is directed toward the *future* (immediate or remote) attainment of an end. . . .Action therefore implies that man *does not have omniscient knowledge of the future*; for if he had such knowledge, no action of his would make any difference. Hence, action implies that we live in a world of an *uncertain*, or not fully certain, future.'' There is certainly enough common ground here for further dialogue.

(B) Expectations

Closely related to historical time is the question of expectations. The Rational Expectations approach has weathered a storm of criticism and may become an established part of the methodology of macroeconomics. As observed by Robert J. Barro:

> I agree with the view that rational vs. nonrational expectations is not per se the key division between Keynesian and non-Keynesian models and, accordingly, is not the essential basis for a division between activist and nonactivist policy conclusions. . . . It is possible to produce Keynesian policy conclusions in models that incorporate rational expectations, but which contain some other departures from sensible behavior, for example, arbitrarily fixed nominal wages, or money illusion either in supply and demand functions or in the form of labor contracts. Thus the nature of the formation of expectations seems to be an important issue within the general context of the efficiency of private arrangements relative to governmental actions, but it is this general concept of relative efficiency that seems to be crucial in evaluations of policy activism.''[2]

The Rational Expectations approach has yet to be fully developed. David K. H. Begg suggests that further research should be undertaken in the following four areas: ''(a) the elaboration of the process of information collection and expectations revision; (b) the development of more sophisticated dynamic structures in which to embed the expectations assumption; (c) the implications for econometric methodology; and (d) the consequences for macroeconometric modelling and policy analysis."[3] Begg's perceptive conclusion is: "We have not reached the end of the Rational Expectations revolution in macroeconomics, nor yet the beginning of the end, but it . . . may mark the end of the beginning."[4] In spite of the profound differences in the approach to probability theory, Post-Keynesians may be able to live with Begg's suggested research program.

(C) Microfoundations of macroeconomics

We have at present a wide variety of models of microfoundations, such as the non-market-clearing models, incomplete-information models, the X-efficiency model, Behaviorist models, implicit contracts models, the neo-Austrian model, the Benassy model, the Fisherian model, and the Post-Keynesian models. They all share some common features. There is yet no canonical microfoundation model. Are we ever going to get such a model in the foreseeable future? Perhaps E. Roy Weintraub has provided us with the answer:

> Looking for such a single model is a foolish way to do science, even economics. The age of the great system builders has passed, not because of a lack of genius to rival Walras or Keynes, but rather because economics has progressed beyond what Kuhn once called the "preparadigm" stage of development as a science. The research programs of modern economic theory, based on the neo-Walrasian synthesis developed many years ago, have transcended their simple beginnings to constitute ongoing activity involving the elaboration of approaches to problem solving.[5]

Notes

Introduction

1. Joan Robinson's Ely Lecture, delivered to the American Economic Association Annual Meeting at New Orleans, December 27, 1971, with J. K. Galbraith being Chairperson.

2. Sir John Hicks, *The Crisis in Keynesian Economics*, Yrjo Jahnsson Lectures (New York: Basic Books, Inc., 1974).

3. Daniel Bell and Irving Kristol, eds., *The Crisis in Economic Theory* (New York: Basic Books, Inc., 1981).

4. Anthony Cutler, Barry Hindess, Paul Hirst, and Athar Hussain, *Marx's Capital and Capitalism Today*, 2 vols. (London: Routledge & Kegan Paul, 1977). Evidence of revisionist economic movements in Socialist countries is common in the daily press. See, for instance, Dan Morgan's article "East Europe Tries Modified Capitalism: Hungary's Economy Sets the Pace," *Washington Post*, May 24, 1982.

5. Cutler, Hindess, Hirst, and Hussain, *Marx's Capital*, p. 2.

6. Frank H. Hahn, "Some Adjustment Problems," *Econometrica*, *38*, 1970, p. 3.

7. Paul Davidson, *Money and the Real World*, 2nd ed. (New York: John Wiley & Sons, 1972, 1978), p. 147.

8. Franklin M. Fisher, *Disequilibrium Foundations of Equilibrium Economics* (New York: Cambridge University Press, 1983).

9. Tjalling C. Koopmans, *Three Essays on the State of Economic Science* (New York: McGraw-Hill Book Co., 1957), p. 179.

10. Fisher, *Disequilibrium Foundations*, p. 21.

11. Ibid., p. 22.

12. Christopher J. Bliss and Roberto F. Cippa, "Temporary Equilibrium with Rationed Borrowing and Consistent Plans," in Mauro Baransini, ed., *Advances in Economic Theory* (New York: St. Martin's Press, 1982), p. 48.

13. Ibid., p. 49.

14. John D. Hey, *Uncertainty in Microeconomics* (New York: New York University Press, 1979), p. 198.

15. K. J. Arrow and F. H. Hahn, *General Competitive Analysis* (San Francisco: Holden-Day, Inc., 1971), pp. 356-357.

16. Frank H. Hahn, *Money and Inflation* (Cambridge, Mass: M.I.T. Press, 1983),

p. 2. First published in 1981 by Basil Blackwell Publisher, England.

17. Ibid., p. 3.

18. Sir John Hicks, *Causality in Economics* (New York: Basic Books, Inc., Publishers, 1979), pp. 101–102.

19. Fisher, *Disequilibrium Foundations*, p. 2.

20. Ibid., p. 16.

21. Jean Michel Grandmont, "Temporary General Equilibrium Theory," *Econometrica, 45* (3), April 1977, pp. 535–572; Allan Drazen, "Recent Developments in Macroeconomic Disequilibrium Theory," *Econometrica, 48* (2), March 1980, pp. 283–306.

22. Jean-Pascal Benassy, *The Economics of Market Disequilibrium* (New York: Academic Press, 1982). His other representative work is "Neo-Keynesian Disequilibrium Theory in A Monetary Economy," *Review of Economic Studies, 42* (4), October 1975, pp. 503–523.

23. Janos Kornai, *Growth, Shortage and Efficiency: A Macrodynamic Model of the Socialist Economy* (Berkeley and Los Angeles: University of California Press, 1982), p. 33. His *Anti-Equilibrium* is published by American Elsevier of New York. The emphasis is ours.

24. James Cicarelli and John Stuck, "Economics: The Next Twenty Years," *Journal of Post Keynesian Economics, 3* (1), Fall 1980, pp. 116–122.

25. Martin Shubik, "A Curmudgeon's Guide to Microeconomics," *Journal of Economic Literature, 8* (2), June 1970, pp. 406–407.

26. Alfred S. Eichner, ed. *A Guide to Post-Keynesian Economics* (Armonk, New York: M. E. Sharpe, Inc., 1978), p. 14.

27. John Cornwall, "Macrodynamics," in Eichner, *A Guide*, p. 29.

28. Benassy, *Economics of Market Disequilibrium*, pp. 71–72.

29. Piero Sraffa, *Production of Commodities by Means of Commodities: Prelude to a Critique of Economic Theory* (London: Cambridge University Press, 1960).

30. Hicks, *Causality in Economics*.

31. Eichner, *Guide to Post-Keynesian Economics*, pp. 11–12.

Chapter 1

1. For lucid discussions of supply-side economics see: James R. Barth, "The Reagan Program for Economic Recovery: Economic Rationale (A Primer on Supply-Side Economics)," *Economic Review*, Federal Reserve Bank of Atlanta, September 1981; John A. Tatom, "We Are All Supply-Siders Now!" *Review*, Federal Reserve Bank of St. Louis, *63* (5), May 1981, pp. 18–30; Robert E. Keleher and William P. Orzechowski, "Supply-Side Effects of Fiscal Policy: Some Historical Perspectives," reviewed in the Federal Reserve Bank of Atlanta, *Economic Review* (February 1981), pp. 26–28; Thomas J. Hailstones, *A Guide to Supply-Side Economics* (Richmond, Va: Robert F. Dame, Inc., 1982); James T. Laney, "The Other Adam Smith," *Economic Review*, Federal Reserve Bank of Atlanta, October 1981, pp. 26–29; Robert M. Dunn, Jr., *Economic Growth among Industrialized Countries: Why the United States Lags* (Washington, D.C.: National Planning Association, 1980); and Arthur B. Laffer and R. David Ranson, "A Formal Model of the Economy," mimeographed (Washington, D.C.: Office of Management and Budget, 1970).

2. See Vivian Walsh and Harvey Gram, *Classical and Neoclassical Theories of General Equilibrium* (New York: Oxford University Press, 1980), p. 5.

3. See J. von Neumann, "A Model of General Economic Equilibrium," *Review of Economic Studies, 13*, 1945–46, pp. 1–9.

4. See Walsh and Gram, *Classical and Neoclassical Theories*, p. 13.

5. Lionel Robbins, *The Theory of Economic Policy in English Classical Political Economy* (London: Macmillan & Co. Ltd., 1952). pp. 56–57.

6. See Karl Polanyi, *The Great Transformation* (Boston: Beacon Press, 1957), Chapter 12, p. 141.

7. Hla Myint, *Theories of Welfare Economics* (New York: Augustus M. Kelley, 1948), p. 12.

8. See Irma Adelman, *Theories of Economic Growth and Development* (Stanford, Ca.: Stanford University Press, 1961), Chapter 3.

9. See Robbins, *Theory of Economic Policy*, pp. 46–47.

10. See Peter J. Stanlis, *Edmund Burke and the Natural Law* (Ann Arbor: The University of Michigan Press, 1965); and *Natural Law and Modern Society* (Cleveland, Ohio: The World Publishing Company, 1966).

11. See Robbins, *Theory of Economic Policy*, p. 47.

12. See Thomas Sowell, *Say's Law* (Princeton, N.J.: Princeton University Press, 1972), pp. 15–17.

13. See David P. Levine, "Aspects of the Classical Theory of Markets," *Australian Economic Papers*, June 1980, p. 4.

14. Robert V. Eagly, *The Structure of Classical Economic Theory* (New York: Oxford University Press, 1974), p. 49.

15. Mark Blaug, *Economic Theory in Retrospect*, rev. ed. (Homewood, Illinois: Richard D. Irwin, Inc., 1968), p. 51.

16. Adam Smith, *The Wealth of Nations* (New York: Random House, 1937, p. 30.

17. Ibid.

18. Myint, *Theories of Welfare Economics*, pp. 19–20.

19. Sir John Hicks, *Capital and Growth* (New York: Oxford University Press, 1965), p. 36.

20. Smith, *Wealth of Nations*, pp. 323–324.

21. David Laidler, "Adam Smith as a Monetary Economist," *The Canadian Journal of Economics*, *14* (2), May 1981, p. 193. The emphasis is ours.

22. Laidler, "Smith as a Monetary Economist," pp. 198–199.

23. Smith, *Wealth of Nations*, p. 817. The emphasis is ours.

24. Ibid., p. 835. The emphasis is ours.

25. Robert E. Keleher, "Historical Origins of Supply-Side Economics," *Economic Review*, Federal Reserve Bank of Atlanta, January 1982, pp. 12–19.

26. Smith, *Wealth of Nations*, p. 879.

27. See Laney, "The Other Adam Smith," p. 27.

28. Richard H. Tawney, *Religion and the Rise of Capitalism* (New York: Harcourt, Brace and Co., 1926) and Max Weber, *Protestant Ethic and the Spirit of Capitalism* (London: G. Allen and Unwin Ltd., 1930).

Chapter 2

1. David Ricardo, *The Principles of Political Economy and Taxation* (London: J. M. Dent & Sons Ltd., 1955), p. 1.

2. Maurice Dobb, *Theories of Value and Distribution Since Adam Smith* (London: Cambridge University Press, 1973), p. 46.

3. Harry G. Johnson, *The Theory of Income Distribution* (London: Gray-Mills Publishing Ltd., 1973), p. 12.

4. Alessandro Roncaglia, *Sraffa and the Theory of Prices* (Chichester, New York: John Wiley & Sons, 1978), translation from Italian by J. A. Kregel, p. 9.

5. Ricardo, *Principles*, p. 5.

6. Ibid., p. 13.

7. George J. Stigler, "Ricardo and the 93 Per Cent Labor Theory of Value," reprinted from the *American Economic Review*, *47*, June 1958, in his *Essays in the History of Economics* (Chicago: University of Chicago Press, 1965), p. 341.

8. Ibid., pp. 339–340.

9. John M. Cassels, "A Re-Interpretation of Ricardo on Value" reprinted from *The Quarterly Journal of Economics*, *49*, May 1935, in Ingrid H. Rima, ed., *Readings in the History of Economic Theory* (New York: Holt, Rinehart and Winston, Inc., 1970), p. 86.

10. Joseph A. Schumpeter, *History of Economic Analysis* (New York: Oxford University Press, 1954), p. 473. It should be noted that Walras, no less than Ricardo, was guilty of the Ricardian vice.

11. For a detailed discussion of the West-Malthus-Ricardo rent theory, see Ingrid H. Rima, *Development of Economic Analysis*, 3rd ed. (Homewood, Illinois: Richard D. Irwin, Inc., 1972), Chapters 6 and 7.

12. Ricardo, *Principles*, p. 38.

13. Mark Blaug, *Ricardian Economics* (New Haven: Yale University Press, 1958), p. 13.

14. Ricardo, *Principles*, p. 45.

15. Nicholas Kaldor, "Alternative Theories of Distribution," reprinted from *Review of Economic Studies*, *23* (2), (1955–6), in his *Essays on Value and Distribution* (Illinois: The Free Press of Glencoe, 1969).

16. William J. Baumol, *Economic Dynamics* (New York: The Macmillan Co., 1951), Chapter 2.

17. Ricardo, *Principles*, p. 23.

18. Ibid.

19. Ibid.

20. Ibid., p. 29.

21. Piero Sraffa, *Production of Commodities by Means of Commodities: Prelude to a Critique of Economic Theory* (London, Cambridge University Press, 1960).

22. Roncaglia, *Sraffa and the Theory of Prices*, p. 24.

23. Ibid., p. xviii.

24. Sraffa, *Production of Commodities*, p. v.

25. Ibid., p. 3.

26. Ibid., p. 10.

27. Ibid., p. 19.

28. Ibid.

29. Ibid.

30. Ibid., p. 18.

31. Ibid.

32. Ibid., p. 20.

33. J. A. Kregel, *Rate of Profit, Distribution and Growth: Two Views* (Chicago: Aldine-Atherton, 1971), p. 24.

34. Ibid., p. 35.

35. Sraffa, *Production of Commodities*, p. 34.

36. J. A. Kregel, *The Reconstruction of Political Economy: An Introduction to Post-Keynesian Economics* (New York: John Wiley & Sons, 1973), pp. 94–95.

37. G. C. Harcourt, *Some Cambridge Controversies in the Theory of Capital* (London: Cambridge University Press, 1972).

38. Joan Robinson's "Foreword," in Alfred S. Eichner, ed., *A Guide to Post-Keynesian Economics* (Armonk, New York: M. E. Sharpe, Inc., 1978), p. xx.

39. Peter Kenyon, "Pricing," in Eichner *A Guide*, p. 37.

40. Alfred S. Eichner, "Introduction to the Symposium: Price Formation Theory," *Journal of Post Keynesian Economics*, 4 (1), Fall 1981, pp. 81–84.

41. Robert J. Barro, "Are Government Bonds Net Wealth?" *Journal of Political Economy*, *85* (1), February 1977, pp. 1095–1117.

42. James M. Buchanan, "Barro on the Ricardian Equivalence Theorem," *Journal of Political Economy*, *84* (2), April 1976, pp. 337–342.

43. James Tobin, *Asset Accumulation and Economic Activity* (Chicago: The University of Chicago Press, 1980), pp. 51–52.

44. Ibid., p. 53.

45. Ricardo, *Principles*, p. 161.

46. Ibid., pp. 163–164.

47. Gerald P. O'Driscoll, Jr., "The Ricardian Nonequivalence Theorem," *Journal of Political Economy*, *85* (1), February 1977, pp. 207–210.

48. Ibid., p. 208.

49. Ricardo, *Principles*, pp. 162–163.

50. Ibid., p. 163.

51. Ibid., p. 95.

52. Thomas Sowell, *Clasical Economics Reconsidered* (Princeton, N.J.: Princeton University Press, 1974), p. 68.

Chapter 3

1. See Mark Blaug, *Ricardian Economics: A Historical Study* (New Haven: Yale University Press, 1958), p. 78.

2. Ibid., p. 80.

3. Ibid., p. 82.

4. See William H. Branson, *Macroeconomic Theory and Policy*, 2nd ed. (New York: Harper & Row, Publishers, 1979), Part II.

5. Luigi L. Pasinetti, *Growth and Income Distribution* (London: Cambridge University Press, 1974), p. 30 note.

6. For more detailed discussions of Malthus's optimum saving theory, see Blaug, *Ricardian Economics*, Chapter 5.

7. See Edmund S. Phelps, *Golden Rules of Economic Growth* (New York: Norton, 1966). For an important discussion of optimal neoclassical growth theory, see Ching-Yao Hsieh, *A Short Introduction to Modern Growth Theory*, with Ahmad A. Abushaikha and Anne Richards (Washington, D.C.: University Press of America, 1978), Chapter 9.

8. See Robert M. Solow, "A Contribution to the Theory of Economic Growth," *Quarterly Journal of Economics*, *70*, February 1956.

9. See Blaug, *Ricardian Economics*, pp. 88–89.

Chapter 4

1. Sir James Jeans, *Physics and Philosophy* (Ann Arbor: University of Michigan Press, 3rd printing, 1966), p. 109. This Laplacian view is known as the fallacy of reductionism.

2. As quoted in Jeans, *Physics and Philosophy*, p. 110.

3. Edwin Burmeister and A. Rodney Dobell, *Mathematical Theories of Economic Growth* (New York: The Macmillan Co., 1970), p. 1.

4. Sir John Hicks, *Causality in Economics* (New York: Basic Books, Inc., Publishers, 1979), p. 8.

5. Sir Arthur Eddington, *The Nature of the Physical World* (Ann Arbor: University of Michigan Press, 1958), p. 295.

6. Hicks, *Causality*, p. 3.

7. Ibid., p. 4.

8. Ibid., p. 38.

9. Quoted in Mark Blaug, *The Methodology of Economics* (London: Cambridge University Press, 1980), p. 57.

10. Adam Smith, *The Wealth of Nations* (New York: Random House, 1937), p. 18.

11. See C. W. J. Granger, "Investigating Causal Relations by Econometric Models and Cross-Spectral Methods," *Econometrica*, July 1969, pp. 424–438, and Christopher A. Sims, "Money, Income and Causality," *American Economic Review*, September 1972, pp. 540–552.

12. Blaug, *Methodology*, p. 58.

13. Paul Anthony Samuelson, *Foundations of Economic Analysis* (Cambridge, Mass.: Harvard University Press, 1948).

14. See Thomas Sowell, *Classical Economics Reconsidered* (Princeton, N.J.: Princeton University Press, 1974), p. 48.

Chapter 5

1. See Alan Coddington, "Keynesian Economics: A Search for First Principles," *Journal of Economic Literature*, *14* (4), December 1976, p. 1265.

2. Sir John Hicks, *Value and Capital* (London: Oxford University Press, 1959) pp. 1–2.

3. See E. Roy Weintraub, "The Microfoundations of Macroeconomics: A Critical Survey," *Journal of Economic Literature*, *15* (1), March 1977, pp. 1–2.

4. See Kenneth J. Arrow and Gerard Debreu, "The Existence of an Equilibrium for a Competitive Economy," *Econometrica*, *22* (3), July 1954, pp. 265–290.

5. Weintraub, "Microfoundations of Macroeconomics," p. 3.

6. Don Patinkin, *Money, Interest and Prices*, 2nd ed. (New York: Harper and Row, 1965).

7. Weintraub, "Microfoundations of Macroeconomics," p. 4.

8. Patinkin, *Money, Interest and Prices*, Part II: Macroeconomics.

9. Ibid., p. 215.

10. Ibid., p. 322.

11. Ibid.

12. Ibid., p. 38.

13. Weintraub, "Microfoundations of Macroeconomics," p. 4.

14. Jean Michel Grandmont, "Temporary General Equilibrium Theory," *Econometrica*, *45* (3), April 1977, p. 535.

15. Don Patinkin, "Price Flexibility and Full Employment," originally appeared in *American Economic Review*, *38*, 1948. This article is reprinted in Don Patinkin, *Studies in Monetary Economics* (New York: Harper & Row, Publishers, 1972), pp. 8–30.

16. Axel Leijonhufvud, *On Keynesian Economics and the Economics of Keynes* (New York: Oxford University Press, 1968), p. 8.

17. Patinkin, *Money, Interest and Prices*, p. 340.

18. Hicks, *Value and Capital*, p. 24.

19. George J. Stigler, *Production and Distribution Theories: The Formative Period*

(New York: Macmillan, 1946), p. 149.

20. For excellent discussions of Böhm-Bawerk and J. B. Clark, see Stigler, *Production and Distribution Theories*, Chapters 8 and 9.

21. See G. C. Harcourt, *Some Cambridge Controversies in the Theory of Capital* (London: Cambridge University Press, 1972), p. 122.

22. See Robert M. Solow, "A Contribution to the Theory of Economic Growth," *Quarterly Journal of Economics*, 70, February 1956.

23. Michio Morishima, *Walras' Economics: A Pure Theory of Capital and Money* (London: Cambridge University Press, 1977), p. 6.

24. Arrow and Debreu, "Existence of an Equilibrium."

25. Ibid., p. 265.

26. Frank Hahn, "General Equilibrium Theory," in Daniel Bell and Irving Kristol, eds., *The Crisis in Economic Theory* (New York: Basic Books, 1981) p. 126.

Chapter 6

1. Robert J. Barro and Herschel I. Grossman, "A General Disequilibrium Model of Income and Employment," *The American Economic Review*, 61 (1), March 1971, p. 82.

2. J. R. Hicks, "Mr. Keynes and the 'Classics': A Suggested Interpretation," *Econometrica*, April 1937; W. B. Reddaway, "The General Theory of Employment, Interest and Money," *Economic Review*, June 1936; J. E. Meade, "A Simplified Model of Mr. Keynes' System," *Review of Economic Studies*, February 1937; Don Patinkin, *Money, Interest and Prices*, 2nd ed. (New York: Harper and Row, 1965).

3. Patinkin, *Money, Interest and Prices*, p. 340.

4. Ibid., pp. 320–321.

5. Ibid., p. 323.

6. Ibid. The emphasis is ours.

7. Barro and Grossman, "General Disequilibrium Model," p. 82.

8. Ibid., pp. 86–87.

9. Ibid.

10. Patinkin, *Money, Interest and Prices*, pp. 323–324.

11. Ibid., p. 343.

12. Barro and Grossman, "General Disequilibrium Model," p. 88.

13. Robert W. Clower, "The Keynesian Counter-Revolution: A Theoretical Appraisal," in F. H. Hahn and F. P. R. Brechling, eds., *The Theory of Interest* (London: Macmillan, 1965), Chapter 5, reprinted in Robert W. Clower, ed., *Monetary Theory* (London: Penguin Modern Economics Readings, 1969), pp. 270–297.

14. Ibid., p. 295.

15. Ibid., pp. 275–276.

16. Barro and Grossman, "General Disequilibrium Model," p. 87.

17. Clower, "Keynesian Counter-Revolution," p. 286.

18. Ibid., p. 287.

19. Barro and Grossman, "General Disequilibrium Model," p. 87.

20. Clower, "Keynesian Counter-Revolution," p. 294.

21. Axel Leijonhufvud, *On Keynesian Economics and the Economics of Keynes* (New York: Oxford University Press, 1968), p. 389.

22. Ibid., p. 50.

23. Kenneth J. Arrow, "Toward A Theory of Price Adjustment," in M. Abramovitz et al., eds., *The Allocation of Economic Resources* (Stanford, California: Stanford University Press, 1959, pp. 41–51.

24. Ibid., pp. 42–43.
25. See Patinkin, *Money, Interest and Prices*, p. 39.
26. Leijonhufvud, *On Keynesian Economics*, p. 53.
27. Sir John Hicks, *Value and Capital* (London: Oxford University Press, 1939) p. 128.
28. Leijonhufvud, *On Keynesian Economics*, pp. 55–56.
29. Ibid., pp. 74–75.
30. Armen A. Alchian, "Information Costs, Pricing and Resource Unemployment," in Edmund S. Phelps, ed., *Microeconomic Foundations of Employment and Inflation Theory* (New York: W. W. Norton & Co., Inc., 1970), pp. 27–52.
31. Ibid., p. 28.
32. Leijonhufvud, *Two Lectures on Keynes's Contribution to Economic Theory* (London: Institute of Economic Affairs, 1969), p. 31.
33. Ibid.
34. Axel Leijonhufvud, "Keynes and the Keynesians: A Suggested Interpretation," *American Economic Review*, 57 (2), 1967, pp. 401–410, reprinted in Clower, *Monetary Theory*, pp. 307–308.
35. See Patinkin, *Money, Interest and Prices*, p. 47.
36. Ibid.
37. Milton Friedman, ed., *Studies in the Quantity Theory of Money* (Chicago: University of Chicago Press, 1956), p. 4.
38. David I. Fand, "A Monetarist Model of the Monetary Process," in William E. Gibson and George G. Kaufman, eds., *Monetary Economics: Readings on Current Issues* (New York: McGraw-Hill Book Co., 1971), p. 75.
39. Irving Fisher's analysis of "Gibson Paradox" (the well-documented empirical association between high market nominal interest rates and high prices) is stated in his *Appreciation and Interest* (London: Macmillan, 1930). Also see J. M. Keynes, *A Treatise on Money* (London: Macmillan, 1930).
40. Milton Friedman, "The Role of Monetary Policy," in Milton Friedman, ed., *The Optimum Quantity of Money and Other Essays* (Chicago: Aldine Publishing Company, 1969), Chapter 5.
41. Ibid., p. 99.
42. Ibid., p. 101.
43. Ibid., p. 100.
44. Ibid., pp. 104–105.
45. See William H. Branson, *Macroeconomic Theory and Policy* (New York: Harper & Row Publishers, 1972), p. 281.
46. Alan S. Blinder and Robert M. Solow, "Does Fiscal Policy Matter?" *Journal of Public Economics*, 2, 1973, pp. 319–337.
47. Ibid, p. 323.
48. Ibid., p. 324 note.
49. Ibid., p. 326.
50. Ibid.
51. James Barth, "Introduction to Crowding Out: Theory and Evidence," in Ching-Yao Hsieh, James Barth, and Salih Neftci, eds., *Macroeconomics: Selected Readings*, rev. ed. (Lexington, Mass.: Xerox Individualized Publishing, 1977), pp. 7–8.
52. Keith M. Carlson and Roger W. Spencer, "Crowding Out and Its Critics," *Review*, Federal Reserve Bank of St. Louis, December 1975, pp. 15–16.
53. Neil Wallace, "Microeconomic Theories of Macroeconomic Phenomena and Their Implications for Monetary Policy," in Thomas J. Sargent and Neil Wallace, eds., *Rational Expectations and the Theory of Economic Policy, Part II: Arguments and*

Evidence (Minneapolis: Research Department, Federal Reserve Bank of Minneapolis, 1976), p. 24.

54. See William H. Branson, *Macroeconomic Theory and Policy* (New York: Harper & Row, Publishers, 1979) 2nd ed., pp. 129–131; also Chapters 4 and 6.

55. Ibid., p. 69.

56. Ibid., p. 125.

57. James Barth, "Notes on Classical, Keynesian and Rational Expecatations Models" (November 1978), unpublished paper, p. 5.

58. Thomas J. Sargent and Neil Wallace, "Rational Expectations and the Theory of Economic Policy," *Journal of Monetary Economics*, 2, 1976, pp. 169–183.

59. Rodney Maddock and Michael Carter, "A Child's Guide to Rational Expectations," *Journal of Economic Literature*, 20 (1), March 1982, p. 49.

60. Israel M. Kirzner, "On the Method of Austrian Economics," in Edwin G. Dolan, ed., *The Foundations of Modern Austrian Economics* (Kansas City: Sheed & Ward, 1976), p. 42.

61. See Ludwig von Mises, *Human Action: A Treatise on Economics* (New Haven: Yale University Press, 1949).

62. Murray N. Rothbard, "Praxeology: The Methodology of Austrian Economics," in Dolan, ed., *Foundations of Modern Austrian Economics*, p. 20. The emphasis is ours.

63. Ludwig von Mises, "Epistemological Relativism in the Science of Human Action," in Helmut Schoeck and James W. Wiggins, eds., *Relativism and the Study of Man* (Princeton, New Jersey: D. Van Vostrand Co., Inc., 1961), p. 129.

64. Friedrich A. Hayek, *The Counter-Revolution of Science* (London: The Free Press of Glencoe, 1955), pp. 26–27.

65. Lionel Robbins, *An Essay on the Nature and Significance of Economic Science* (London: Macmillan & Co., Ltd., 1952), pp. 24–25.

66. Israel M. Kirzner, "Equilibrium versus Market Process," in Dolan, ed., *Foundations of Modern Austrian Economics*, pp. 119–120.

67. See G. L. S. Shackle, *Epistemics and Economics* (Cambridge: Cambridge University Press, 1972), p. 3.

68. G. L. S. Shackle, "Imagination, Formalism, and Choice," in Mario J. Rizzo, ed., *Time, Uncertainty, and Disequilibrium* (Lexington, Mass.: D. C. Heath & Co., 1979), p. 22. The emphasis is ours.

69. S. C. Littlechild, "Comment: Radical Subjectivism or Radical Subversion," in Rizzo, ed., *Time, Uncertainty, and Disequilibrium*, p. 46. The emphasis is ours.

70. Ludwig M. Lachmann, "On the Central Concept of Austrian Economics: Market Process," in Dolan, ed., *Foundations of Modern Austrian Economics*, p. 131.

71. Edwin G. Dolan, "Austrian Economics as Extraordinary Science," in Dolan, ed., *Foundations of Modern Austrian Economics*, p. 9.

72. Rizzo, *Time, Uncertainty, and Disequilibrium*, p. 3.

73. Kirzner, "On the Method of Austrian Economics," p. 49.

74. Sir John Hicks, "Capital Controversies: Ancient and Modern," *American Economic Review*, May 1974, p. 315.

75. Israel M. Kirzner, "The Theory of Capital," in Dolan, ed. *Foundations of Modern Austrian Economics*, p. 137. The emphasis is ours.

76. Ibid., p. 138.

77. Ludwig M. Lachmann, "On Austrian Capital Theory," in Dolan, ed., *Foundations of Modern Austrian Economics*, p. 150.

78. Ibid., p. 145.

Chapter 7

1. Sir John Hicks, *Causality in Economics* (New York: Basic Books), p. 65.
2. Sir John Hicks, *Value and Capital* (London: Oxford University Press, 1939), pp. 74–75.
3. Ibid., p. 75.
4. Ibid., p. 82.
5. See Milton Friedman, "A Monetary Theory of Nominal Income," *Journal of Political Economy*, March/April, 1971.
6. K. J. Arrow and F. H. Hahn, *General Competitive Analysis* (San Francisco: Holden-Day Inc., 1971), pp. 356–357.
7. Paul Davidson, *Money and the Real World*, 2nd ed. (New York: John Wiley and Sons, 1978), p. 147.
8. See Milton Friedman, *The Optimum Quantity of Money and Other Essays* (Chicago: Aldine Publishing Company, 1969), Chapter 1.

Chapter 8

1. K. R. Ranadive, *Income Distribution: The Unsolved Puzzle* (Bombay: Oxford University Press, 1978), p. 211.
2. Ibid., pp. 212–213.
3. See G.C. Harcourt, *Some Cambridge Controversies in the Theory of Capital*, (London: Cambridge University Press, 1972), Chapter 4. For a survey of this question, see Ching-yao Hsieh, Ahmad A. Abushaikha, and Anne Richards, *A Short Introduction to Modern Growth Theory* (Washington, D.C.: University Press of America, 1978), Chapter 11.
4. A. Bhaduri, "On the Significance of Recent Controversies on Capital Theory: A Marxian View," *Economic Journal*, 79, 1969, pp. 532–539; reprinted in G. C. Harcourt and N. F. Laing, eds., *Capital and Growth*, Penquin Modern Economic Readings (Middlesex, England: Penguin Books, Ltd.,1971), pp. 255–256.
5. See Paul A. Samuelson, "Parable and Realism in Capital Theory: The Surrogate Production Function," *Review of Economic Studies*, 39, 1962, pp. 193–206.
6. See P. Garegnani, "Heterogeneous Capital, the Production Function and the Theory of Distribution," *Review of Economic Studies*, 37 (3), 1970, pp. 407–436.
7. Bhaduri, "Significance of Recent Controversies," pp. 256–257.
8. J. A. Kregel, "Income Distribution," in Alfred S. Eichner, ed., *A Guide to Post-Keynesian Economics* (Armonk, N.Y.: M. E. Sharpe, Inc., 1979), p. 53.
9. Nicholas Kaldor, "Alternative Theories of Distribution," originally published in *Review of Economic Studies*, 23 (2), 1955–56, reprinted in Kaldor's *Essays on Value and Distribution* (Illinois: The Free Press of Glencoe, 1969), p. 229.
10. Luigi L. Pasinetti, *Growth and Income Distribution* (London: Cambridge University Press, 1974), pp. 101–102.
11. Kaldor, "Alternative Theories of Distribution," p. 232.
12. Ibid., p. 233.
13. Joan Robinson, *Essays in the Theory of Economic Growth* (New York: St. Martin's Press, Inc., 1962), p. 26.
14. Ibid., p. 34.
15. Ibid., pp. 51–59.
16. Ibid., p. 47.
17. Ibid., p. 48.
18. Michal Kalecki, *Selected Essay on the Dynamics of Capitalist Economy* (Cam-

bridge: Cambridge University Press, 1971), p. 165.

19. Paul Davidson, *Money and the Real World* (New York: John Wiley and Sons, 1978), pp. 120–129.

20. Robinson, *Essays*, p. 49.

21. Ibid., p. 67.

22. R. M. Solow, "Investment and Technical Progress," in K. J. Arrow, S. Karlin, and P. Suppes, eds., *Mathematical Methods in Social Sciences* (Stanford, California: Stanford University Press, 1960), Chapter 7. For a simplified version of Solow's model, see Hsieh, Abushaikha, and Richards, *A Short Introduction to Modern Growth Theory*, Chapter 6.

23. F. M. Fisher, "Embodied Technical Change and the Existence of an Aggregate Capital *Stock,"Review of Economic Studies*, *32*, October 1965, pp. 263–287.

24. R. D. G. Allen, *Macroeconomic Theory* (New York: St. Martin's Press, 1967), p. 283.

25. Nicholas Kaldor and James A. Mirrlees, "A New Model of Economic Growth," *Review of Economic Studies*, *29*, June 1962, pp. 174–192, reprinted in Harold R. Williams and John D. Huffnagle, eds., *Macroeconomic Theory: Selected Readings* (New York: Appleton-Century-Crofts, 1969), pp. 504–527.

26. Ibid., p. 510.

27. Ibid., p. 522.

28. Alfred S. Eichner and J. A. Kregel, "An Essay on Post-Keynesian Theory: A New Paradigm in Economics," *Journal of Economic Literature*, *13* (4), December 1975, p. 1296.

29. K. J. Arrow and F. H. Hahn, *General Competitive Analysis* (San Francisco: Holden-Day Inc., 1971) p. 357.

30. Sir John Hicks, "Some Questions of Time in Economics," in A. M. Tang, F. M. Westerfield, and J. S. Worley, eds., *Evolution, Welfare and Time* (Lexington, Mass.: Lexington Books, 1976), p. 136.

31. Robert W. Clower, "The Anatomy of Monetary Theory," *American Economic Review*, Papers and Proceedings of the 89th Annual Meeting, September 16–18, 1976 (February 1977), p. 206.

32. Davidson, *Money and the Real World*, p. 144.

33. Paul Davidson, "The Dual-faceted Nature of the Keynesian Revolution; Money and Money Wages in Unemployment and Production Flow Prices," *Journal of Post Keynesian Economics*, *2* (3), Spring 1980, p. 298.

34. Ibid., p. 299.

35. Ibid.

36. Ibid., p. 300.

37. See Sidney Weintraub, "The Missing Theory of Money Wages," *Journal of Post Keynesian Economics*, *1* (2), Winter 1978–79, pp. 59–78.

38. Ibid., p. 61.

39. Paul Davidson, "Why Money Matters: Lessons from a Half-Century of Monetary Theory," *Journal of Post Keynesian Economics*, *1* (1), Fall 1978, p. 61.

40. Ibid., pp. 61–62.

41. See Basil J. Moore, "The Endogenous Money Stock," *Journal of Post Keynesian Economics*, *2* (1) Fall 1979; and Hyman P. Minsky, *John Maynard Keynes* (New York: Columbia University Press, 1975).

42. Davidson, *Money and the Real World*, p. 270.

43. Moore, "The Endogenous Money Stock," pp. 132–134.

44. Hyman P. Minsky, "The Financial Instability Hypothesis: An Interpretation of Keynes and an Alternative to 'Standard' Theory," *Challenge*, *20*(1), March/April 1977, p. 24.

45. Ibid., p. 25.

46. Minsky, *John Maynard Keynes*, p. 162.

47. Ibid.

48. Davidson, "The Dual-faceted Keynesian Revolution," p. 306.

49. The dynamization of Leontief's closed model resembles the von Neumann model. See Robert Dorfman, Paul A. Samuelson, and R. M. Solow, *Linear Programming and Economic Analysis* (New York: McGraw Hill, 1958), Chapter 11; and Frank H. Hahn and R. C. O. Mattews, "The Theory of Economic Growth: A Survey," *Economic Journal, 74*, December 1964. Reprinted in *Surveys of Economic Theory*, Vol. 2 (St. Martin's Press, 1965).

50. Alfred S. Eichner, "Introduction to the Symposium of Price Formation," *Journal of Post Keynesian Economics, 4* (1), Fall 1981, p. 81.

51. See Michal Kalecki, *Theory of Economic Dynamics* (New York: Monthly Review Press, 1968), Alfred S. Eichner, *The Megacorp and Oligopoly* (Cambridge: Cambridge University Press, 1976), Joseph Steindl, *Maturity and Stagnation in American Capitalism* (New York: Monthly Review Press, 1976), and David P. Levine, *Economic Theory*, Vol. 2 (London: Routledge & Kegan Paul, 1981).

52. J. A. Kregel, *Rate of Profit, Distribution and Growth: Two Views* (Chicago: Aldine-Atherton, 1971), pp. 99–100.

53. Kalecki, *Theory of Economic Dynamics*, p. 11.

54. Ibid., pp. 12–13.

55. Robert T. Averitt, *The Dual Economy* (New York: W. W. Norton & Co., Inc., 1968), p. 1.

56. Nina Shapiro, "Pricing and the Growth of the Firm," *Journal of Post Keynesian Economics, 4* (1), Fall 1981, p. 85.

57. Averitt, *The Dual Economy*, p. 12.

58. See Alfred Marshall, *Principles of Economics*, 8th ed. (London: Macmillan, 1953), p. 315.

59. Nai-Pew Ong, "Target Pricing, Competition, and Growth," *Journal of Post Keynesian Economics, 4* (1), Fall 1981, p. 103.

60. Peter Kenyon, "Pricing," in Eicher, ed., *A Guide*, p. 34.

61. Shapiro, "Pricing and the Growth of the Firm," p. 99.

62. Eileen Appelbaum, "Post-Keynesian Theory: The Labor Market," *Challenge, 21* (6), January/February 1979, p. 44.

63. Michael J. Piore, "Unemployment and Inflation: An Alternative View," *Challenge, 21* (6), January/February 1979, p. 25.

64. Sidney Weintraub, *Capitalism's Inflation and Unemployment Crisis* (Reading, Mass: Addison-Wesley, 1978), Chapter 5. Portions of the chapter are reprinted in Weintraub, "The Missing Theory of Money Wages."

65. Weintraub, "The Missing Theory of Money Wages," p. 76.

66. The reader is referred to an excellent survey of this literature by Glen G. Cain— "The Challenge of Segmented Labor Market Theories to Orthodox Theory: A Survey," *Journal of Economic Literature, 14* (4), December 1976, p. 1215.

67. Ibid., p. 1222.

68. Ibid.

69. Ibid., p. 1223.

70. Davidson, *Money and the Real World,* p. 13.

71. Sir John Hicks, *Causality in Economics* (New York: Basic Books, 1979), p. 88.

72. Ibid., p. 91.

73. Arrow and Hahn, *General Competitive Analysis*, p. 357.

74. Hicks, *Causality*, p. 94.

75. Paul Davidson, "*Casuality in Economics*: A Review," *Journal of Post Keynes-*

ian Economics, 2 (4), Summer 1980, p. 582.
    76. Hicks, *Causality*, pp. 101–102.

Chapter 9

1. Surveys of some of the important literature have been made by Jean Michel Grandmont, "Temporary General Equilibrium Theory," *Econometrica*, 45(3), April 1977, pp. 535–572, Allan Drazen "Recent Developments in Macroeconomic Disequilibrium Theory," *Econometrica*, 48 (2), March 1980, pp. 283–306, John D. Hey, Economics in Disequilibrium (New York: New York University Press, 1981), Hal R. Varian, "Non-Walrasian Equilibria," *Econometrica*, 45 (3), April 1977, and E. Roy Weintraub, *Microfoundations: The Compatibility of Microeconomics and Macroeconomics* (New York: Cambridge University Press, 1979).
    2. J. P. Benassy's work is quite extensive. Some of his better known articles are: "Neo-Keynesian Disequilibrium Theory in a Monetary Economy," *Review of Economic Studies*, 42, October 1975, pp. 503–523; "The Disequilibrium Approach to Monopolistic Price Setting and General Monopolistic Equilibrium," *Review of Economic Studies*, 43, 1976, pp. 69–81, "On Quantity Signals and the Foundations of Effective Demand Theory," *Scandinavian Journal of Economics*, 79, 1977, pp. 153–168, and *The Economics of Market Disequilibrium* (New York: Academic Press, 1982).
    3. H. I. Grossman, "Money, Interest and Prices in Market Disequilibrium," *Journal of Political Economy*, 79 (5), September/October 1971, pp. 943–961.
    4. Robert Clower, "A Reconsideration of the Microfoundations of Monetary Theory," *Western Economic Journal*, 6, 1967, pp. 1–9.
    5. Axel Leijonhufvud, *Information and Coordination: Essays in Macroeconomic Theory* (New York: Oxford University Press, 1981), p. 119.
    6. See Benassy, "Neo-Keynesian Disequilibrium Theory in a Monetary Economy," p. 505, and Benassy, *Economics of Market Disequilibrium*, pp. 19–24.
    7. Mark Casson, *Unemployment: A Disequilibrium Approach* (New York: John Wiley & Sons, 1981), pp. 41–42.
    8. Benassy, *Economics of Market Disequilibrium*, p. 62.
    9. Ibid., p. 83.
    10. Ibid., p. 14.
    11. Ibid.
    12. Ibid., p. 64.
    13. Ibid., p. 67.
    14. Ibid., p. 73.
    15. Ibid. The emphasis is ours.
    16. Ibid., p. 85.
    17. Ibid., p. 98.
    18. See Armen A. Alchian, "Information Costs, Pricing, and Resource Unemployment," in E. S. Phelps, ed. *Microeconomic Foundations of Employment and Inflation Theory*, Chapter 1 (New York: W. W. Norton, 1970). Leijonhufvud's discussions on the same subject can be found in his *Information and Coordination*.
    19. William J. Baumol, *Economic Theory and Operations Analysis*, 4th ed. (Englewood Cliffs, N.J.: Prentice-Hall, Inc., 1977), Chapter 23.

Chapter 10

1. See Sir John Hicks, *Value and Capital* (Oxford: Oxford University Press, 1939), Chapter 5.

2. Paul A. Samuelson, *Foundations of Economic Analysis* (Cambridge, Mass.: Harvard University Press, 1958), p. 263.

3. Ibid.

4. Michael D. Intriligator, *Mathematical Optimization and Economic Theory* (Englewood Cliffs, N.J.: Prentice-Hall, Inc., 1971), p. 242.

5. Ibid.

6. Franklin M. Fisher, *Disequilibrium Foundations of Equilibrium Economics* (New York: Cambridge University Press, 1983), p. 25.

7. K. J. Arrow and L. Hurwicz, "On the Stability of the Competitive Equilibrium, I," *Econometrica*, 26, October 1958, and K. J. Arrow, H. D. Block, and L. Hurwicz, "On the Stability of the Competitive Equilibrium, II," *Econometrica*, 27, January 1959.

8. E. Roy Weintraub, *Microfoundations: The Compatibility of Microeconomics and Macroeconomics* (New York: Cambridge University Press, 1979), pp. 32–33.

9. Lionel W. McKenzie, "Stability of Equilibrium and the Value of Positive Excess Demand," *Econometrica*, 28, 1960.

10. Weintraub, *Microfoundations*, pp. 109–110.

11. Intriligator, *Mathematical Optimization*, pp. 469–470.

12. See Frank H. Hahn, "A Stable Adjustment Process for a Competitive Economy," *Review of Economic Studies*, 29, 1962, pp. 62–65; Frank H. Hahn, "On the Stability of Pure Exchange Equilibrium," *International Economic Review*, 3, 1962, pp. 206–213; Frank H. Hahn and T. Negishi, "A Theorem on Non-Tâtonnement Stability," *Econometrica*, 30, 1962, pp. 179–186; H. Uzawa, "The Stability of Dynamic Process," *Econometrica*, 29, 1961, pp. 317–331; and U. Uzawa, "On the Stability of Edgeworth's Barter Process," *International Economic Review*, 3, 1962, pp. 218–282.

13. Fisher, *Disequilibrium Foundations*, p. 26.

14. Ibid., p. 27.

15. See Hahn and Negishi, "A Theorem on Non-Tâtonnement Stability," and Uzawa, "On the Stability of Edgeworth's Barter Process."

16. Vivian Walsh, *Introduction to Contemporary Microeconomics* (New York: McGraw-Hill Book Co., 1970), Chapter 16.

17. Ibid., pp. 160–161.

18. Ibid., p. 162.

19. Weintraub, *Microfoundations*, p. 130.

20. Weintraub, *Microfoundations*, Chapter 8, and K. J. Arrow and F. H. Hahn, *General Competitive Analysis* (San Francisco: Holden-Day, Inc., 1971), p. 185.

21. Weintraub, *Microfoundations*, p. 142.

22. Leo Hurwicz, Roy Radner, and Stanley Reiter, "A Stochastic Decentralized Resource Allocation Process, Parts I and II," *Econometrica 43* (2), March 1975, pp. 187–221; 43 (3), pp. 363–394.

23. Daniel A. Graham and E. R. Weintraub, "On Convergence to Pareto Allocations," *Review of Economic Studies*, July 1975, *42* (3), pp. 469–472.

24. Fisher, *Disequilibrium Foundations*, p. 31.

25. Ibid., p. 32.

26. Ibid., p. 34.

27. Ibid.

28. Ibid., p. 94.

29. Ibid., p. 85.

30. Ibid., p. 90.

31. Ibid., p. 196.

32. Ibid.

33. Ibid., p. 197.
34. Ibid., p. 14. Note that Fisher's position in this respect is very much Post-Keynesian in spirit.
35. Ibid., p. 15.
36. Ibid., pp. 115–116.
37. Kenneth J. Arrow, "Toward a Theory of Price Adjustment," in M. Abramovitz et al., eds., *The Allocation of Economic Resources* (Stanford: Stanford University Press, 1959), pp. 41–51.
38. Ibid., p. 47.
39. Ibid., pp. 214, 218.

Chapter 11

1. Alfred S. Eichner, "Introduction to the Symposium: Price Formation Theory," *Journal of Post Keynesian Economics*, 4 (1), Fall 1981, p. 82.
2. See Nina Shapiro, "Pricing and the Growth of the Firm," Nai-Pew Ong, "Target Pricing, Competition, and Growth," both in *Journal of Post Keynesian Economics*, 4 (1), Fall 1981, pp. 85–116; Josef Steindl, *Maturity and Stagnation in American Capitalism* (New York: Monthly Review Press, 1976).
3. Eichner, "Introduction," p. 82.
4. Shapiro, "Pricing and Growth," p. 85.
5. Ibid., p. 86.
6. Ibid., pp. 93–94.
7. Ibid., p. 99.
8. Ibid.
9. David K. H. Begg, *The Rational Expectations Revolution in Macroeconomics* (Baltimore: Johns Hopkins University Press, 1982), p. 1.
10. Paul Davidson, "Rational Expectations: A Fallacious Foundation for Studying Crucial Decision-Making Processes," *Journal of Post Keynesian Economics*, 5 (2), Winter 1982–1983, p. 184.
11. James R. Wible, "The Rational Expectations Tautologies," *Journal of Post Keynesian Economics*, 5 (2), Winter 1982–83, pp. 199–207.
12. Davidson, "Rational Expectations," p. 188.
13. See Paul Davidson, *"Causality in Economics*: A Review," *Journal of Post Keynesian Economics*, 2 (4), Summer 1980, p. 580.
14. G. L. S. Shackle, "Probability and Uncertainty," *Metroeconomica*, 1, 1949, reprinted in *Uncertainty in Economics and Other Reflections* (London: Cambridge University Press, 1955), reprinted 1968, pp. 6–7.
15. G. L. S. Shackle, *Time in Economics* (Amsterdam: North-Holland Publishing Co., 1958) p. 13.
16. Ludwig M. Lachmann, "From Mises to Shackle: An Essay on Austrian Economics and Kaleidic Society," *Journal of Economic Literature*, 14 (1), March 1976, p. 58.
17. Ibid.
18. Shackle, *Time in Economics*, p. 35.
19. Douglas Vickers, "Uncertainty, Choice, and the Marginal Efficiencies," *Journal of Post Keynesian Economics*, 2 (2), Winter 1979–80, p. 252.
20. Shackle, *Time in Economics*, p. 52. The emphasis is ours.
21. Paul Davidson, *Money and the Real World*, 2nd ed. (New York: John Wiley & Sons, 1978), p. 147.

22. Arthur Eddington, *The Nature of the Physical World* (Ann Arbor: The University of Michigan Press, 1958), pp. 51–52.

23. Harvey Leibenstein, "A Branch of Economics Is Missing: Micro-Micro Theory," *Journal of Economic Literature*, *17* (2), June 1979, pp. 477–502.

24. Ibid., p. 478.

25. Harvey Leibenstein, "The General X-Efficiency Paradigm and the Role of the Enterpreneur," in Mario J. Rizzo ed., *Time, Uncertainty, and Disequilibrium* (Lexington, Mass.: Lexington Books, 1979), p. 130.

26. Ibid., p. 129.

27. Harvey Leibenstein, "X-Efficiency: From Concept to Theory," *Challenge*, September/October, 1979, p. 16.

28. See Joan Robinson, "The Production Function and the Theory of Capital," in *Collected Economic Papers*, Vol. 2 (London: Blackwell, 1965), pp. 114–131.

29. Leibenstein, "The General X-Efficiency Paradigm," pp. 135–136.

30. Israel M. Kirzner, "Comment: X-Inefficiency, Error, and the Scope for Entrepreneurship," in Mario J. Rizzo (ed.), *Time, Uncertainty, and Disequilibrium* (Lexington, Mass.: Lexington Books, 1979), p. 142.

31. Ibid.

32. Leibenstein, "The General X-Efficiency Paradigm," p. 483.

33. Richard Day, "Review of Cyert and March, *A Behavioral Theory of the Firm*," *Econometrica*, *32* (3), July 1964, pp. 461–465; and Richard Day, *Behavioral Economics* Madison: University of Wisconsin, Social System Research Institute, 1975).

34. Leibenstein, "The General X-Efficiency Paradigm," p. 481. Leibenstein observes further that the Carnegie school ideas have "not resulted in an alternative to the existing neoclassical paradigm, although it may contain the raw materials for constructing one or more such alternatives" (p. 481).

35. Richard M. Cyert and James G. March, *A Behavioral Theory of the Firm* (Englewood Cliffs, New Jersey: Prentice-Hall, Inc. 1963), p. 16.

36. Ibid., p. 17.

37. Ibid.

38. Ibid., p. 19.

39. Ibid., p. 27.

40. Ibid., p. 81.

41. Herschel I. Grossman, "Why Does Aggregate Employment Fluctuate?" *American Economic Review*, Papers and Proceedings of the 91st Annual Meeting, August 29–31, 1978, *69* (2), May 1979, pp. 64–69.

42. Ibid., p. 65.

43. Armen A. Alchian, "Information Costs, Pricing, and Resource Unemployment," in Edmund S. Phelps, ed., *Microeconomic Foundations of Employment and Inflation Theory* (New York: W. W. Norton, 1970), pp. 27–52.

44. Phelps, ed., "Introduction," *Microeconomic Foundations*, pp. 6–7.

45. Dale T. Mortensen, "A Theory of Wage and Employment Dynamics," in Phelps, ed., *Microeconomic Foundations*, pp. 167–211.

46. Charles C. Holt, "How Can the Phillips Curve Be Moved to Reduce Both Inflation and Unemployment?" in Phelps, ed., *Microeconomic Foundations*, pp. 224–256.

47. Robert E. Lucas, Jr., and Leonard A. Rapping, "Real Wages, Employment, and Inflation," in Phelps, ed., *Microeconomic Foundations*, pp. 257–305.

48. Phelps, ed., *Microeconomic Foundations*, pp. 22–23.

49. See Frank H. Hahn, "On Non-Walrasian Equilibria," *Review of Economic Studies*, *45*, February 1978, pp. 1–17.

50. Ibid., p. 1.

51. Ibid., p. 14.
52. Ibid., p. 2.
53. Ibid., p. 15.
54. Allan Drazen, "Recent Developments in Macroeconomic Disequilibrium Theory," *Econometrica*, *48*(2), March 1980, p. 299.
55. Grossman, "Why Does Aggregate Employment Fluctuate?" p. 66.
56. Ibid., p. 64.
57. Arthur M. Okun, "The Invisible Handshake and the Inflationary Process," *Challenge*, January/February, 1980, p. 6.
58. Ibid.
59. Benjamin Klein, "Contract Costs and Administered Prices: An Economic Theory of Rigid Wages," *American Economic Review*, Papers and Proceedings of the 96th Annual Meeting of the American Economic Association, December 28–30, 1983, p. 332. Klein points out that, with regard to workers' risk aversion, important theoretical contributions have been made by Martin Neal Baily ("Wages and Employment Under Uncertain Demand," *Review of Economic Studies*, *41*, January 1974, pp. 37–50.), Costas Azariadis ("Implicit Contracts and Underemployment Equilibria," *Journal of Political Economy*, *83*, December 1975, pp. 1183–1202), and Donald Gordon ("A Neoclassical Theory of Keynesian Unemployment," *Economic Inquiry*, *12*, December 1974, pp. 431–459.) For contrary views in the spirit of Klein's analysis, see Michael Wachter and Oliver Williamson ("Obligational Markets and the Mechanics of Inflation," *Bell Journal of Economics*, Autumn 1978) and David Mayers and Richard Thaler ("Sticky Wages and Implicit Contracts," *Economic Inquiry*, *17*, October 1979, pp. 55–74.) The reference to Robert Hall's contribution can be found in Hall's paper, "Employment Fluctuations and Wage Rigidity," *Brookings Paper on Economic Activity*, *1*, 1980, pp. 91–123.
60. Klein, "Contract Costs," p. 334.
61. Ibid.
62. Okun, "The Invisible Handshake," p. 8.
63. Ibid., p. 7.
64. Bengt Homstom, "Contractual Models of the Labor Market," *American Economic Review*, Papers and Proceedings of the 93rd Annual Meeting, September 5–7, 1980, p. 309.
65. Okun, "The Invisible Handshake," p. 8.
66. Ibid., p. 12.

Chapter 12

1. Franklin M. Fisher, *Disequilibrium Foundations of Equilibrium Economics* (New York: Cambridge University Press, 1983), p. 22. The emphasis is ours.
2. Robert J. Barro, "Second Thoughts on Keynesian Economics," *American Economic Review*, Papers and Proceedings of the 91st Annual Meeting, August 29–31, 1978 (May 1979), p. 56.
3. David K. H. Begg, *The Rational Expectations Revolution in Macroeconomics* (Baltimore: John Hopkins University Press, 1982), p. 262.
4. Ibid., p. 265.
5. E. Roy Weintraub, *Microfoundations: The Compatibility of Microeconomics and Macroeconomics* (New York: Cambridge University Press, 1979), p. 159.

Bibliography

Adelman, Irma. *Theories of Economic Growth and Development* (Stanford: Stanford University Press, 1961).

Alchian, Armen A. "Information Costs, Pricing and Resource Unemployment," in Edmund Phelps, ed., *Microeconomic Foundations of Employment and Inflation Theory* (New York: W. W. Norton, 1970).

Allen, R. D. G. *Macroeconomic Theory* (New York: St. Martin's Press, 1967).

Appelbaum, Eileen. "Post-Keynesian Theory: The Labor Market," *Challenge*, *21* (6), January/February 1979.

Arrow, K. J. "Toward a Theory of Price Adjustment," in M. Abramovitz et al. (eds.), *The Allocation of Economic Resources* (Stanford: Stanford University Press, 1959).

————. "Samuelson Collected," *Journal of Political Economy*, 1967.

————. "The Limitations of the Profit Motive," *Challenge* September/October 1979.

Arrow, K. J., and Debreu, Gerard. "The Existence of an Equilbrium for a Competitive Economy," *Econometrica*, *22* (3), July 1954.

Arrow, K. J., and Hahn, F. H. *General Competitive Analysis* (San Francisco: Holden-Day, Inc., 1971).

Arrow, K. J., and Hurwicz, L. "On the Stability of the Competitive Equilibrium, I," *Econometrica*, *26*, October 1958.

Arrow, K. J.; Block, H. D.; and Hurwicz, L. "On the Stability of the Competitive Equilibrium, II," *Econometrica*, *27*, January 1959.

Averitt, Robert T. *The Dual Economy* (New York: W. W. Norton, 1968).

Azarladis, Costas. "Implicit Contracts and Underemployment Equilibria," *Journal of Political Economy*, *83*, December 1975.

Baily, Martin Neal. "Wages and Employment Under Uncertain Demand," *Review of Economic Studies*, *41*, January 1974.

Barro, R. J. "A Theory of Monopolistic Price Adjustment," *Review of Economic Studies*, 1972.

————. "Are Government Bonds Net Wealth?" *Journal of Political Economy*, *85* (1), February 1977.

————. "Second Thoughts on Keynesian Economics," *American Economic Review*, May 1979.

Barro, R. J., and Grossman, H. I. "A General Disequilibrium Model of Income and Employment," *American Economic Review*, *61* (1), March 1971.

————. *Money, Employment and Inflation* (New York: Cambridge University Press, 1976).

Barth, James R. "Introduction to Crowding Out: Theory and Evidence," in Ching-Yao Hsieh, James Barth, and Salih Niftci, eds., *Macroeconomics: Selected Readings* (Lexington, Mass.: Xerox Publishing, 1977).

————. "Notes on Classical, Keynesian and Rational Expectation Models" (George Washington University, mimeograph, November 1978).

————. "The Reagan Program for Economic Recovery: Economic Rationale (A Pioneer on Supply-Side Economics)," *Economic Review*, Federal Reserve Bank of Atlanta, September 1981.

Baumol, William J. *Economic Dynamics* (New York: MacMillan, 1951).

————. *Economic Theory and Operations Analysis*, 4th ed. (Englewood Cliffs, N. J.: Prentice-Hall, 1977).

Bausor, Randall. "Time and the Structure of Economic Analysis," *Journal of Post Keynesian Economics*, 5 (2), Winter 1982–83.

Begg, D. K. H. *The Rational Expectations Revolution in Macroeconomics* (Baltimore: John Hopkins University Press, 1982).

Bell, Daniel, and Kristol, Irving. *The Crisis in Economic Theory* (New York: Basic Books Inc., 1981).

Benassy, Jean-Pascal. "Neo-Keynesian Disequilibrium Theory in a Monetary Economy," *Review of Economic Studies*, 42, October 1975.

————. "The Disequilibrium Approach to Monopolistic Price Setting and General Monopolistic Equilibrium," *Review of Economic Studies*, 1976.

————. "Regulation of the Wage-Profit Conflict and the Unemployment-Inflation Dilemma in a Dynamic Disequilibrium Model," *Economic Appliquee*, 1976.

————. "A Neo-Keynesian Model of Price and Quantity Determination Disequilbrium," in G. Shcwodiauer, ed., *Equilibrium and Disequilibrium in Economic Theory* (D. Reidel Publishing, 1977).

————. "Cost and Demand Inflation Revisited: A Neo-Keynesian Approach," *Economic Appliquee*, 1978.

————. *The Economics of Market Disequilibrium* (New York: Academic Press, 1982).

Bhaduri, A. "On the Significance of the Recent Controversies on Capital Theory: A Marxian View," *Economic Journal*, 79, 1969.

Blaug, Mark. *Ricardian Economics* (New Haven: Yale University Press, 1958).

————. *Economic Theory in Retrospect* (Homewood, Illinois: Irwin, 1968).

————. *The Methodology of Economics* (London: Cambridge University Press, 1980).

Blinder, Alan S., and Solow, Robert M. "Does Fiscal Policy Matter?" *Journal of Public Economics*, 2, 1973.

Bliss, Christopher J., and Cippa, Roberto F. "Temporary Equilibrium with Rationed Borrowing and Consistent Plans," in Mauro Baransini, ed., *Advances in Economic Theory* (New York: St. Martin's Press, 1982).

Branson, William H. *Macroeconomic Theory and Policy*, 2nd ed. (New York: Harper and Row, 1979).

Brunner, Karl, and Meltzer, Allan. "Money, Debt and Economic Activity," *Journal of Political Economy*, 80, September–October 1972.

Buchanan, James. "Barro on the Ricardian Equivalence Theorem," *Journal of Political Economy*, 84 (2), April 1976.

Buiter, W. "The Macroeconomics of Dr. Pangloss: A Critical Survey of the New Classical Macroeconomics," *Economic Journal*, 1980.

Burmeister, Edwin, and Dobell, A. Rodney. *Mathematical Theories of Economic Growth* (New York: Macmillan, 1970).

Cain, Glen G. "The Challenge of Segmented Labor Market Theories to Orthodox

Theory: A Survey," *Journal of Economic Literature, 14* (4), December 1976.

Caldwell, B. *Beyond Positivism: Economic Methodology in the Twentieth Century* (London: George Allen and Unwin, 1982).

Carvalho, Fernando. "On the Concept of Time in Shacklean and Sraffian Economics." *Journal of Post Keynesian Economics, 6* (2), Winter 1983–84.

Casson, M. *Unemployment: A Disequilibrium Approach* (New York: John Wiley, 1981).

Chick, V. *Macroeconomics After Keynes* (Cambridge, Mass: MIT Press, 1983).

Cicarelli, James, and Stuck, John. "Economics: The Next Twenty Years," *Journal of Post Keynesian Economics, 3* (1), Fall 1980.

Clower, Robert. "The Keynesian Counter-Revolution: A Theoretical Appraisal," in F. H. Hahn and F. Brechling, eds., *The Theory of Interest Rates* (London: Macmillan, 1965).

————. "A Reconsideration of the Microfoundations of Monetary Theory," *Western Economic Journal, 6,* 1967.

————. "The Anatomy of Monetary Theory," *American Economic Review,* February 1977.

Coddington, A. "Keynesian Economics: A Search for First Principles," *Journal of Economic Literature, 14* (4), December 1976.

Cornwall, John. "Macrodynamics," in Alfred S. Eichner, ed., *A Guide to Post-Keynesian Economics* (Armonk, N.Y.: M. E. Sharpe Inc., 1978).

Corry, Antony; Hindess, Barry; Hirst, Paul; and Hissain, Athar. *Marx's Capital and Capitalism Today* (London: Routledge and Kegan Paul, 1977).

Cyert, Richard M., and March, James G. *A Behavioral Theory of the Firm* (Englewood Cliffs, N.J.: Prentice-Hall, 1963).

Davidson, Paul. *Money and the Real World,* 2nd ed. (New York: John Wiley & Sons, 1978).

————. "Why Money Matters," *Journal of Post Keynesian Economics, 1* (1), Fall 1978).

————. "The Dual-faceted Nature of the Keynesian Revolution: Money and Money Wages in Unemployment and Production Flow Prices," *Journal of Post Keynesian Economics, 4* (3), Spring 1980.

————. "Rational Expectations: A Fallacious Foundation for Studying Crucial Decision-making Processes," *Journal of Post Keynesian Economics,* Winter 1982–83.

Day, Richard. "Review of Cyert and March: *A Behavioral Theory of the Firm,*" *Econometrica, 32* (3), July 1964.

————. *Behavioral Economics* (Madison, Wis.: University of Wisconsin, 1975).

Dobb, Maurice. *Theories of Value and Distribution Since Adam Smith* (London: Cambridge University Press, 1973).

Dolan, Edwin G., ed. *The Foundation of Modern Austrian Economics* (Kansas City: Sheed & Ward, 1976).

Domar, E. D. "Expansion and Employment," *American Economic Review, 37,* 1947.

————. "Capital Expansion, Rate of Growth and Employment," *Econometrica,* 1946.

Drazen, Allan. "Recent Developments in Macroeconomic Disequilibrium Theory," *Econometrica, 48* (2), March 1980.

Dreze, J. "Existence of an Equilibrium under Price Rigidity and Quantity Rationing," *International Economic Review,* 1975.

Dunn, Robert M., Jr. *Economic Growth among Industralized Countries: Why the United States Lags* (Washington, D. C.: National Planning Association, 1980).

Eagly, Robert V. *The Structure of Classical Economic Theory* (New York: Oxford

University Press, 1974).

Eckstein, O., ed. *The Econometrics of Price Determination* (Washington, D. C.: Science Research Council, 1972).

Eddington, Sir Arthur. *The Nature of the Physical World* (Ann Arbor: University of Michigan Press, 1958).

Eichner, A. S. *The Megacorp and Oligopoly* (Cambridge: Cambridge University Press, 1976).

————. *A Guide to Post-Keynesian Economics* (Armonk, N.Y.: M. E. Sharpe, Inc., 1978).

————. "Introduction to the Symposium: Price Formation Theory," *Journal of Post Keynesian Economics*, 4 (1), Fall 1981.

Eichner, A. S., and Kregel, J. A. "An Essay on Post-Keynesian Theory: A New Paradigm in Economics," *Journal of Economic Literature*, 13 (4), December 1975.

Fand, David I. "A Monetarist Model of the Monetary Process," in William Gibson and George Kaufman, eds., *Monetary Economics: Readings on Current Issues* (New York: McGraw-Hill, 1971).

Ferguson, Charles E. *The Neoclassical Theory of Production and Distribution* (London: Cambridge University Press, 1969).

Fisher, Franklin M. "Embodied Technical Change and the Existence of an Aggregate Capital Stock," *Review of Economic Studies*, 32, October 1965.

————. "On Price Adjustment Without an Auctioneer," *Review of Economic Studies*, 39 (1), January 1972.

————. *Disequilibrium Foundations of Equilibrium Economics* (New York: Cambridge University Press, 1983).

Fisher, Irving. *Appreciation and Interest*, (London Macmillan, 1930).

Frenkel, J. A. "Inflation and the Formation of Expectations," *Journal of Monetary Economics*, 1975.

Friedman, Milton. *The Optimum Quantity of Money and Other Essays* (Chicago: Aldine, 1969).

————. "A Monetary Theory of Nominal Income," *Journal of Political Economy*, April 1971.

————."Comments on the Critics," *Journal of Political Economy*, 80, September–October 1972.

Friedman, Milton, ed., *Studies in the Quantity Theory of Money* (Chicago: University of Chicago Press, 1956).

Garegnani, P. "Heterogeneous Capital, the Production Function and the Theory of Distribution," *Review of Economic Studies*, 37 (3), 1970.

Georgescu-Roegen, Nicholas. *The Entropy Laws and the Economic Process* (Cambridge, Mass.: Harvard University Press, 1971).

Gordon, Donald. "A Neo-classical Theory of Keynesian Unemployment," *Economic Inquiry*, 12, December 1974.

Gordon, Robert J. "Output Fluctuations and Gradual Price Adjustment," *Journal of Economic Literature*, 13 (2), June 1970.

Gordon, Robert J., and Wilcox, James A. "The Monetarist Interpretation of the Great Depression: An Evaluation and Critique," in Kan Brunner, ed., *The Great Depression Revisited* (Martinus Nijhoff, 1981).

Graham, Daniel A., and Weintraub, E. R. "On Convergence to Pareto Allocations," *Review of Economic Studies*, 42 (3), July 1975.

Grandmont, J. M. "Temporary General Equilibrium Theory," *Econometrica 45* (3), April 1977.

Granger, C. W. J. "Investigating Causal Relations by Econometric Models and Cross-Spectral Methods," *Econometrica*, July 1969.

Green, Jerry R., and Majundar, Mukul. "The Nature of Stochastic Equilibria," *Econometrica*, *43*, 1975.

Grossman, H. I. "Money Interest and Prices in Market Disequilibrium," *Journal of Political Economy*, *79* (5), September–October 1971.

————. "Why Does Aggregate Employment Fluctuate?" *American Economic Review*, *69* (2), 1979.

Haberler, G. "Critical Notes on Rational Expectations," *Journal of Money, Credit and Banking*, 1980.

Hahn, Frank H. "On the Stability of Pure Exchange Equilibrium," *International Economic Review*, *3*, 1962.

————. "A Stable Adjustment Process for a Competitive Economy," *Review of Economic Studies*, *29*, 1962.

————. "Some Adjustment Problems," *Econometrica*, *38*, 1970.

————. "On Non-Walrasian Equilibria," *Review of Economic Studies*, *45*, February 1978.

————. *Money and Inflation* (Cambridge, Mass: MIT Press, 1983).

Hahn, Frank H., and Negishi, T. "A Theorem on Non-Tâtonnement Stability," *Econometrica*, *30*, 1962.

Hailstones, Thomas J. *A Guide to Supply-Side Economics* (Richmond, Va.: Robert Dame Inc., 1982).

Hall, Robert E. "Employment Fluctuations and Wage Rigidity," *Brookings Paper on Economic Activity*, 1980.

Hansen, B. *A Survey of General Equilibrium Systems* (New York: McGraw-Hill, 1970).

Harcourt, G. C. *Some Cambridge Controversies in the Theory of Capital* (London: Cambridge University Press, 1972).

Harrod, R. F. *Towards a Dynamic Economics* (London: Macmillan, 1948).

Hayek, Fredrick A. *The Counter-Revolution of Science* (London: Free Press of Glencoe, 1955).

Hey, J. D. *Uncertainty in Microeconomics* (New York: N.Y.U. Press, 1979).

————. *Economics in Disequilibrium* (New York: N.Y.U. Press, 1981).

Hicks, Sir John. "Mr. Keynes and the 'Classics': A Suggested Interpretation," *Econometrica*, April 1937.

————. *Value and Capital* (London: Oxford University Press, 1959).

————. *Capital and Growth* (New York: Oxford University Press, 1965).

————. "Capital Controversies: Ancient and Modern," *American Economic Review*, May 1974.

————. *The Crisis in Keynesian Economics* (New York: Basic Books, 1974).

————. "Some Questions of Time in Economics," in A. M. Tang, F. M. Westerfield, and J. S. Worley, eds., *Evolution, Welfare, and Time* (Lexington, Mass: Lexington Brooks, 1976).

————. *Casuality in Economics* (New York: Basic Books, 1979).

Hilhorst, J. G. M. *Monopolistic Competition, Technical Progress and Income Distribution* (Rotterdam University Press, 1968).

Hollander, Samuel. *The Economics of Adam Smith* (Toronto and Buffalo: University of Toronto Press, 1973).

Holt, Charles C. "How Can the Phillips Curve Be Moved to Reduce Both Inflation and Unemployment?" in Edmund S. Phelps, ed., *Microfoundations of Employment and Inflation Theory* (New York: W. W. Norton, 1970).

Hsieh Ching-Yao; Abushaikha, Ahmad A.; and Richards, Anne. *A Short Introduction to Modern Growth Theory* (Washington D. C., University Press of America, 1978).

Humphrey, T. M. *Essays on Inflation*, 3rd ed. (Richmond: Federal Reserve Bank, 1982).

Hurwicz, L.; Radner, R.; and Reiter, S. "A Stochastic Decentralized Resource Allocation Process, Parts I and II," *Econometrica*, *43* (2), March 1975.

Intriligator, Michael D. *Mathematical Optimization and Economic Theory* (Englewood Cliff, N. J.: Prentice-Hall, 1971).

Ito, T. "Methods of Estimation for Multi-Market Disequilibrium Models," *Econometrica*, 1980.

Iwai, K. "The Firm in Uncertain Markets and Its Price, Wage and Employment Adjustment," *Review of Economic Studies*, 1974.

————. *Disequilibriuim Dynamics* (New Haven: Yale University Press, 1981).

Jeans, Sir James. *Physics and Philosophy* (Ann Arbor: University of Michigan Press, 1966).

Johnson, Harry G. *The Theory of Income Distribution* (London: Gray-Mills, 1973).

Kaldor, Nicholas. "Alternative Theories of Distribution," *Review of Economic Studies*, *23* (2), 1955-56.

————. *Essays on Value and Distribution* (Illinois: Free Press of Glencoe, 1960).

————. "The Irrelevance of Equilibrium Economics," *Economic Journal*, December 1972.

Kaldor, Nicholas, and Mirrlees, James A. "A New Model of Economic Growth," *Review of Economic Studies*, *29*, June 1962.

Kalecki, Michal. *Selected Essays on the Dynamics of a Capitalist Economy* (Cambridge: Cambridge University Press, 1971).

Kelcher, Robert E., and Orzechawski, William P. "Suppy-Side Effects of Fiscal Policy: Some Historical Perspectives," reviewed in *Economic Review*, Federal Reserve of Atlanta, February 1981.

Kenyon, Peter. "Pricing," in A. S. Eichner, ed., *A Guide to Post Keynesian Economics* (Armonk, N.Y.: M. E. Sharpe, Inc., 1978).

Keynes, John Maynard. *A Treatise On Money* (London: Macmillan, 1930).

————. *The General Theory of Employment, Interest, and Money* (London: Macmillan, 1951).

Kirzner, Israel M. "Equilibrium versus Market Process," in Edwin Dolan, ed., *The Foundation of Modern Austrian Economics* (Kansas City: Sheed & Ward, 1976).

————. "Comment: X-Inefficiency, Error, and the Scope of Entrepreneurship," in Mario J. Rizzo, ed., *Time, Uncertainty, and Disequilibrium* (Lexington, Mass.: Lexington Books: 1979).

Klein, Benjamin. "Contract Costs and Administered Prices: An Economic Theory of Rigid Wages," *American Economic Review*, Papers & Proceedings of Annual Meeting, December 28-30, 1983.

Kline, Morris. *Mathematics in Western Culture* (New York: Oxford University Press, 1964).

Koopmans, Tjalling C. *Three Essays on the State of Economic Science* (New York: McGraw-Hill, 1957).

Kornai, Janos. *Anti-Equilibrium* (New York: American Elsevier, 1971).

————. *Growth, Shortage and Efficiency: A Macrodynamic Model of the Socialist Economy* (Berkeley and Los Angeles, University of California Press, 1982).

Kregel, J. A. *Rate of Profit, Distribution and Growth: Two Views* (Chicago: Aldine Atherton, 1971).

————. *The Reconstruction of Political Economy: An Introduction to Post-Keynesian Economics* (New York: John Wiley & Sons, 1973).

Lachmann, Ludwig M. "From Mises to Shackle: An Essay on Austrian Economics and Kaleidic Society," *Journal of Economic Literature*, *14* (1), March 1976.

Laffer, Arthur B., and Ranson, R. David. "A Formal Model of the Economy" (Washington, D. C.: Office of Management and Budget, 1970).

Laidler, David. "Adam Smith as a Monetary Economist," *The Canadian Journal of Economics*, *14* (2), May 1981

————. *Monetarist Perspectives* (Cambridge, Mass.: Harvard University Press, 1982).

Laney, James T. "The Other Adam Smith," *Economic Review*, Federal Reserve Bank of Atlanta, October 1981.

Lange, O. *Price Flexibility and Employment* (The Principia Press, 1944).

Leibenstein, Harvey. "A Branch of Economics Is Missing: Micro-Micro Theory," *Journal of Economic Literature*, *17* (2), June 1979.

————. "The General X-Efficiency Paradigm and the Role of the Enterpreneur," in Mario J. Rizzo ed., *Time, Uncertainty and Disequilibrium* (Lexington, Mass: Lexington Books, 1979).

————. "X-Efficiency: From Concept to Theory," *Challenge*, September/October, 1979.

Leijonhufvud, Axel. "Keynes and the Keynesians: A Suggested Interpretation," *American Economic Review*, *57* (2), 1967.

————. *On Keynesian Economics and the Economics of Keynes* (London: Oxford University Press, 1968).

————. *Two Lectures on Keynes' Contribution to Economic Theory* (London: Institute of Economic Affairs, 1969).

————. *Information and Coordination: Essays in Macroeconomic Theory* (New York: Oxford University Press, 1981).

Levine, A. L. "This Age of Leontief . . . And Who?" *Journal of Economic Literature*, *12* (3), September 1974.

Levine, David P. "Aspects of the Classical Theory of Markets," *Austrialian Economic Papers*, June 1980.

————. *Economic Theory*, Vol. 2 (London: Routledge & Kegan Paul, 1981).

Lindahl, Eric. *Studies in the Theory of Money and Capital* (1939).

Lorie, H. R. "A Model of Keynesian Dynamics," *Oxford Economic Papers*, 1977.

————. "Price-Quantity Adjustments in a Macro-Disequilibrium Model," *Economic Inquiry*, 1978.

Lucas, Robert E., Jr., and Rapping, Leonard A. "Real Wages, Employment and Inflation," in Edmund Phelps, ed., *Microfoundations of Employment and Inflation Theory* (New York: W. W. Norton, 1970).

Mack, Ruth P. "New Ideas in Pure Theory," *American Economic Review*, *60*, May 1970.

Maddock, Rodney, and Carter, Michael. "A Child's Guide to Rational Expectations," *Journal of Economic Literature*, *20* (1), March 1982.

Malinvaud, E. *Theory of Unemployment Reconsidered* (New York: John Wiley & Sons, 1977).

Marshall, A. *Principles of Economics*, 8th ed. (New York: Macmillan, 1953).

May, J. "Period Analysis and Continuous Analysis in Patinkin's Macroeconomic Model," *Journal of Economic Theory*, 1970.

Mayers, David, and Thaler, Richard. "Sticky Wages and Implicit Contracts," *Economic Inquiry*, October 1979.

McCullum, B. T. "Rational Expectations and Macroeconomic Stabilization Policy: An Overview," *Journal of Money, Credit and Banking*, 1980.

McKenzie, L. W. "Stability of Equilibrium and the Value of Positive Excess Demand," *Econometrica*, *28*, 1960.

Meade, J. E. "A Simplified Model of Mr. Keynes' System," *Review of Economic*

Studies, February 1937.

Minford, P., and Peel, D. "The Natural Rate Hypothesis and Rational Expectations— A Critique of Some Recent Developments," *Oxford Economic Paper*, 1980.

Minsky, Hyman P. *John Maynard Keynes* (New York: Columbia University Press, 1975).

————. "The Financial Instability Hypothesis: An Interpretation of Keynes and an Alternative to 'Standard' Theory," *Challenge*, 20 (1), March/April 1977.

Mises, Ludwig von. *Human Action: A Treatise on Economics* (New Haven: Yale University Press, 1949).

————. "Epistemological Relativism in the Science of Human Action," in Helmut Schoeck and James W. Wiggins, eds., *Relativism and the Study of Man* (Princeton: D. Van Vostrand Co., 1961).

Moore, Basil J. "The Endogenous Money Stock," *Journal of Post Keynesian Economics*, 2 (1), Fall 1979.

Morgan, B. *Monetarists and Keynesians* (Halstead Press, 1978).

Morishima, Michio. *Walras' Economics: A Pure Theory of Capital and Money* (London: Cambridge University Press, 1977).

Muellbauer, J., and Portes, R. "Macroeconomic Models with Quantity Rationing," *Economic Journal*, 1978.

Muth, John F. "Rational Expectations and the Theory of Price Movements," *Econometrica*, 29, July 1961.

Myint, Hla. *Theories of Welfare Economics* (New York: Augustus M. Kelley, 1948).

Nagatani, K. *Macroeconomic Dynamics* (Cambridge: Cambridge University Press, 1981).

Neary, J. P., and Roberts, K. W. S. "The Theory of Household Behavior under Rationing," *European Economic Review*, 1980.

Neary, J. P., and Stiglitz, J. E. "Toward a Reconstruction of Keynesian Economics: Expectations and Constrained Equilibria," *Quarterly Journal of Economics*, 1983.

Neumann, J. von. "A Model of General Economic Equilibrium," *Review of Economic Studies*, 1945–46.

Ng, Y. K. "Macroeconomics with Non-Perfect Competition," *Economic Journal*, 1980.

Nordhaus, W. D. "Recent Development in Price Dynamics," in O. Eckstein, ed., *The Econometrics of Price Determination*, 1972.

O'Driscoll, Gerald P., Jr. "The Ricardian Nonequivalence Theorem," *Journal of Politcal Economy*, 85 (1), February 1977.

Okun, Arthur M. "The Invisible Handshake and the Inflationary Process," *Challenge*, 22 (6), January/February 1980.

Ong, Nai-Pew. "Target Pricing, Competition, and Growth," *Journal of Post Keynesian Economics*, 4 (1), Fall 1981.

Parrinello, S. "The Price Level Implicit in Keynes' Effective Demand," *Journal of Post Keynesian Economics*, 3 (1), Fall 1980.

Pasinetti, Luigi L. *Growth and Income Distribution: Essays in Economic Theory* (London: Cambridge University Press, 1974).

Patinkin, D. "Price Flexibility and Full Employment," *American Economic Review*, 38, 1948.

————. *Money, Interest, and Prices*, 2nd ed. (New York: Harper and Row, 1965).

————. *Studies in Monetary Economics* (New York: Harper and Row, 1972).

Peterson, Wallace C. "Institutionalism, Keynes and the Real World," *Challenge*, 20 (2), May/June 1977.

Phelps, Edmund S. *Golden Rules of Economic Growth* (New York: Norton, 1966).

Phelps, Edmund S., ed. *Microeconomic Foundations of Employment and Inflation*

Theory (New York: W. W. Norton. 1970).

Piore, Michael J. "Unemployment and Inflation: An Alternative View," *Challenge*, *21* (6), January/February 1979.

Polanyi, Karl. *The Great Transformation* (Boston, Beacon Press, 1957).

Ranadive, K. R. *Income Distribution: The Unsolved Puzzle* (Bombay: Oxford University Press, 1978).

Reddaway, W. B. "The General Theory of Employment, Interest, and Money," *Economic Review*, June 1936.

Ricardo, David. *The Principles of Political Economy and Taxation* (London: J. M. Dent & Sons, 1955).

Riker, William H., and Ordeshook, Peter C. *An Introduction to Positive Political Theory* (New Jersey: Prentice-Hall, 1973).

Rima, Ingrid H. *Development of Economic Analysis* (Homewood, Illinois: Richard D. Irwin, 1972).

Rizzo, Mario J., ed. *Time Uncertainty, and Disequilibrium* (Lexington, Mass.: D. C. Heath, 1979).

Robbins, Lionel. *An Essay on the Nature and Significance of Economic Science* (London: Macmillan, 1952).

―――. *The Theory of Economic Policy in English Classical Political Economy* (London, Macmillan, 1952).

―――. *The Theory of Economic Development in the History of Economic Thought* (New York: St. Martin's Press, 1968).

Robinson, Joan. *Essays in the Theory of Economic Growth* (New York: St. Martin's Press, 1962).

―――. *Economic Philosophy* (Chicago: Aldine, 1963).

―――. "The Production Function and the Theory of Capital," in *Collected Economic Papers*, Vol. 2 (London: Blackwell, 1965).

―――. "The Second Crisis of Economic Theory," *American Economic Review*, May 1972.

―――. *Contributions to Modern Economics* (New York: Academic Press, 1978).

Roncaglia, Alessandro. "The Sraffian Revolution," in Sidney Weintraub, ed., *Modern Economic Thought* (Philadelphia: University of Pennsylvania Press, 1977).

―――. *Sraffa and the Theory of Prices* (New York: John Wiley, 1978).

Rothbard, Murray N. "Praxeology: The Methodology of Austrian Economics," in Edwin G. Dolan, ed., *The Foundations of Modern Austrian Economics*, 1976.

Samuels, Warren J. *The Classical Theory of Economic Policy* (Cleveland: World Publishing, 1966).

Samuelson, P. A. *Foundations of Economic Analysis* (Cambridge, Mass: Harvard University Press, 1948).

―――. *Economics*, 6th ed. (New York: McGraw-Hill, 1964).

―――. *The Collected Scientific Papers of Paul Anthony Samuelson*, Vol. 2 (Boston: MIT Press, 1966).

―――. "Understanding the Marxian Notion of Exploitation: A Summary of the So-Called Transformation Problem Between Marxian Values and Competitive Prices," *Journal of Economic Literature*, *9* (2), June 1971.

―――. "Parable and Realism in Capital Theory: The Surrogate Production Function," *Review of Economic Studies*, *39*, 1962.

Sargent, Thomas, and Wallace, Neil. "Rational Expectations and the Theory of Economic Policy," *Journal of Monetary Economics*, *2*, 1979.

Schodiauer, G., ed. *Equilibrium and Disequilibrium in Economic Theory* (D. Reidel Publishing, 1977).

Schumpter, Joseph. *History of Economic Analysis* (New York: Oxford University Press, 1954).

Seligman, Ben B. *Main Currents in Modern Economics* (New York: Free Press of Glencoe, 1962).

Shackle, G. L. S. "Probability and Uncertainty," *Metroeconomics, 1*, 1949, reprinted in *Uncertainty in Economics and Other Reflections*, (Cambridge: Cambridge University Press, 1955).

———. *Time in Economics* (Amsterdam: North-Holland, 1958).

———. *Epistemics and Economics* (Cambridge: Cambridge University Press, 1972).

———. "Imagination, Formalism, and Choice," in Mario J. Rizzo, ed., *Time, Uncertainty, and Disequilibrium* (Lexington, Mass.: D. C. Heath, 1979).

Shapiro, Nina. "Pricing and the Growth of the Firm," *Journal of Post Keynesian Economics, 4* (1), Fall 1981.

Sheffrin, S. M. *Rational Expectations* (New York: Cambridge University Press, 1983).

Shubik, Martin. "A Curmudgeon's Guide to Microeconomics," *Journal of Economic Literature*, June 1970.

Sims, Christopher A. "Money, Income and Causality," *American Economic Review*, September 1972.

Skouras, T. "A Post-Keynesian Alternative to 'Keynesian' Macromodels," *Journal of Economic Studies*, 1979.

Smith, Adam. *The Wealth of Nations* (New York: Random House, 1937).

Sneessens, H. R. *Theory and Estimation of Macroeconomic Rationing Models* (Springer-Verlag, 1981).

Solow, R. M. "A Contribution to the Theory of Economic Growth," *Quarterly Journal of Economics, 70* February 1956.

———. "Investment and Technical Progress," in K. J. Arrow, S. Karlin, P. Suppes, eds., *Mathematical Methods in Social Sciences* (Stanford: Stanford University Press, 1960).

———. "What to Do (Macroeconomically) when OPEC Comes," in S. Fischer, ed., *Rationing Expectations and Economic Policy* (University of Chicago Press, 1980).

Sowell, Thomas. *Say's Law* (Princeton: Princeton University Press, 1972).

———. *Classical Economics Reconsidered* (Princeton: Princeton University Press, 1974).

Spraos, J. "New Cambridge Macroeconomics, Assignment Rules, and Interdependence," in R. Z. Aliber, ed., *The Political Economy of Monetary Reform* (Allanheld, Osmun & Co., 1977).

Sraffa, Piero. *Production of Commodities by Means of Commodities: Prelude to a Critique of Economic Theory* (London: Cambridge University Press, 1960).

Stanlis, Peter J. *Edmund Burke and the Natural Law* (Ann Arbor: University of Michigan Press, 1965).

Steigum, E., Jr. "Keynesian and Classical Unemployment in an Open Economy," *Scandinavian Journal of Economics*, 1980.

Stein, J. *Monetarist, Keynesian and New Classical Economics* (New York: New York University Press, 1982).

Steindl, Joseph. *Maturity and Stagnation in American Capitalism* (New York: Monthly Preview Press, 1976).

Stigler, George J. *Production and Distribution Theories: The Formative Period* (New York: Macmillan, 1946).

———. "Ricardo and the 93 Percent Labor Theory of Value," *American Economic Studies, 47*, 1958.

Swamy, P. A. V. B.; Barth, James R.; and Tinsley, P. A. "The Rational Expectations Approach to Economic Modeling," *Journal of Economic Dynamics and Control*, 1982.

Tatom, John A. "We Are All Supply-Siders Now," *Review*, Federal Reserve Bank of St. Louis, *63* (5), May 1981.

Tawney, Richard H. *Religion and the Rise of Capitalism* (New York: Harcourt, Brace and Co., 1926).

Taylor, L. *Structuralist Macroeconomics* (New York: Basic Books, 1983).

Tobin, James. *Asset Accumulation and Economic Activity* (Chicago: University of Chicago Press, 1980).

Uzawa, H. "The Stability of Dynamic Process," *Econometrica, 29,* 1961.

———. "On the Stability of Edgeworth's Barter Process," *International Economic Review,* 1962.

Varian, Hal R. "Non-Walrasian Equilibiria," *Econometrica, 45* (3), April 1977.

Vickers, Douglas. "Uncertainty, Choice, and the Marginal Efficiencies," *Journal of Post Keynesian Economics, 2* (2), Winter 1979-80.

Viner, Jacob. *Studies in the Theory of International Trade* (New York: Harper & Brothers, 1937).

Wachter, Michael, and Williamson, Oliver. "Obligational Markets and the Mechanics of Inflation," *Bell Journal of Economics,* Autumn 1978.

Wallace, Neil. "Microeconomic Theories of Macroeconomic Phenomena and Their Implications for Monetary Policy," in Thomas J. Sargent and Neil Wallace, *Rational Expectations and the Theory of Economic Policy: Part II* (Minneapolis: Federal Reserve, 1976).

Walras, Leon. *Element of Pure Economics or Theory of Social Wealth,* 1874.

Walsh, Vivian. *Introduction to Contemporary Microeconomics* (New York: McGraw-Hill, 1970).

Walsh, Vivian, and Gram, Harvey. *Classical and Neoclassical Theories of General Equilibrium* (New York: Oxford University Press, 1980).

Weber, Max. *Protestant Ethic and the Spirit of Capitalism* (London: G. Allen and Unwin, 1930).

Weintraub, E. Roy. "The Microfoundations of Macroeconomics: A Critical Survey," *Journal of Economic Literature, 15* (1), March 1977.

———. *Microfoundations: The Compatibility of Microeconomics and Macroeconomics* (New York: Cambridge University Press, 1979).

Weintraub, E. R., and Weintraub, S. "The Full Employment Model: A Critique," *Kyklos,* 1972.

Weintraub, S. *Capitalism's Inflation and Unemployment Crisis* (Addison-Wesley, 1978).

———. *Keynes, Keynesians, and Monetarists* (Philadelphia: University of Pennsylvania Press, 1978).

———. "The Missing Theroy of Money Wages," *Journal of Post Keynesian Economics, 1* (2), Winter 1978-79.

Wible, James R. "The Rational Expectations Tautologies," *Journal of Post Keynesian Economics, 5* (2), Winter 1982-83.

Wilson, Robert. "The Game Theoretic Structure of Arrow's General Possibility Theorem," *Journal of Economic Theory,* August 1972.

About the Authors

Ching-Yao Hsieh is Professor of Economics at George Washington University. He is the author (with J. Aschiem) of *Macroeconomics Income and Monetary Theory* and *A Short Introduction to Modern Growth Theory*.

Stephen L. Mangum is Assistant Professor in the Faculty of Management and Human Resources, The Ohio State University. He is the coauthor of *The Lingering Crisis of Youth Unemployment* and the author of *Job Search: A Literature Review*.